Crash!

The Story of Information Technology

Ludovic Smith

First published in Great Britain by Corrillium Press 2006

ISBN 0955263409

This edition published by Exposure Publishing, 2007
ISBN 978 1846855832

A record of this publication is available from the British Library

Table of Contents

1 Pre-History

19th Century London

For someone who would go on to hold the same professorship as Isaac Newton, Charles Babbage proved to be a somewhat impish student. He was known to persuade the servants at his lodgings to concoct sick notes on his behalf and have them delivered to his Cambridge college. The college kitchens would take sympathy on the ailing youth and dispatch provisions for his fortification. The food would be promptly loaded onto a boat and Babbage, in rude good health, would set off with a number of friends for a pleasant few days messing about on the River Cam. On other occasions, he and his acquaintances formed a 'Ghost' society to undertake extra-curricular investigations into the supernatural. They even formed an 'Extractors' society which would club together to 'rescue' any of its members from mental asylums should their families see fit to incarcerate them.

Another of his japes turned into something more substantive. When Babbage was at Cambridge, between 1810 and 1814, there was an on-going battle between the supporters of the different printed forms of the Bible. One camp wanted a version published that provided commentary

1

and discussion for those with a less theological education. The rival camp considered this heretical and insisted that the Bible should only be published in its original form untainted by progressive interpretations. There was no agreement in sight and the opposing factions would distribute tracts filled with high powered invective aimed at the other side.

Babbage saw parallels between this and his own beliefs on more temporal matters. He was studying mathematics, at the center of which stood the topic of calculus. The concepts behind calculus had been developed independently over a century earlier by Newton at Cambridge and Leibniz at Hanover. That's what we know now but in Babbage's day it was believed in Britain, and in particular Newton's Alma Mater, Cambridge University, that Newton had invented calculus and that Leibniz had later stolen it. Newton's feud with Leibniz had been taken up by his colleagues and continued long after his death. By the time of the Napoleonic wars, which raged whilst Babbage was at Cambridge, it was seen as deeply unpatriotic to champion anything 'continental' including anything to do Leibniz's take on calculus. This was unfortunate for Babbage who saw many benefits in the way Leibniz approached the topic and, in particular, its notation (which is the one we normally use today and uses 'd' rather than Newton's dots) seemed to him to be superior.

Taken by one of his fits of mischief, he knocked up a satirical pamphlet in the style used by the Bible activists. It extolled the virtues of Leibniz's notation and condemned those who would look no further than Newton's dots as sinners who would know no redemption. His friends found it very amusing and together they formed yet another society, the Analytical Society, which took up the task of attempting to change the perceptions of continental maths. This they did with moderate success though it took a number of years for the transformation to take full effect. It was partially as a result of his efforts with the Analytical Society that Babbage was elected a fellow of the Royal Society of London within 2 years of his graduation from Cambridge University: an accolade normally reserved for people of more senior years.

Babbage's experience in maths wasn't restricted to calculus. He would regularly run up against the every day problems of mathematicians of his era. Whilst in modern times any practical application of maths requires at least the use of a pocket calculator, in his day the equivalent calculations required the use of mathematical tables. The feeling of monotony when applying tables to longhand calculations was only matched by the feeling of uncertainty over whether the values in the tables were correct. Calculations were, at best, only as accurate as the tables used to perform them and this, in many cases, was not good.

Tables were compiled by what would best be described as amateur gentlefolk. The mainstay of the table publishing process was the country parson and part-time science enthusiast who would spend many hours in solitary calculation, laboriously working out all the thousands of values with pen and ink. After a large number of values had been prepared they would be sent to the publishing house who would compare the values with a set of supposedly identical calculations made but another bored vicar in another parish. Conflicting values were sent back for checking. Matching values were transcribed and sent to the printers for typesetting. The steps of transcription and typesetting were both prone to errors themselves. Disreputable publishing houses, or bored or incompetent staff, would make matters worse by skipping the double-checking step rendering the results of all the effort somewhat dubious.

This was not entirely an academic issue. In the early 19th century, the world was opening up to commerce, and trade by sea needed accurate navigation. Accurate navigation in turn needed accurate navigational tables. Errors in tables could result in ships striking off on the wrong course and either arriving late or in extreme circumstances running aground before arrival. It was a practical problem that was begging to be solved as Babbage was all too aware.

In 1819, he undertook a tour of Europe to explore developments in continental science and during a visit to Paris he was introduced to the work on the preparation of mathematical tables by Baron Gaspard de Prony. At the end of the previous century, de Prony had supervised the creation of an entirely new set of mathematical tables which had been triggered by the move to the then all-new metric system imposed after the French Revolution. De Prony had used the system of 'division of labor', as set out by Adam Smith, to make his huge task more manageable. The table making group of his 'Bureau du Cadastre', equivalent to the Ordinance Survey, was organized into three levels: at the top were a small group of true mathematicians who determined how the calculations were to be performed; at the bottom were the human 'computers' who performed the repetitive calculations. 'Complex' functions, such as logarithm and cosine, were reduced to repeated additions or subtractions using a technique known as the 'method of differences'. In turn this meant that the human 'computers' required no more skills than basic numeracy and a tolerance for large doses of tedium. It is reported that many of the 'computers' were in fact former hairdressers to the aristocracy whose ostentatious creations were in significantly lower demand in the post-revolution age of the guillotine.

Babbage saw that in the 30 years since de Prony had organized his team, the way of applying the 'division of labor' had changed subtly. Instead of repetitive tasks being performed by humans, they were by his day being performed by machine. If only the computer's task could be performed by machine, thought Babbage, numerical errors could be eradicated.

Babbage went to work. He devised such a machine, prepared a small demonstration model and by 1823 was attempting to raise funds for his 'Difference Engine', so called after the method of differences it employed. The Difference Engine would, like de Prony, reduce complex calculations to repetitive additions and subtractions. These simple operations had already been automated, to a limited extent, by Blaise Pascal nearly 200 years earlier. It would also be able to print out the results so that there would be no risk of transcription and printing errors. The proposed machine would however be on an unprecedented scale and would require components to be manufactured to accuracies near the limits of those possible by the craft-workers of his day. He met with the Chancellor of the Exchequer to seek public funds for his venture and received initial funding of £1,500.

Work continued fitfully for over a decade with large chunks of money being thrown at the project periodically. Babbage performed a study on the manufacturing techniques available at the time and insisted that only one Joseph Clement could perform the work to the required accuracy. Work of this standard did not come cheap and there were constant complaints about outrageous bills. The final dispute was over compensation that Babbage had agreed to pay Clement to move his workshop closer to Babbage's home. Clement downed tools and work stopped long before the device was complete.

To compound his 'industrial relations' difficulties, Babbage could not stop himself constantly changing the design. The initial demonstration Difference Engine modeled a 2nd order 'polynomial' with every value being worked out to six decimal places. Shortly before work stopped,

Babbage refused to work on anything less than a 6th order 'polynomial' with 20 decimal places. That was until he was taken with another idea: his Analytical Engine. In 1834, he proposed abandoning the incomplete Difference Engine to start work on the 'simpler' but more powerful Analytical Engine. Babbage hinted that it would cost more to get the Difference Engine working than to build his new Analytical Engine from scratch. This was not a good way to persuade the politicians to hand over more cash. Decisions never come easy to them and they ended up dithering for a total of 8 years.

The original Difference Engine project was formally dropped by the British government in 1842, nearly 20 years after it had been kicked off. The government had spent £17,500 on it, enough to build and equip a small flotilla of warships. Babbage had also invested around £6,000 of his own money in the scheme. Babbage's critics were quick to point out that even though they had spent a small fortune, the government did not even have a 'clever toy' to show for it.

It has to be said that the concepts behind the Difference Engine were sound. The problems lay in what would now be called project management. It was in a sense an early government-funded technology fiasco. It wasn't long before an alternative team had come up with an effective solution. George and Edvard Scheutz, a Swedish father and son team, had been intrigued by published accounts of Babbage's calculating machine and set about building their own as early as 1834, the year that work stopped on Babbage's original. It took continual adaptations and improvements over a period of 20 years before it worked reliably. It was selected as the gold medal winner in the 1855 Paris Great Exhibition. The Scheutz's machine got further down the road of implementation than Babbage's but even it wasn't too successful. Only two were ever made. One went to the Dudley Observatory in Albany, New York to produce astronomical tables. The director of the observatory was fired shortly afterwards for his general extravagance and the machine was rarely used. The second replica was bought by the British Registrar's office for use in preparing actuarial tables. It cost £1,200, less than the initial installment from the exchequer for Babbage's engine.

The Difference Engines of Babbage and Scheutz are only of passing interest in the history of computing. There have been many such specialist calculating machines over the centuries of which they are but two. Babbage's more remarkable achievement was in coming up with the concept of the Analytical Engine which would operate on similar principles to the computers of today. Its design had five main components: store (memory), mill (processor), control (program), input and output. The input and output was to be by a punched card device, similar to that employed on a Jacquard loom. It was however more of a developing concept than a single design and there was no serious attempt to fund the construction of the device. The politicians after all had become weary of Babbage and his wonder machines especially given that they had more pressing matters such as strikes and riots to contend with.

The conceptual development of the Analytical Engine did suggest several improvements to the original Difference Engine (known as No. 1). These improvements were included in 'Difference Engine No. 2' which was designed between 1847 and 1849 incorporating a number of the Analytical Engine's components. Whilst the abandoned Difference Engine No. 1 would have had 25,000 moving parts, Difference Engine No. 2 had only 4,000 moving parts yet it was designed to perform exactly the same task. Again, there was no attempt during Babbage's lifetime to build Difference Engine No. 2 but a version was built against Babbage's original drawings by the London Science Museum to be ready for an exhibition marking the bicentennial of his birth in 1991. It worked perfectly with only two minor changes to Babbage's blueprints.

Given the countless rejections Babbage received when he sought funding for his machines, it is not surprising that as he grew older he became more and more embittered. Even before work had stopped on Difference Engine No. 1 he had published a book entitled "Reflections on the Decline of Science in England". He would later go on to attack the nay-sayers he encountered every day:

> Propose to an Englishman any principle, or any instrument, however admirable, and you will observe that the whole effort of the English mind is directed to find a difficulty, a defect, or an impossibility in it. If you speak to him of a machine for peeling a potato, he will pronounce it impossible: if you peel a potato with it before his eyes, he will declare it useless, because it will not slice a pineapple.

He clearly felt a great resentment that they had ignominiously rejected his great works: the Difference and Analytical Engines. He turned down the offer to be made a baronet, insisting that he be given the higher honor of a life peerage. By the 1850s his best years were behind him. He had focused his formidable faculties on many topics over the years but now all he wanted was peace and quiet. He couldn't understand why, on proposing a parliamentary bill to outlaw the nuisance of street musicians, ordinary folk found this amusing. He certainly couldn't understand why they chose to persecute him for it. His neighbors would hire street musicians to play broken wind instruments outside his house. On one occasion a brass band turned up and conducted a 5 hour marathon concert with minimal breaks.

In his day he had been the toast of London society but when he died in 1871 he had disappeared from the public consciousness. Only a handful of mourners attended his funeral with a single carriage following the hearse bearing his coffin.

1880s Washington

As a child, Herman Hollerith showed promise. He was generally bright, except that is for his spelling. It came to the point that he became so anxious to avoid his over-zealous teacher's attentions that he became known for missing school and ended up being educated by the local Lutheran minister. Despite all his difficulties, he graduated from New York's Columbia University at the tender age of 19 and was introduced to the US Census office by one of his old professors.

The US census had been instituted to provide solid population figures that could be used as the basis for the allocation of seats in the House of Representatives but by 1880 the process was in trouble. With the explosive growth in the population of the United States during a period of mass migration and the increasing scope of data collected for each individual, the act of collating the census results was becoming unmanageable. The compilation of the 1870 census required 438 clerks. Ten years later, for the 1880 census, 1495 clerks would be employed and the final census report wouldn't be ready for 7 years. Clearly, if this trend continued the results of the 1890 census would not be available before the 1900 census was under way.

Hollerith saw this at first hand whilst working at the Census Bureau but it wasn't until he was working as an instructor at Massachusetts Institute of Technology a couple of years later that he started trying to find a solution to the problem: mechanizing the act of counting and collating. He started his experiments by using paper tape with holes punched in it to record the characteristics of individuals. This proved troublesome. His machine had to start and stop whilst counting took place which made it a tricky, inaccurate and slow process. In the end he settled on the idea of recording all the information against an individual on a single punched card with a machine that counted each time it saw a certain combination of holes. This was similar to the mode of operation of the Jacquard looms that had been the inspiration behind Babbage's analytical engine's input and output capabilities.

Life as an academic did not suit Hollerith and in 1884 he moved to work at the US Patent Office. Here he submitted the first of 30 patents in his own name, this time for the ideas he had developed whilst at MIT for the construction of a tabulating machine for use with punched cards. By 1887, the machine had been built and was being used to generate the mortality statistics for first Baltimore and then New York City.

As the 1890 census approached, a new superintendent, Robert Porter, was installed at the Census Bureau. Porter had many facets including a flair for journalism and an enthusiasm for statistics. He knew full well that the system of 'tally sheets' used in the previous censuses had to be replaced. It was too slow and cumbersome. As a journalist, he had written of Hollerith's machinery and knew well of its power but as the census superintendent, he couldn't be seen to simply anoint a preferred replacement. Instead he set up a competition, open to all comers, with an independent commission choosing the final system for the tabulation of the 1890 census. That way he could not be accused of favoritism. In the end, three groups put forward solutions. One involved using colored ink on white cards. The second involved using black ink on colored cards. The third was Hollerith's punched card and machine mechanism. When it came to recording the characteristics of each individual, all three mechanisms came out evenly. When it came to counting the number of individuals with a given set of characteristics the Hollerith system won hands down with the tabulating phase being 10 times faster than the more traditional methods. The commission unanimously selected the Hollerith system for the 1890 census.

Six weeks into the count, the population total of 62,622,250 was announced. This was below what many commentators felt was right for a nation of such standing. The media decried the efforts of the Census Bureau with headlines such as 'Slip Shod Work Has Spoiled the Census' being printed by the New York Herald but their thinking may have been colored by the fact that Robert Porter, the new superintendent, was the founder and editor of the rival New York Press.

Once the furor had died down, the Census Bureau quietly got into a steady rhythm and the originally leased 56 Hollerith machines were increased to 100. The 26,408 page census report was published after two and a half years effort at a cost of $11.5 million: $5 million less than the estimated cost of using manual labor. The original disputed population count had been confirmed as accurate and Hollerith machines were seen as a great success. They were successfully used in censuses in other counties in the following years and were used once again in the 1900 US census but by this time Hollerith, who had by now formed his 'Tabulating Machine Company', was demanding more money to supply the machines than was saved by automating the process.

This left a bitter taste in the mouth of the Census Bureau's management and in time for the 1910 census they had arranged for an alternative and generally superior tabulating machine to be developed along the same principles as Hollerith's but circumventing his patents. The developer, one James Powers, was for some reason permitted to patent the publicly developed improvements in his own name and formed the Powers Tabulating Machine Company. Over the following decade it went on to take a significant chunk of the tabulating machine market away from Hollerith's incumbent. The concept of tabulating machine was a success but Hollerith's Tabulating Machine Company was showing signs of strain.

1880s Dayton, Ohio

The cash register started out as a very basic device for the paranoid small businessman. James Ritty, a restaurateur in Dayton, Ohio was convinced his staff were defrauding him. He created a device that showed on a display the cash value of items being sold for all to see and simultaneously recorded the amount on a roll of paper. In this scenario, the customer also played the role of policeman. If the amount displayed was not what they were being asked to pay they would complain. This made sure that the cashiers recorded the correct amount. At the end of the day the proprietor could add up the recorded sales and compare this to the amount of cash in the drawer. As long as the cashier hadn't stolen any money, the total in the drawer should be the same as the total of the individual transactions. Ritty made an attempt to manufacture and market his 'Incorruptible Cashier' but gave up after only managing to sell a solitary device to a local coal merchant.

Fortunately for Ritty, his sole customer John H. Patterson liked the product so much he eventually bought the company and, in short order, was selling over a thousand of the machines a year. The products of Patterson's new company, National Cash Register, were not even indispensable: most retailers managed perfectly well without one. What made National Cash Register successful was its revolutionary sales techniques.

First came the understanding that cash registers, like encyclopedias, were 'sold not bought'. It was very unlikely that a retailer would spontaneously seek out a purveyor of cash registers. A direct sales force was necessary to confront the retailers in their shops.

It was accepted that only a few customers would purchase a cash register based on a cold call. This was built into the economics of the business but meant a salesman could easily become dispirited after repeated rejections. In order to keep them motivated, NCR paid them a good basic salary and generous commission based on the amount of product sold. Each salesman was given a demanding but not impossible target. Those that met their sales target became members of the 'Hundred Point Club' and were invited to an annual get-together for the best salesmen at the NCR headquarters, in Dayton, Ohio.

In order to support those new to the trade of selling, and to ensure a consistent approach, a sales school was held for new recruits. The sales school taught the process of selling: how to approach prospects, the standard pitch, demonstrating the machine, handling queries, closing a sale. Sales people were thus not on their own during a sales call; all they had to do was to repeat the line of attack taught in the sales school. Sales ceased to be seen as a grubby occupation where you did what you could to foist some pointless contraption onto an off-guard customer before making off as swiftly as possible.

The salesmen were also backed up by large quantities of what would now be called sales collateral: brochures and pamphlets extolling the virtues of NCRs products. Some items were even mailed out to prospective customers in an early example of direct marketing.

NCRs success was not however based entirely on quiet, virtuous hard work. Paterson had a fearsome and by all accounts well deserved reputation as a dirty operator. In addition to what would later become the industry standard sales practices described above, NCR would dish-out a wide variety of torment to rivals and their customers using any number of underhand tricks from spying and sabotage to predatory pricing and intimidation.

Into this dynamic and growing, if somewhat unethical, company stepped Thomas Watson, a 21-year-old former piano salesman and failed butcher. He had pestered his local NCR sales manager to take him on as a kind of apprentice in 1896 and within a few months he had passed through the NCR sales school. He went on to become a highly effective NCR salesman, turning around the previously loss making sales office at Rochester, New York. Before long he had been marked out for special duties.

In 1903 Patterson summoned the star-salesman Watson to the Dayton HQ to invite him to lead a new wave of deceit. By this time NCR had already railroaded countless commercial competitors from the market place and about the only serious competition to new NCR machines came from second-hand NCR machines offered through small independent outlets. Watson was given $1 million and told to orchestrate a nationwide campaign to close down the small trading posts by fair means or foul. His techniques were simple. He would open a shop trading second-hand cash registers very close to that operated by an incumbent. Before long the prices in his emporium would be significantly below that which allowed his competitor's operation to survive. He would strike up a friendly relationship with the rival and buy out his business, often commiserating about the state of the trade generally and generously paying slightly more than the business was worth. Before long both shops would be closed and the Watson caravan would move on to set up shop near the next victim. Ruses such as these had their desired effect and the second-hand market dissolved in the face of the co-ordinated and well funded assault.

Once his mission was complete, Watson was welcomed back to NCR and within 5 years he had become the overall sales manager of the company. His brisk rise up the hierarchy was checked however when, in 1912, Patterson, Watson and several other NCR executives ended up in court for the then relatively new offense of 'anti-trust' law violation. All were convicted, fined and sentenced to 1 year in prison. They, of course, appealed. (The verdict was indeed overturned in 1915 on a technicality.) Whist the appeal was pending, Patterson gradually made it plain that a number of the members of his original inner circle were no longer welcome. It seems Patterson wanted a clean break from the past and Watson had to go. The separation does not appear to have been acrimonious. In spring 1913, Patterson gave the 40-year-old Watson a large country house near his own as a wedding present and by the end of the year Watson had left the company with a generous severance package.

1914 New York

Watson looked around for his next opportunity. Whilst he was acknowledged to be a highly effective sales manager he did have the ticklish problem of being a convicted monopolist. One individual that wouldn't hold that against him was Charles Flint. He was an arch-monopolist, who had grown rich forming and operating trusts. Trusts are groups of companies that would corner a market and exclude all others. Unlike now, in the early 20th century this was not universally seen as a bad thing. Flint had formed yet another small grouping, the Computing-Tabulating-Recording (C-T-R) company, which brought together, amongst other units, a manufacturer of retailers scales (computing), the struggling Hollerith Tabulating Machine Company (tabulating) and a manufacturer of factory time-clocks (recording). The different groups were not integrating well and showed no signs of forming a cohesive unit let alone a monopoly. Flint invited Watson to consider joining his tiny operation as general manager. At the time, none of the companies operated in the ruthless systematic manner of NCR and Watson saw an opportunity to transform the business and make himself a fortune in the process. He wanted not just to be a hired manager but to share in the benefits of success. He negotiated a pay packet of a small base salary plus 5% of any profits. Given the small profits and uncertain future of the group, at the time this was not too much to ask.

Watson set about applying the lessons he had learned whilst at NCR. What would now be called a product development group was set up to incrementally improve products. This was unusual in the early 20th century. A sales school was instituted. Sales territories, targets and commissions were defined and the hundred-per-cent-club inaugurated as a carrot to motivate the salesmen. Just as at NCR, Watson became known for his inspirational speeches and especially his exhortation to 'THINK'. He demanded absolute loyalty from his staff and rewarded them with, for the time, excellent pay and conditions.

Predictably sales grew steadily and in 1924, Watson dropped the name 'Computing-Tabulating-Recording Company' and chose the more elegant moniker 'International Business Machines'. On the basis of solid rather than exciting products, constantly improved by small incremental steps, marketed ruthlessly by a highly trained and regimented sales force, IBM grew. Even during the depression of the early 1930s, Watson made the bold claim that he would not force anyone out of a job. He was true to his word, ending up with massive stocks of unused tabulating machinery. This turned out to be to IBM's advantage when they were released into highly profitable service when in 1935 the US government Social Security Act kicked in. The employment records of 26 million people had to be managed somehow and IBM tabulators were ideal. Ten years after the change of name Watson's 5% of profits amounted to over a third of a million dollars a year and he was officially the highest paid manager in America. IBM was on its way to world domination.

1930s Berlin

IBM specialized in selling tabulating machinery to help businesses and governments manage their data processing. All they did was count punched cards. The problems of automating the mathematics that Babbage had been attacking a century before had still not been cracked. That did not mean that the problems had gone away. In fact if anything they had become worse. In the early 1930s, a young German called Konrad Zuse was studying to become a civil engineer at a technical university in Berlin and was fed up plowing though endless simultaneous equations for his stress calculations. He resolved to develop a device to help with those calculations and started work developing the machine in his parents' living room. By 1938, his first machine, known as the Z1, finally worked – sort of. The machine could generally be coaxed, one way or another, to produce the required answer but reliable it was not. It was a pure mechanical computer like that proposed by Babbage – unlike Babbage's, it was based on the binary system which kept the mechanisms relatively simple. It should be said that Zuse was not aware of the work of Babbage or indeed anyone else in the field. He came up with the ideas on his own in order to save him doing boring repetitive calculations.

The 'success' of the Z1 spurred Zuse on to replace the less reliable parts of his design with alternative solutions but in 1939, war was declared and Zuse was called up to the German military. He was sent to the infantry but was later re-assigned as a stress analyst on flying bomb development which left him some spare time to continue with his work on calculating machines. Working when he could, he completed the Z3 with the help of similarly-minded friends and in 1941 the Z3, the first functioning program-controlled calculating machine, was demonstrated to the aircraft construction authorities. They were impressed but simultaneously underwhelmed: this device was not going to win the war. There was no obvious point in improving it or replicating it for pure military reasons. Nevertheless, the Z3 was used by the German Aircraft Research Institute in solving a number of problems, most notably that of 'wing flutter', but the research institute was not a high enough priority to allow Zuse to be released from his day job of stress analysis.

The Z3 he demonstrated was an 'electro-mechanical' device based on relays. Relays are similar, in a sense, to a domestic door-bell where a plunger is moved by an electro-magnet to hit a chime. In a relay the electrical contacts are used to move a switch. A single relay on its own is an extremely dumb device. In order to make a machine that can perform a complex task, many relays have to be wired together so that they can interact. The Z3 contained around 2600 interconnected relays, each wired to make decisions based on the settings of others.

The drawback of using relays in calculating machines is that they are restricted by Newton's laws of motion. It takes time for the contacts to move between 'on' and 'off' states and performing one calculation involves many, many such electro-mechanical decisions. Users of relay based computers had better have a good book to hand and be prepared to wait. The Z3 could only perform 3 additions per second or one multiplication every 5 seconds.

In 1942, work started on the Z4, an improved Z3. Work was hampered by the lack of resources due to war. High quality paper was in short supply so the program input tapes were made from used 35 mm celluloid film, presumably from movies no-one wanted to watch. In the closing weeks of the war, as the allies closed on Berlin, the incomplete machine was loaded onto a railway truck and began an Odyssey to safety in the south. Tension was high when the British and Americans finally sought out the then mysterious 'V4' (V stood for experimental). They were concerned that this was the big brother to the unmanned 'Vengeance' flying bombs, the V1 and V2, that caused devastation as they rained down on London during the late stages of the war. There was universal relief when they discovered it was nothing but a seemingly useless mass of electrical components.

1940s Harvard

In no way could IBM's chief executive, Thomas Watson, be described as a technologist or a techo-fan. He was a businessman pure and simple, but a highly effective one. Throughout the 1930s, he pushed IBM to grow based on a range of solid punched card equipment. He did however allow himself to stray occasionally. One of IBM's first forays away from commercial record keeping, the normal use of punched card equipment, was at Columbia University in New York. In 1928, Watson was prevailed upon to donate three truck loads of punched card equipment to a group examining the possibility of using them to mark exam papers on a large scale. This of course could have given rise to whole new applications of punched card equipment, with resulting new sales for IBM, and thus the donation was not entirely altruistic. The relationship between IBM and Columbia matured and in 1931, the company developed a set of special 'difference tabulators' which could be used in the scientific work at the university. This was in sharp contrast to the extreme difficulty that all other IBM customers had in persuading the company to adapt its machines. At the time the machines were all leased and not sold so IBM had to approve any changes. Something it very rarely chose to do. Before long, the donated punched card equipment was regularly used for scientific calculations but it was neither advanced nor high speed. It did however show IBM there was a market for calculation machinery. Watson, an inveterate collector of honors and awards, saw the relationship as beneficial and a couple of years later he was made a trustee of Columbia. In return, he invited the college president to join IBM's board of directors.

One of the many academics in the first half of the 20th century who would dearly have loved a fully functioning calculating machine was Howard Aiken, in 1936, a 36-year-old pursuing a PhD in theoretical physics at Harvard. To make progress with his thesis on the 'theory of space charge conduction' (how electronic vacuum tubes worked), he found himself having to solve a non-linear differential equation. Whilst

15

so-called 'ordinary differential equations' can generally be solved elegantly and cleanly (known as 'analytically'), 'non-linear differential equations' can be solved in one of two ways. The first is inspired guesswork. If a skilled and experienced mathematician plays with the equation for long enough they might deduce a 'function' that solves the equation. Or they might not. The second approach is the so-called numerical-methods. This is what a cryptographer would describe as a 'brute force' attack on the problem. The equation is evaluated at hundreds or even thousands of points (the more points, the more accurate the result) and then all the results collated to give an answer. Each evaluation performed by a human, even with a mechanical calculator like the one Aiken used in the late 1930s, runs the risk of error. All these errors add up to mean that the results of a manual calculation are dubious at best. Aiken proposed that it would be possible to create an automatic calculating machine using a collection of commercial punched card machines – just like the set-up at Columbia. A number of modifications would be required but the resulting integrated machine would deliver answers to the type of scientific and engineering problems he was looking into at that time. He received 'rather limited enthusiasm' from those around him in the Harvard faculty and the plan was dropped for a time. It was not the place of graduate students to come up with such an expensive, risky and resource-intensive novelty. The circulation of the report did have one interesting effect, however. A technician in the department took Aiken to a store where he presented a small fragment of a machine that had been designed a hundred years before to mechanize calculation. It was none other than a dismembered section of Babbage's original difference engine which had been donated to Harvard in 1886 by Babbage's son. It was, the technician pointed out, intended for the same purpose as Aiken's proposed machine.

Given the lukewarm reception from within Harvard, Aiken tried to tempt outside organizations to help build his machine. First he sought assistance from the Monroe Calculating Machine Company but they declined to help. A colleague suggested that he should try having a word with IBM. It was known that one of the professors in the Harvard Business School, one T. H. Brown, was familiar with the IBM president, the legendary Thomas Watson. Aiken made inquiries and was introduced to Watson who agreed to assist in the building of his device at the IBM plant in Endicott, New York. $15,000 was initially committed to developing such a device though the anticipated cost had risen to $100,000 within months.

IBM provided four of their most experienced engineers to build the device and as time went on ever increasing amounts of cash. The design was started in 1939 with construction commencing in summer 1941. Unlike Zuse who got 'hands on' with his devices, Aiken was content to provide a design and leave the implementation to the IBM engineers. This was just as well as Aiken moved to active service as a Naval Commander after the declaration of war by the US.

The war gave new application to the nascent computing device: naval gunnery. Battleships of the era could send a one ton shell of high-explosives up to 20 miles. This was all very impressive but of little use if they did not hit their target. Even if a spotter close to the target could radio back how close one salvo had been, the gun operators on a ship could only guess how to adjust his guns to make the next attack more accurate. To help the gun operators in their task, tables of trajectories were prepared in advance for each type of gun and munition. These would indicate to the operators how to adjust the guns to have the desired effect. Engineers could create sets of equations to model the dynamics of shells under the influence of explosive propulsion, gravity, air resistance, atmospheric conditions, cross winds and even the rotation of the earth whilst the shell was in flight. Unfortunately, using the equations meant that differential equations had to be solved. The process would have to be done for each type of shell, for each type of gun, for each gun elevation/angle, for each set of atmospheric conditions, etc. A single gunnery table would require up to 3000 entries which would tie up a team of 100 human computers for up to a month. Armies of human 'computers', normally young women who had been studying maths before the war, were employed to churn through calculations. Given the shear scale of the task though there just wasn't enough trainable humans to keep up with the prolific output of new weapons. The IBM Automatic Sequence-Controlled Calculator, or Harvard Mark I as it came to be known, was thus re-assigned during its development to work on creating naval gunnery tables.

Like the Zuse machines, the Mark I was a pure relay device. As mentioned, relays have mechanical components meaning that they are inherently slow. A single multiplication took the Mark I six seconds and working out a trigonometry function took over a minute. They were also noisy. According to one visitor the machine in operation sounded 'like a roomfull of ladies knitting'.

The Mark I could not remember its program. This was held on a paper tape which was threaded continually through a tape reader. It could only remember 72 numbers, and these could only be used in certain ways. It was a limited device but one that was useful: to a certain extent. The original rationale for the device had been the same as Babbage's – to produce mathematical tables. Within a few years, however, it became clear that the days of maths tables were numbered. Who needed a mathematical table when the machines doing the calculations could generate the values on the fly.

As the project neared completion, Aiken and IBM's Watson did not see eye to eye. The construction of the device at IBM Endicott was complete by early 1943 but it wasn't producing table data in a Harvard Basement until May 1944 because of disagreements over who could take credit for the work and the related patent rights. The Mark I was unusual for the time as the whole project was performed in the public domain, not shrouded in military secrecy. Announcements were made during the design and construction culminating in a formal public 'dedication' in August 1944. For this event, Watson insisted that the device was clad in stainless steel and glass, not easily procured at a time of war, to project a professional image. Aiken meanwhile thought this was unnecessary and would only hinder maintenance. As so often happened, Watson got his own way and, as intended, the pictures of a 'clinically clean' Mark I contrast very well with the wire strewn anarchy of other machines of the time.

For the dedication ceremony, Watson traveled to Boston by train. He arrived on the Sunday evening, the day before the event itself. As a benefactor who had gifted Harvard with a machine that had ended up costing in the region of $500,000, he expected to be greeted by senior members of the university. Instead the only person waiting for him at the train station was a local IBM branch manager. On the way to his hotel, Watson was shown the Sunday papers. Splashed across the front pages were extensive details of the Mark I with adulatory references to Aiken and Harvard but hardly any mention of IBM. Not only had Harvard released details of the machine early but they had also neglected to give any account of IBM's long-term commitment. Understandably, Watson was livid. In a fit of pique, he announced that he was not going to attend the dedication ceremony but was eventually persuaded to do so by a high level delegation from the University that had been summoned to calm him down. He managed to make it through the scheduled events without causing embarrassment to himself or his hosts but left determined to show the world that IBM had created the device and that it could create an even better one without the meddling of Howard Aiken.

Six months after the Harvard Mark I snub, Watson established the 'Watson Computer Laboratory' at the Ivy League University he had the closest ties to, Columbia. It was to develop a 'super-calculator', later to become known as the Selective Sequence Electronic Calculator, or SSEC. The SSEC would be an improvement over the Mark I but had no real target user group and was not technically noteworthy: it gave IBM some experience in electronics, it was a significant PR asset but it had not been built to perform any specific task. It did use electronics for certain core functions but other devices had done this, and more, years before. It was, however, the first machine that had enough spare capacity in its schedules that it could be rented by the 'paying public' for $300 a hour. In order to garner maximum publicity, it was installed on the ground floor of the IBM New York offices in full view of passers-by who would be able to watch the flashing neon lights, 23,000 relays and 13,000 vacuum tubes in full flight. Should maintenance be required that necessitated access to the machine's guts, floor-to-ceiling curtains would be drawn to preserve its modesty and maintain its mystique. It had a relatively short life, being dismantled in 1952, only 5 years after its inauguration.

1940s Buckinghamshire

Whilst the Harvard Mark I started out as a device for general calculations and ended up being used by the military, the machine that took the next step towards the modern computer was designed and built for purely military purposes. It was used to break codes and the process that led to its emergence was triggered by the rise to power of the Nazis in Germany in the mid-1930s.

The people of Poland understandably felt under a significant threat from their aggressive new neighbors. If there was going to be a conflict, the Poles would need all the help they could get against the might of the German military machine. Knowing the plans of their enemy might just enable them to stay one step ahead. In order to work out the Germans' intentions they were prepared to put a large amount of effort into breaking the codes that were used by their military.

In the 1930s, the German military used a system known as 'Enigma', a cipher machine developed shortly after the First World War to automate the process of securing communication. The machine, which looked like a large typewriter, would accept a message typed into a keyboard. As each letter was typed, it would be scrambled and the 'encoded' letter illuminated on a display board. The encoded letters would be written down as they were illuminated and either sent in written form or, more normally, radioed using Morse Code. When the encoded message arrived at its destination an Enigma machine would be set up in an identical manner and the newly arrived cryptic message typed in. This time the original text would be illuminated on the display board.

The special feature that made Enigma seem so secure was that it could be set up in so many different ways. Techniques such as 'cross wired' encoding rotors, plug boards and reflectors meant that there was up to 107,458,687,327,250,619,360,000 ways to set it up. If you knew the way that the sending machine was set up, it would be easy to reconstruct the message. If you did not know how the machine was set up, you would have a lot of combinations to try. In the days before electronic computers, it was just not possible to try that many combinations individually. The makers of the machine, and the German cipher specialists, believed it to be impregnable.

In the years between the wars, the British, French and American cipher analysts all agreed. They had a look at the possibility of breaking the Enigma system but quickly gave up. When the very existence of your country is at risk from a neighboring fascist dictatorship, desperation can give you a different perspective. The Poles did not just give up on Enigma but hired a number of mathematicians to attempt to break into the messages it created. Initially, they didn't make much progress, the task was just too big, until they had a helping hand from the French.

The French assistance took the form of more traditional espionage. A member of the German cypher bureau was, in the words of the head of the French code-breaking operation, 'fond of money, which he needed because he was fonder still of women'. The French were only too happy to indulge their German spy's vices – in return for Enigma artifacts that is. With this new information, which included operational procedures and technical documentation, the French make their own attack on Enigma but quickly gave up. It was passed on to the Poles as a gesture of goodwill. The French didn't expect them to have much use for it.

The Poles took more care with the information; they deduced the internal workings of the German military Enigmas and found a weakness in the system. If you attacked the problem in a certain way you could effectively remove the effect of the 'plug board' reducing the set-up possibilities to 105,456. By analyzing intercepted messages, it was noticed that each set-up had a characteristic 'signature'. Over the period of a year, the Poles prepared an index of 'signatures' for each of the 105,456 Enigma set-ups. Each day, after analyzing a number of intercepted messages, they could determine the 'signature' and deduce the Enigma settings from the index.

The technique allowed the Poles to read the encrypted German messages for several years until in September 1938, in preparation for the annexation of the so-called Sudetenland, Germany changed their procedures. Overnight, the index of signatures had become useless. If the Poles attempted to generate another set of indexes, this too could easily be swept away by minor changes to the Enigma system. Instead of constantly reacting to minor changes with huge organizational efforts to recreate the index, a special electro-mechanical machine called a 'Bomby' was developed to test each of the possible Enigma set-ups against the signature. It served the Polish cipher bureau well until early 1939 when the Germans distributed additional Enigma rotors to increase security. This had the effect of increasing the complexity by a factor of 10. In order to break the code, 10 times the number of Bombys would be needed – well beyond the resources available to the Polish cypher bureau.

On September 1 1939, German invaded Poland. With the German Army's advance, the focus of code-breaking activity moved to Bletchley Park in the UK. The Poles had passed their knowledge of Enigma on to the French and British who, over time, adapted the process and redesigned the Bomby, partly to improve the process, partly because the Germans were being more inventive in their use of Enigma. The British cracked the German Army and Luftwaffe codes almost every day from 1941 until the end of the war with the help of the Bombes (as the redesigned Bomby were known).

The German Navy, apparently suspicious that the impregnable Enigma had been compromised, continually increased the complexity of their system. By 1943, the standard British Bombes could not reliably cope with the increased complexity of the Navy cipher. Regular heavy bombing raids had left industrial resources in the UK heavily stretched by 4 years of war and attempts at delivering upgraded Bombes to handle the changes did not go well. Under heavy pressure from their American allies, the British Bombe designs were reluctantly passed to the US Navy code breakers in Washington. With the American industrial complex relatively unscathed by war, the Bombes were once again redesigned, this time in a section of NCR's factory at Dayton, Ohio that had been requisitioned for war work. The option of redeveloping the device using electronic vacuum tubes was considered but discounted due to the tubes' inherent unreliability. The resulting improved electro-mechanical device, operating around 30 times faster than the British Bombes, broke the German Navy traffic on a regular basis often meaning that U-boat messages could be read in Washington and London at the same time as Berlin.

The Germans used cypher machines other than Enigma to encrypt their messages. The Lorenz machine, based on the then common teleprinter, was used by the high command and was considered by the Germans to be even more secure than Enigma. In August 1941, a Lorenz operator was asked to send a 4000 character message from Athens to Berlin. The transmission was not understood by the target station and a resend was requested. The lazy operator ignored all the procedures he would have been taught, reset his machine in exactly the same way as for the initial message and resent the same long message. Both transmissions were intercepted by a British listening post and after a herculean effort over a number of months, just from these two messages, the workings of the Lorenz machine cypher was deduced.

Yet another specialist electro-mechanical device, known as a Robinson (after Heath Robinson, the British illustrator of ridiculous makeshift devices, much akin to the American Rube Goldberg) was devised. Unfortunately, it had difficulty reading the message data fast enough to make use of it and when it did manage to read the data, it didn't always give the right answer. A young engineer called Tommy Flowers, from the Post Office Research Station at Dollis Hill, North London, was asked if he could assist in solving the problems with Robinson. It quickly became clear to Flowers that "Robinson was never going to work". Just like the US Navy's consideration of electronic valves to speed up the Bombes, Flowers proposed a new machine based on vacuum tubes to perform the work of Robinson. The lack of moving parts would mean that it could work far faster than the semi-mechanical Robinson, and using electronics would allow the message data to be read using light, rather than mechanical sensors, which would mean that input tapes could be read without error at a higher speed. Just like the US Navy's decision, the Bletchley Park code-breakers decided against a vacuum tube machine: it would take too long to build to be useful for the war and its valves would be too unreliable.

Flowers, however, was convinced that Robinson was not going to work very well. He set about building his vacuum tube based machine back at the Dollis Hill research station, at times paying for components out of his own pocket. After 10 months work, in early December 1943, the device now known as Colossus was demonstrated at Bletchley Park. It contained 1500 valves and read Lorenz messages from a paper tape punched with holes. The machine operated on statistical principles, comparing the Lorenz encoded message with what the code-breakers thought would be in the message. After about 20 minutes of thought it would display its statistical analysis on banks of primitive indicators. It was then up to the code-breakers experience and intuition to finish off the cracking manually.

By the end of the war, there were 10 improved Colossus II in operation, each containing 2500 valves and running five times faster than the original. This is currently thought to be the first use of an advanced electronic device to perform useful work.

The term 'currently thought' has to be used because both the Bombes and Colossus were considered highly secret and their existence, let alone details of their operation, was kept confidential until 1974. During the execution of the war, if Germany found out about the code breaking they would immediately drop Enigma as a communication tool, rendering all the work on code breaking useless.

1940s Pennsylvania

At the end of 1940, after the fall of Poland and whilst Bletchley Park was struggling to get their Bombes fully operational, a physicist called John Mauchly gave a talk on computing at the conference of the American Association for the Advancement of Science. As the USA hadn't yet entered World War II, the subject matter was not of military interest but related to a device Mauchly had developed to help in the study of his favorite topic: weather forecasting. Mauchly's device was a basic version of what is known as an analog computer and followed in the footsteps of other machines that had been built to attempt to automate calculations. In the audience for the presentation was one John V Atanasoff, a physics professor from Iowa State University. Atanasoff was also advanced in building a prototype for a device to perform a different kind of calculation: solving simultaneous equations. This was the same task that had goaded Zuse into building his machines in Berlin a few years previously. After Mauchly's talk had finished, Atanasoff introduced himself and the two talked about their shared passion.

Atanasoff's device was to become known as the ABC – the Atanasoff Berry Computer – in honor of Atanasoff himself and Clifford Berry who assisted in its construction. What was unique about Atanasoff's machine was that it used digital electronics to perform logic. His machine could 'think' without having to wait for some component, be it linkage or a relay, to physically move.

Mauchly was captivated by the idea and the following year even traveled to Iowa to have a look at the machine. Whilst Atanasoff's approach was revolutionary, it wasn't heavily documented and the prototype had reliability issues. The machine could normally perform the task it was set but couldn't be easily reprogramed and had to be handled carefully by those who knew its temperament. In its early days, the only way to enter data into the machine was to tap a capacitor with a charged wire. Antanasoff's enthusiasm gradually faded. After he left for war work, the prototype was left in the basement of the Iowa physics department until it was dismantled when the space was needed for other purposes.

Mauchly on the other hand remained hooked on the notion of using machines to aid calculations but it wasn't until over a year after his visit to Atanasoff that he could start to do something about it. With the USA entering the war after Pearl Harbor, Mauchly left his college job teaching physics and signed up to a war-related cross-training program. In the summer of 1942, he arrived at the Moore School, an engineering college attached to the University of Pennsylvania, to study electrical engineering. Here it was clear that the US Navy was not the only entity that was having difficulty generating firing tables for heavy guns. Unsurprisingly, the US Army had a similar problem. Their efforts were based at the Ballistics Research Laboratory at the Aberdeen Proving

Ground in Maryland with academic back-up from the nearby Moore School in Philadelphia.

The US Army had two means of working out shell trajectories. The first was the time honored 'human calculator' approach. The second was to use a 'differential analyzer' developed before the war by Vannevar Bush. This was an 'analog computer', like Mauchly's original weather forecasting effort, where distances, forces and other 'variables' were represented by physical movement within the machine. The machine essentially simulated the physical word: as a shell rose in the simulation, gears would turn and linkages would rise; as a shell fell in the simulation, the gears would turn some more and the linkages would fall. A problem was not so much 'worked out' as 'acted out'. This technique did produce results, about one every half hour, but due to the size and complexity of the machine, the research station only had access to two examples: one in the Moore School basement and one at the Aberdeen Proving Ground. When a new type of shell or size of gun was to be modeled, different sized components had to be fitted into the machine requiring hours of work. Whilst this was going on, the machine was unusable.

In order to speed up the calculations, Mauchly proposed building a large calculating machine using electronic components. Instead of acting out the scenario, it would calculate the answers to the differential equations just like the human computers and the Harvard Mark I did. Unlike its predecessors, because it was electronic, it would be able to perform 10 multiplications every second, many times faster than the Mark I.

His initial proposals were comprehensively ignored. Except that is by a young army officer, Lieutenant Herman Goldstine, allocated the role of liaison between the BRL and the Moore School. Goldstine, with a PhD in mathematics, was able to grasp what Mauchly was proposing and had a far more open mind than the pressured bureaucrats the original proposal had been sent to. He was also far more politically savvy than Mauchly and given his position he was trusted to a far greater extent by those managing the institutions. With the arrival in North Africa of the US Army in 1943, the pressure for more firing tables grew even stronger. It had become clear that the normal tables were inadequate for use in the dessert terrain and dry atmosphere. Goldstine grasped the opportunity. The top brass could well be willing to throw money at a speculative venture like an electronic computer if it had even a remote possibility of taking the pressure off them. With Mauchly, he worked on a revised submission. Goldstine prepared the ground within the army through informal discussion so that when a formal proposal was made, it was viewed with interest. Phrases were chosen to make the proposal less frightening. 'Digital Computor' was dropped in favor of 'Electronic Diff. Analyzer' the last two words of which were comfortingly familiar to all those working on the firing tables. In the spring of 1943, project PX was approved to create the 'Electronic Numerical Integrator and Calculator' or ENIAC. It was funded, of course, by the US Army.

Whilst Mauchly was the visionary behind the project, he was always viewed as being untrustworthy by those in power. Untrustworthy that is in the sense of being a dreamer who was unfocused, lazy and unmotivated to deliver. The delivery of the ENIAC would be placed in the hands of a recent Moore School graduate called J. Presper Eckert who had worked with Mauchly many times before. Eckert was an archetypal engineer. He was highly rational and a master of whatever technical specialty caught his attention but he was unforgiving of human foibles. Over the next 3 years, he drove himself and his team hard to get the machine built whilst it would still be useful.

Like the ABC, the ENIAC would use vacuum tubes: 18,000 of them. Vacuum tubes of this era were not reliable. In many ways they were like a domestic light bulb and had an unfortunately tendency to burn out. With 18,000 of them, all interdependent, they could expect several failures daily. This was a big problem in the early days of development but it was soon realized that, just like domestic light bulbs, valves were most vulnerable when their heating element was being switched on and warmed up. A reasonable reliability could be achieved by the simple expedient of not switching the computer off and running the tubes below their designed voltage.

The computer ran its first useful program at the end of 1945. Given its lack of moving parts, it was hundreds of times faster than the previous electro-mechanical computers, such as Harvard Mark I, and it was pointed out at its public unveiling in early 1946 that it could calculate a shell's trajectory faster than the shell would take to travel it. This was unheard of calculating power for the time.

By the time ENIAC was entering active use, it was already known to be suboptimal. The reliability of the vacuum tubes was a constant annoyance, though the team became well practiced at dealing with failures. The machine did not store its program in memory. It was hard-wired into the circuits. Thus when the problem being worked on was completed and it was time to move on, the wiring of several large 'plug boards', similar to the old style telephone operators switch board, had to be manually re-configured. A single change-over could take hours or days – much the same time as Vannevar Bush's analogue machine.

A number of design improvements made themselves obvious but by 1944, the design of ENIAC was frozen in order to avoid a Babbage-style debacle where physical construction would never catch up with a constantly changing design: It is better to have one inferior but functioning machine than the design for an improved machine that's 'not quite ready yet'. A plan was made to build an improved computer, the EDVAC (Electronic Discrete Variable Automatic Computer), to perform the same task. The ENIAC's circuits would be simplified (18,000 tubes down to 4,000), reducing the amount of time spent hunting down blown vacuum tubes whilst also simplifying the programing task. The program would be read in and stored in computer memory avoiding the time-consuming physical re-plugging. The ENIAC's approach of having 20 separate small number stores, each simultaneously working on their own calculations before being collated together, would be dropped. Instead there would be one processing unit and one large store. Instead of the decimal system that ENIAC (and Babbage/Harvard Mark 1) used, the new machine would operate on the binary number system that's more natural for computers (like Zuse). The design of the next generation of machines gradually took shape as construction continued.

Enter John von Neumann, international mathematical star. Von Neumann, like Charles Babbage, was the son of a leading banker, this time from Budapest, Hungry. After a stellar academic career in Europe, where he had laid the groundwork for quantum mechanics amongst much else, he emigrated to the United States in 1930. In 1933, at the age of 30, he was invited to join Princeton's Institute of Advanced Study as a founding professor, alongside one Albert Einstein.

In 1940 he became a member of the Scientific Advisory Committee to the BRL and 3 years later a consultant to the Los Alamos National Laboratory where the first nuclear weapons were developed. His initial work for the Ballistics Research Laboratories was not much related to the ENIAC, so the story goes, until he was accosted on the local train station platform one day in June 1944 by Goldstine, the Moore School liaison officer. Goldstine was more interested in having a chat with an international celebrity than in pushing his own project but as the conversation moved to what ENIAC and its successor could do, he would later recall

> ... the whole atmosphere changed from one of relaxed good humor to one more like the oral examination for the doctor's degree in mathematics.

Von Neumann could instantly see how an automated computer could help solve the more intractable problems he was working on at Los Alamos. Within a few months he was acting as a consultant to the ENIAC team and wrote a paper summarizing the planned improvements that would be incorporated in its successor, the 'EDVAC'. 'First Draft of a Report to the EDVAC' is a milestone in computer history because it summarizes the fundamental components required in a computing machine: a memory, a calculating unit, a control unit, etc. The framework it described is still valid today.

According to the academic supervisor of the work on EDVAC, von Neumann had written the paper as a summary of the team's thinking. It was considered a draft for internal discussion within the project. Within months, it became apparent that the incomplete and supposedly internal draft document had found its way to other groups in the US and even one group in the UK. Mauchly and Eckert were not happy. Firstly, the report contained many of their ideas, formulated before von Neumann arrived, yet they were not mentioned as contributors. Only von Neumann's name was on the paper. Secondly the 'publishing' of the report meant that the design principles it contained, which they felt that they had created, could be considered to be in the public domain and meant they could not be effectively patented.

The controversy continues to this day. Who distributed the report and what were their motives? It's thought unlikely that Goldstine would have done it himself without approval whilst an internationally acclaimed academic such as von Neumann did not need the kudos that could be derived from a limited distribution of a half finished document. It's unlikely the answer to the question will ever be known but whoever did distribute the document, the structure of the machine developed at the Moore School in the mid-1940s is now universally known as the 'von Neumann Architecture'.

With the end of the war and the delivery of ENIAC to the US Army, the atmosphere changed. A senior academic, returning to the Moore School after spending the war working on projects at MIT, decided to update the small school's patent policy to match that of larger institutions. Mauchly and Eckert were given the ultimatum that if they wished to continue working at the Moore School, they would have to sign over their patent rights to the University. Today this would not be considered unusual but in 1943 when the ENIAC project was starting off, the University had so little faith in the scheme that they declined to get involved in patents and left it to Mauchly and Eckert to sort themselves out. Given the about face by the university and the high-handed way the edict was applied, both Mauchly and Eckert resigned.

Goldstine, on leaving the army at the end of the war, became von Neumann's assistant at the Institute of Advanced Study in Princeton. They continued to work on the application of computers to scientific problems building their own EDVAC-like computer to the principles contained in the 'first draft'. Of course, with the contents of the document being in the public domain, they were free to do so without risk of any disputes over intellectual property rights. Their efforts at the IAS were characterized by a great openness. Information and design principles were passed freely to visitors. Goldstine and von Neumann saw the computer as a fundamental aid to 'applied mathematics' and that the rules of academia should apply.

A New Age Dawns

By the summer of 1946, the world still did not have a device that could be called a computer by today's standards.

The machines built in Germany during the war by Zuse were all electro-mechanical in some way. The original Z3 had been blown up in an allied bombing raid in 1943 and the Z4 would languish incomplete for several years after the end of the war due to lack of resources. Over time, the situation improved and by 1950, the machine was in action at the technical university in Zurich. It was finally retired from a French research establishment in 1960.

At the end of the war, the British and Americans kept their code-breaking activities secret. It was not generally known that Enigma and Lorenz had been broken and their mechanisms for encrypting messages continued to be used by many other countries in the years that followed, sometimes at the suggestion of the British. By keeping quiet about their abilities, the British and Americans could read the diplomatic and military messages of these countries without much effort. The successor organization to Bletchley Park, GCHQ, was still running Colossus into the 1960s and even into the mid-1980s was threatening to imprison workers who wrote about their experiences.

The Colossus was not, however, a computer as we know it today. It was intended to perform specialist statistical operations and could not work on differential equations let alone be freely programed.

Over at Harvard, Howard Aiken continued to build computers but without IBM's involvement. Aiken remained wedded to the technologies of relays, decimal arithmetic and a program executed directly from tape, techniques that would be dropped by everyone else before too long. He is renowned for his prophesy that the US would only require a handful of computers to service its entire needs. He said this at a time when he firmly believed that computers would be used to generate mathematical tables that would then be used in the time honored fashion. It wouldn't be too long before this would seem like a quaint, old-fashioned view of the world.

Like the Zuse machines, the Mark I was electro-mechanical. All of the units had to be strictly synchronized. This was achieved using a single rotating shaft that ran the length of the machine driven by a 5 horsepower electric motor. This forced the machine to be built in a straight line. Whilst it was over 50 feet long, it was only 2 foot deep.

Computers of this type were also open to an unusual form of 'attack'. One day a window was left open and shortly after the nearby computer stopped functioning. The team moved through the diagnostic procedure and in short order a stunned moth was retrieved from one of the relay contacts. The moth was taped to the machine's log book for posterity along with the caption 'first actual case of a bug being found'. This is believed to be the first time the word bug was written down in relation to a computer fault, although the term was previously used informally.

As a result of IBM's publicity for Harvard Mark I, it is often seen as one of the first modern computers. It could, however, be seen as just a well-executed application of Babbage's Analytical Engine for the age of electricity.

Just as Colossus couldn't do differential equations, the ENIAC at the Moore School couldn't do statistics. It was more flexible than Colossus but you did not so much reprogram it as rewire it. It was withdrawn from service in 1955.

The key deficiency of all the machines was their inability to hold their program, their list of instructions if you will, in their own memory. The programs were all either hard wired (ENIAC, Colossus) or read from some kind of tape (Z3, Mark I). Not having the entire program available at one time meant that it wasn't possible for the device to make decisions. To make decisions, it would be necessary to leap about the program and execute different set of instructions based on what choice had been made. When the machine was executing its program from a tape it would be necessary for the tape reader to zoom up and down searching for a specific set of instructions. As the tape sped past it would be easy to miss the target instruction or more likely for the tape to snap. As a result, the early machines were very rigid and stubborn. All they would do was execute the same list of instructions in a pre-arranged order, over and over again without deviating. This was adequate for solving differential equations or correlation studies but would hamper anything that required more flexibility.

The conceptual leap to enable the next generation of computers was first made at the Moore School as part of the EDVAC design. This was to store the program in the computer's memory along with the numbers being worked on. Leaping around the program would merely involve pointing to a different memory location inside the machine. This could be done in a flash and with complete accuracy. For the first time, it would be possible to use words like 'if' and 'when' in a computer program.

The 'stored program' concept was the main conceptual leap of the 'first draft on the EDVAC'; it was this that took it beyond the ideas of Babbage's Analytical Engine. As the document was circulated more widely, interest grew. The ENIAC was also well publicized, unlike the Zuse machines and Colossus, which lead to the Moore School becoming a focal point for the worldwide computing effort. The college was inundated with requests from researchers asking to visit so that they could learn about the machine. Those that did visit all asked the same questions and took up the time of the staff that were supposed to be working on the ENIAC replacement, the EDVAC. Most of the key staff,

Eckert, Mauchly, von Neumann and Goldstine, were also leaving the project. The dean of the Moore School decided that it would be wise to arrange a formal event to bring the wider community together and explain how ENIAC and EDVAC worked. It would be the farewell performance of those departing for new pastures and would be of great benefit to the academic community as a whole. It would also allow the Moore School to move on.

A summer school was arranged in July and August 1946 at the Moore School to summarize the state of knowledge in computing to a select group of invited researchers. A total of 48 lectures were presented by contributors from far and wide: Howard Aiken came from Harvard, von Neumann and Goldstine came from the Princeton IAS and one of the UK's foremost computer authorities Douglas Hartree came from Manchester University in the UK. Even Eckert and Mauchly returned to their former employer to go over their areas of expertise. 28 participants from the US and two from the UK sat through several hours of lectures every morning and participated in a free-for-all seminar in the afternoon. When the end came after 8 weeks, they all shook hands, thanked their hosts for their troubles and returned to their respective homes. Now they all had the same foundation of understanding on which to build their first computer. The race was on.

2 Hardware

1940s Cambridge

Not everyone's path to the Moore School lectures was smooth. Before the war, Maurice Wilkes had been working at the newly established 'mathematical laboratory' at Cambridge University intended to offer a calculating service to academics and researchers. Its many toys included a differential analyzer, like the one in the basement of the Moore School, and a number of mechanical calculating machines. As soon as war broke out, Wilkes was moved to the British radar research center known as the Telecommunications Research Establishment in Malvern where he remained until he could return to Cambridge in 1945. He made his way back to the mathematical laboratory, this time as director, to try and regenerate what momentum had built up before the outbreak of hostilities.

Whilst Wilkes would be very familiar with the state of the art of radar research he would have had no knowledge of the top secret electronics work undertaken at Bletchley Park or, more specifically, Colossus. From what he heard from the US, the age of the digital computer was approaching and it was high time that the Cambridge Mathematical

Laboratory got involved. This was not just to jump on the bandwagon but because it clearly offered a far superior way of performing the kind of advanced calculations that the lab was supposed to perform for the rest of the university.

In May 1946 whist a visiting academic was staying at the nearby St John's College he had access to a copy of von Neumann's EDVAC report but only for a single evening. Given that photocopiers were not available at the time, he sat up late into the night pouring over the document. The logic and conclusions of the report were beyond question and in his memoirs he would recall:

> I recognized this at once as the real thing, and from that time on I never had any doubt as to the way computer development would go.

In the following weeks, he received a telegram from the Dean of the Moore School inviting him to the summer school on electronic computers. There was no time to go through the formal procedure for approving transatlantic business travel and so he decided to pay his own way and hope that he would get his money back later. To further complicate matters, shipping was closely managed in the aftermath of the war and he had to apply to the University Grants Committee for permission to sail to the USA. It took some time for this to be forthcoming and in the end the best the bureaucrats could do was to offer him a sailing at the beginning of August, several weeks after the start of the course. A few weeks of attendance would be better than none at all and so Wilkes reluctantly agreed.

He set sail on the Drakensberg Castle on the 2nd of August. The ship, an elderly cargo vessel, would only normally carry 12 passengers but given the economic situation was carrying 35 on this trip. Wilkes had to share a cabin, intended for single occupancy, with two fellow passengers. The discomfort was however balanced by the excellent food that was available: the ship was not subject to food rationing that still cast a shadow over life ashore. The ship experienced boiler trouble and spent a full day adrift in the middle of the Atlantic Ocean and, to add insult to injury, was diverted without warning or explanation from its original destination of Philadelphia to New York. Wilkes finally arriving at Philadelphia on the 18th August 1946 with only 2 weeks of the summer school left to run.

As far as the design of the new EDSAC went, he didn't miss much because there was not too much to miss. With the disintegration of the ENIAC's team, the design hadn't progressed much beyond a number of paper exercises. His attendance was useful nonetheless because the afternoon seminars allowed him to meet with the leading figures of the day in computing and discuss the merits of the various new ideas. Before his return passage he visited Howard Aiken at Harvard to view the work on his new and improved relay computer and also to MIT to see the construction of a new and improved differential analyzer. Compared to the devices discussed at the Moore School, these were relics of a bygone era. He set off home with his original hunch confirmed: the stored program digital computer was the way to go.

Wilkes took the approach that he wanted to build a working computer quickly rather than build the best possible computer eventually. He was not interested in expanding the limits of computer technology. He just wanted the equations that researchers submitted solved quickly and accurately. The main technical challenge for all the groups attempting to build computers at the time was that of how to store numbers and programs. Wilkes chose the most ponderous and unwieldy of the alternative solutions simply because he had access to the know-how to construct it, not because it was best. His computer was to use something called 'acoustic delay line' storage. These were slow to operate and used vats of liquid mercury which are never very convenient to construct or maintain. They had been studied extensively for use with radar on both sides of the Atlantic during the war and it so happened that one of the UK's experts on the topic had since, like Wilkes, moved to Cambridge. A working delay line was in action within 6 months of his return from Philadelphia.

Wilkes was also able to move forward quickly because he, as director, was in a position to divert the research funds of the maths lab to the new computer project. There was no need to fish for funding. It did however mean that funds were tight. A situation that was alleviated to an extent by an unexpected contributor:

I was rung up one day by a genial benefactor in the Ministry of Supply who said that he had been charged with the disposal of surplus stocks, and what could he do for me. The result was that with the exception of a few special types we received a free gift of enough [vacuum] tubes to last the life of the machine.

The complete computer would run its first serious program on 6th May 1949 and in the days following become the first stored-program electronic computer to perform useful work.

1940s Philadelphia

After being ejected from the Moore School when they would not give up their patent rights, the ENIAC pioneers Mauchly and Eckert looked for opportunities elsewhere. There were tentative talks about joining von Neumann and Goldstine at the Institute of Advanced Studies to help build their new EDVAC-like computer. There were talks about them joining a fledgling company called ERA in St Paul (which we will shortly hear more about). IBM even suggested setting up a research lab for computers under their direction. None of the deals got very far. All the groups were interested in the engineering powerhouse of Eckert and had little time for the lotus-eating Mauchly. At IBM, Watson was even heard to say:

> This guy Mauchly wears these loud socks. I wouldn't want him in my business anyway.

Eckert himself had far more respect for his long-time collaborator and declined all their advances, setting off instead with Mauchly on an adventure of their own.

They formed a company, originally called 'Electronic Control Company' but quickly renamed to 'Eckert-Mauchly Computer Corporation'. Their aim was to commercially exploit the concepts that had been developed during their time at the Moore School and, in particular, attempt to build an EDVAC-like computer for sale to paying customers. From the very early days, the idea was to sell the machines not only to the traditional customers of these devices such as spies and academics but also to ordinary businesses. Mauchly, in particular, had spent a considerable amount of time thinking about possible applications of computers to the likes of banks and insurance businesses that made heavy use of punched card installations. He decided that the original EDVAC design would need to be adapted to make it more suitable. The general purpose business computer would be called the UNIVAC (UNIVersal Automatic Calculator).

The primary difference between the scientific and business applications was that the former did very complicated things to a small amount of data whilst the latter did very simple things to a large amount of data. The ability to read and output large amounts of information was therefore crucial for the business market. Unfortunately, as no non-electronic device of the era could even approach the speed of the new computers, there were no suitable input or output devices available on the market to buy. EMCC would have to build their own input and output equipment. High on its list of priorities was the creation of machines that could read information from magnetic tape rather than punched cards and a printer that could print fast enough so that it would not get in the way of the central processor.

Funding was sought from any possible source to get the work under way. Unfortunately, the concept of venture capital did not yet exist and the government military funding that kick-started many other computing efforts was not forthcoming because of paranoia that Mauchly and a number of other employees were in some way a security risk. The US National Bureau of Standards was kind enough to give them a grant of $75,000 to develop various peripheral devices for their new computer but it wasn't until October 1947 that the first contract for a computer was received from the Northrop Aircraft Company.

This was for the BINAC (Binary Automatic Computer) a small device and the first of Eckert and Mauchly's to use binary arithmetic. It worked fitfully in testing and was finally shipped to Northrop, nearly 18 months late, in September 1949 where, according to many reports, it was never seen to work again. The blame was placed on careless transportation. The project was notable for two reasons: firstly it is said to be the first stored-program computer to work in North America (though only in testing) and secondly it was wildly unprofitable. The contract with Northrop was for a price of $100,000 but delivering it cost Eckert–Mauchly $278,000.

The combination of the focused, highly-talented engineer and the conceptual thinking physicist lead to a highly technically capable enterprise that was, to put it kindly, commercially naive. The most notable feature of the following 5 years was the sizable gulf between the price customers paid for work and the cost to EMCC of actually performing it. Eckert and Mauchly hoped to recoup their early losses from the profits that would arrive when their computers were sold in volume. Unfortunately, the application of this strategy always had the edge of blind desperation: poor cost control continued unchecked for years. Between 1947 and 1950, EMCC picked up a number of orders to deliver computers to the Census Bureau, Air Force & Army Map service, but true to form, they spent far more on attempting to deliver the contracts than they were ever going to earn from them.

In 1948, during one of their periodic lows, a vice president of the American Totaliser Board called Harry Strauss took an interest in EMCC. His organization made the machines that were used to look after on-course betting for horse races and Strauss could see not only the general uses of a computer but also a potential application to the Totaliser Board's business. $500,000 was injected in return for 40% of the company's stock. Unfortunately Strauss was killed in a plane crash in October 1949 and no more money was forthcoming. By the end of 1949, The Eckert-Mauchly Computer Corporation was short of cash and in a perilous state.

1940s Minnesota

Whilst the end of the war indirectly triggered Eckert and Mauchly's departure from the Moore School, it caused many others to think about their future. Two officers in the US Navy's code-breaking office in Washington, Howard Engstrom and William Norris, didn't know what lay in store for them. One thing they did know was that they didn't want to spend peacetime in a government research lab. Their boss, Captain Joseph Wegner, who had been responsible for the building of the high-speed Enigma bombes for the US Navy a few years previously, was becoming uncomfortable that the considerable expertise that had been built during the war would be lost. Wegner urged Engstrom and Norris to form their own private company that could then sell their skills back to the US Navy. Like Eckert and Mauchly, they had many unsuccessful encounters with investors before a match was found after a big shove from the Navy.

John Parker, a veteran investor who owned a factory in St Paul, Minnesota, had a problem. His factory made the wooden gliders used to silently transport troops behind enemy lines on operations such as the D-Day landings. Unless there was a remarkable surge in the peace time demand for engineless wooden aircraft, his St Paul factory would have to be closed. This would not only disrupt the lives of its workers but would be financially painful to himself. This troubled him. One of his contacts suggested that he might wish to have a talk to the Navy in Washington who could have an unspecified solution to his problem.

Parker turned up one day to discuss the mysterious opportunity with Navy 'Officials'. The first of these officials turned out to be Admiral Chester Nimitz, the former commander of the US Navy in the Pacific. Apparently the Navy wanted to keep a special group of people together and thought Parker could help. No one would be specific about what the new venture would do beyond 'research into electronics' but it was clear that the Navy was going to be the main customer and that the 'big guns' were being rolled out to get the project moving. Parker agreed to put half the capital into a new venture, 'Engineering Research Associates', to be based at the St Paul glider factory. This had the benefit that Parker's glider company could be used as a front for government contracts with ERA doing the real work at the same location. Making ERA jump through the hoops to become an approved government supplier would bring attention to what was intended to be a secret operation.

Like many of the military organizations that used technology at the time, the navy code-breaking outfit in Washington had sent one of their number to the Moore School lectures. That individual became convinced that the way forward was to create code-breaking devices that could, unlike the Bombes and Colossus, be freely reprogramed. By 1947, the US Navy code breakers, Engstrom and Norris's former employer, ordered its first general purpose computer from ERA, to become known as Atlas. The first Atlas was delivered to what had become the NSA (National Security Agency – the US equivalent of GCHQ) in December 1950 with a second in March 1953. The Atlas was the first computer operational in the US that could store its program internally – BINAC never became operational, the original ENIAC was hard wired and EDVAC was not yet complete.

Shortly before the first Atlas was delivered, a newspaper column highlighted the unusual relationship between the US Navy and ERA. Auditors were appointed and started to examine the ERA organization. There was also conflict between ERA and the US Government over Parker's expense account. He eschewed commercial airlines and commuted from Washington to St Paul in his own Cessna aircraft, charging the expenses back to the Navy as an overhead. He also held a number of parties to 'entertain' the Navy which were charged back. The

Navy pointed out that they had a long-standing relationship, had signed contracts and did not 'need entertaining'.

To expand the business to take advantage of the pioneering work on Atlas, as Norris wanted, Parker guessed that he would have to raise $5 to 10 million in capital. All this at a time when the relationship with the Government was becoming strained to say the least. Parker started to look around for alternatives.

Remington Rand

The Remington Company had far more sturdy roots than the young upstarts. It started out in the 19th century as a manufacturer of pistols and rifles but the end of the American Civil War meant there was a serious drop in demand for its products. To fill the gap, it started the manufacture of the newly patented typewriter with 'QWERTY' keyboard. Launched in 1874, the product initially flopped with less that 5,000 sold. Four years later, the decorative casing had gone and a shift key, to allow upper and lower case characters to be typed, had been added to leave the 'Remington No 2'. Within a decade, the product had taken off with, amongst others, Mark Twain being an early convert.

In the closing years of the 19th century, as the sales of the 'Remington No 2' were maturing, a former bank clerk from New York State, James Rand Sr introduced his 'Visible Ledger' office stationary range to the public. Sales grew strongly for 10 years at which point James Rand Sr was joined in the family business by his recently graduated son James Rand Jr. As with many head-strong young executives, junior became frustrated. In his case, the company was not interested in following up his idea of supplying branded metal cabinets along with the Visible Ledger cards. He resigned, borrowed $10,000 and started a rival company, the 'American Kardex Company', which also grew rapidly. For 10 years, from 1915 to 1925, James Rand Sr faced off against his son James Rand Jr in what appears to be friendly competition, even adopting a similar range of products to those rejected a few years before. As Rand Sr approached retirement in 1925, and at the instigation of his mother, Rand Jr agreed to merge the two family firms into the Rand Kardex Company.

It wasn't long before another merger was, so to speak, 'on the cards'. In 1927, the Powers Accounting Machine Company, the rival to Hollerith's punched card machines that was created out of the work done for the 1910 census, and the Remington Typewriter Company merged with Rand Kardex to form the 'Remington Rand Corp'. This allowed each company's products to be marketed to the customers of the other.

By the end of the 1940s, James Rand Jnr, by then chairman of Remington Rand, could see that computing had at least the potential to take over the office functions performed by his punched card tabulators. To get into the market, he could create a computer operation from scratch or he could take over another company already in existence. A small but struggling computer company which appeared to have some good ideas but also poor commercial execution, the Eckert-Mauchly Computer Corporation, would be a good place to start. In February 1950, Remington Rand bought the EMCC. The founders and staff received a total of $100,000 whilst the American Totaliser Board, whose remaining executives brokered the deal, received most of their original $500,000 back. An unfair deal but it was the only one available to the struggling computer company.

EMCC was focused on commercial computing: using electronic devices to perform business tasks. At the time, the main focus in the computing field, and the largest number of juicy contracts, was in the defense arena. In order to push further into this market, James Rand Jr approached Parker, the man who put the original cash into Engineering Research Associates, suggesting that Remington Rand purchase the company to add to their growing technology stable. Looking at the major funding needed to expand the ERA business, the growing gulf with the government, and the potential appreciation of his investment (his shares had risen from an initial $0.10 to the offered price of $8.00 in under 6 years), Parker sold out.

Once under the Remington Rand umbrella, Eckert-Mauchly and ERA continued to focus on their respective markets in almost complete isolation. Remington Rand's management managed to prevail upon two of UNIVAC's commercial customers, the Prudential and AC Nielsen, to abandon their optimistically priced contracts. This, and additional funding from the parent company, allowed the first UNIVAC to be 'delivered' to the Census Bureau in 1951. Delivered in a contractual sense but not physical. The actual computer remained in the UNIVAC factory to avoid the disruption and possible delay in getting the device working at the Census Bureau. It's interesting to note that the first major use of an electronic computer was by the same institution that had been the first to use the punched card tabulator.

After a shaky start, the Eckert-Mauchly group started to deliver UNIVACs to customers at the rate of one every 2 weeks. By 1956, about 46 UNIVAC Is had been delivered. This was around the same number of computers as had been created in the whole world outside the United States. The era of commercial computing was truly off and running.

Whilst Eckert-Maunchly, driven by the technically adventurous and perfectionist Eckert, made spectacular and consistent losses, ERA, driven by the technical competent but hands off Norris, was quietly and consistently profitable. During the implementation of the Atlas series for the NSA, ERA decided to prepare a range of computers for sale to defense organizations based on the Atlas design. A design for the UNIVAC 1101 was prepared (by 1954, all Remington Rand's computers were designated UNIVACs) but no customers could be found. Approval was sought from the Remington Rand management to market the UNIVAC 1103 as a rival to IBM's newly announced 701. After years of battling IBM's punched card machines and often being seen as the inferior, James Rand saw this as his opportunity to get even. The go-ahead was given for battle to commence.

IBM

In the post war years, all office equipment companies had the same task: to update their products to take advantage of war-related technology before their competitors did. It was important however not to frighten the horses. All this had to be done at the same time as maintaining a profitable business. IBM unsurprisingly chose to focus on updating its venerable and profitable punched card machines into the age of electronics. Creating a whole new class of electronic business machines would have to wait. In the late 1940s, it did put in train two low priority projects: the magnetic drum calculator and the tape processing machine.

The tape processing machine, as the name implies, would use magnetic tape as input rather than the bulky and clumsy punched cards. The TPM would be suitable for large-scale data processing centers and offer high performance with concomitant high cost. It was targeted squarely at the same market as the UNIVAC.

The magnetic drum calculator, also as the name implies, would use a magnetic drum to store data. Magnetic drums were cheap but slow which made them unsuitable for the largest of enterprises. The MDC would thus offer relatively cheap and cheerful computing to the mid market. Something that no UNIVAC product would do for some years.

By 1950, with the onset of the Korean War, Watson decided to focus on high-performance computers for the defense market. He saw this more as an act of patriotism than commercial instinct. With only a limited amount of development funding available, work on both the TPM and MDC was halted. A new high performance computer, to become known as the IBM 701 'defense calculator', would be developed and would become a successful product in its narrowly defined scientific and military market.

IBMs complacency that punched cards would remain the way forward for business was shaken not long after the decision was taken to focus on the 701. Watson's son, Thomas Watson Jr, who by this time had risen to a senior executive role in IBM, claimed it was the announcement of the sale of a UNIVAC to the Census Bureau that triggered his conviction that before long business would be starting to talk about getting one of these 'UNIVACs'. (At the time the brand was a generic term for computer just like 'Hoover' remains a generic term for vacuum cleaner.) If no action was taken, all IBM could do was attempt to sell the inappropriate defense calculator. This was not good enough. Inside IBM the feeling was that if they had not already missed the boat they were about to do so. Hastily the TPM and MDC were resurrected and polished up. Customers would be offered the high performance 702 (a renamed TPM) or the more basic but far cheaper 650 (the renamed MDC).

Many commentators say the design of the first IBM machines were not as elegant as that of the UNIVAC, that the powerful central processor could perform more work than it could either read in or write out. That is to say it could 'chew far more than it could bite off'. The IBM machines were however more 'solid' and built in a more business friendly way. For example, they were designed in modules that would fit through normal doors. Sadly, the same could not be said of UNIVACs.

IBM had hundreds of development engineers skilled in the workings of electro-mechanical punched card equipment. This paid off in unexpected ways. Whilst the CPU was the realm of electronics engineers, input and output devices, which proved to be the limiting factor in early computer installations, still had a heavy mechanical bias. The tape machines and printers that IBM could put together quickly were a class apart from those created by the small electronics-lead UNIVAC team.

The reliability of the overall IBM system was thus higher than the best UNIVAC could deliver.

In mid 1955, UNIVAC was still leading the sales race with 30 UNIVACs to 24 large IBM machines but just 1 year later, IBM had shot past with 66 installations to 46 UNIVACs and with three times as many IBM machines on order.

The factors that lead to IBM dominance in punched cards were leading to the same result in the nascent computer industry. Solid but unspectacular engineering meant IBM products would not frighten the customers. Ruthlessly organized and executed salesmanship would drive home the benefits of IBM kit whilst leaving all the drawbacks obscured. No potential sale was left unclosed.

Nor was any public relations opportunity left unseized. The old semi-mechanical SSEC, created in a fit of pique after Aiken upset Watson at the Harvard Mark I inauguration, was replaced in the window of the New York Office with a 701 and the press invited to come and have a look. IBM also made sure that in 1956 it was an IBM 701 that was used to predict the results during the television coverage of the Presidential election.

The US public's introduction to computers had been on election night 4 years previously in 1952. To IBM's chagrin, the computer had been a UNIVAC. During the TV coverage, the UNIVAC used the first available sets of results to predict that there would be a Eisenhower landslide. Unfortunately, the exit polls indicated that the election 'was too close to call'. Those operating the computer feared that their program had made a huge blunder and so adjusted it to produce output that was acceptably vague. As the night wore on it became clear that Eisenhower had indeed won by a landslide and the UNIVAC staff sheepishly went on air to own up to their panic adjustments. It turned into a propaganda coup for UNIVAC that Watson made sure would not be repeated in 1956.

The story was different at Remington Rand. Like IBM, historically they had a large sales force for punched card equipment. Unlike IBM they were not told to start selling computers and continued to push punched card equipment often in competition with their own computer salesmen. There was not even one group of computer salesmen; the old Eckert-Mauchly band in Philadelphia and the former ERA group in Mineapolis continued to operate more or less independently and some might say counter-productively.

Whilst in many cases the UNIVAC products of the early 1950s were technically superior to IBMs, the people occupying the key positions at customer organizations often did not know the difference between a good and a bad computer: they just bought from the company that could generate the greatest 'warm feeling'. Remington Rand told them to either upgrade their punched card set-up or buy a computer and then left them to sink or swim on their own. IBM told them to lease a computer, finance included, and then offered software, training and technical support services.

In 1955, Remington Rand merged with Sperry Gyroscope to form Sperry Rand. The two competing computer divisions, the old EMCC and ERA, were merged in what by all accounts was a very clumsy manner. One of the original ERA founders from code-breaking days, William Norris, left. He was later to suggest that the company had descended into a maelstrom of "confusion, indecision, conflict of orders, organization line breaches, constant organizational change, fighting and unbridled competition between divisions". This was not a recipe for success.

Norris started another computer company 'Control Data Corporation', more commonly known as CDC, and over the following months a number of the old ERA staff joined him, including one young and promising designer called Seymour Cray. Like ERA they focused on the military and scientific market, and specifically on large computers intended for demanding mathematics.

By the end of the 1950s, the computer industry had formed itself into what had become known as 'Snow White and the seven dwarfs'. Snow White was, of course, IBM with the vast majority of all computer sales with seven smaller competitors, Sperry Rand (with its UNIVAC brand), Burroughs, NCR, RCA, Honeywell, GE and CDC, picking up customers where they could. The smaller competitors tended to concentrate on a small number of industries where they could focus their efforts rather than expose themselves to the all-encompassing marketing might of IBM.

The computer interests of RCA, Honeywell and GE were small parts of huge industrial groups each with, at the time, revenues far greater than IBM's. They did not, however, have the background that the office-machines companies had in selling to business managers and would soon abandon the computer market as unprofitable.

Technologies

After the Moore School lectures in 1946, virtually all the teams building computers chose the same 'Von Neuman' approach and were faced with a common set of problems. They needed to find viable technologies that allowed them to perform the core functions of a computer (memory, processor, input/output and storage) with adequate reliability and at reasonable cost.

Memory

The stored-program concept of the von Neumann approach gave rise to a need for a relatively large memory. In the likes of the ENIAC and Colossus, the program was wired into the machine. All the memory had to hold was a few numbers that were required during calculation. The memory of a programable computer would have to be developed to hold both data and program and be able to retrieve its values reliably and, even more importantly, quickly.

By 1950, three mechanisms had been developed. The cheapest and slowest was the magnetic drum. This consisted of a spinning drum with a magnetic coating. A read/write head could be moved up and down the drum as it spun reading and storing values. The problem was that if you were picky and wanted to read a specific value, you would have to wait while the read/write head moved to the correct part of the drum and then for the drum to spin round to the correct spot. Whilst this was going on the rest of the computer would be at a standstill. This was not a problem when the rest of the computer was cheap and cheerful as well. Drum storage was used in the low performance, low price computers such as the IBM 650 and the early ERA Atlas which typically ran 100 times slower than their bigger cousins.

In the late 1940s and early 1950s, high performance computers tended to use a mercury delay line as a store. This, as the name implies, was a tube of mercury. An electrical pulse would be converted to a shock-wave at one end of the tube and, if the mercury was kept at the same temperature and pressure, would flow through the liquid metal at a certain, constant speed. When the signal reached the far end of the tube, it would be converted back into an electrical pulse and routed back to the start of the tube via an external electrical circuit. Once back at the start of the tube it would start its journey again, constantly looping until intentionally changed or the power was switched off. Whilst this shock-wave was making its journey through the mercury, more pulses could be converted into waves to travel behind the original. In all it was normal to have up to 1000 pulses in flight at once, each looping through the tube hundreds of times a second without interfering with others.

The delay line was first developed as part of radar research during the war as a means of removing hills and stationary obstacles from radar displays. Each sweep of the rotating radar produced a signal that could be held in the mercury lines until the next pass and then compared. Any object that was found in the same place in both the stored and the fresh radar signature could be removed as uninterestingly stationary. This was how hills and trees were removed from radar signals. Computer groups that could call on wartime radar expertise, like the Cambridge EDSAC team, had a head start in developing delay lines for use with their computers. Eckert had also been working on them at the Moore School before being diverted to work on the ENIAC.

An alternative means of storing radar signals had been the cathode ray tube (CRT), more commonly recognized as the traditional fat TV screen or computer monitor. It was a former radar engineer, Freddy Williams, that took the design further and succeeded in getting it working as a storage device for computers. Williams had spent the war at the same TRE radar research center that Wilkes, the prime driver behind the Cambridge EDSAC, had worked at. He moved to Manchester University at the end of 1946 and along with another former TRE worker Tom Kilburn developed the 'Williams–Kilburn tube'.

Physically, the original Williams–Kilburn tube was a non-specialist, commercially available CRT. In order to update a memory location, which was stored on the surface of the CRT, all that was required was to direct the CRT electron beam to that location. This could be done in a flash, much quicker than the drum and mercury line options.

The drawback was it was flaky: very flaky. Even some years after the original demonstration, when installed in a commercial product, it had reliability problems. At the public inauguration of one manufacturer's machine, the tube was sent haywire by reporters' cameras. The old-style camera flashguns were inducing false readings and confusing the machine.

One demonstration of the Williams Tube did however mark the beginning of the modern computer age. By the end of 1947, Williams and his assistants had demonstrated that their CRT device could store values for a number of hours. They still needed to show that it could be used as the memory store for a real computer. The only drawback was that there was no stored-program computer in existence. A member of the Manchester University faculty had attended the Moore School lectures and was happy to take them through the principles of such a machine. They created a small computer that would read its program and data from the Williams tube and write an answer back. After many weeks of trials, on 21st June 1948, the machine finally settled on the correct answer. It was the first computer to execute an internally stored program. It has to be said though that the Manchester 'Baby', as it became known, was not a practical computer and was little more than a test rig. It had no acceptable means of accepting input or displaying output. The values on the Williams tube were entered in binary by flicking switches for each individual digit and there was no output device other than reading patterns of blobs from the surface of the Williams–Kilburn tubes.

The Williams–Kilburn tubes went on to form the memory for a full-sized machine at Manchester which was taken by the electronics company Ferranti as the basis for their first range of computers. It would also be licensed by IBM for use in their first electronic stored program offering, the 701 defense calculator.

Core Memory

Certain demanding applications could not use any of these techniques. The prime examples of these were real-time systems. Real-time systems have to respond to events as they happen, 'in real time'. Probably one of the most pressing examples of a real-time system in the 1940s was the creation of flight simulators. Basic simulators had been used during World War II to train pilots without the expense or danger of leaving the ground. By today's standard they were however rather rudimentary. They included an array of cockpit instruments and the simulator assembly, where the trainees sat, which could pitch and wallow to a limited extent. It was however all that was necessary to give rookie pilots their first taste of flight. All this was managed by something similar to an analog computer but each type of aircraft required a brand new simulator to mimic its dynamics. In 1943, a project was kicked off at MIT to create a more flexible universal aircraft trainer.

Things moved slowly at first with plans based on a set-up similar to the traditional simulator but with an expanded analog computer. It became apparent that an analog computer would be too slow to cope with the calculations required to handle mimicking the flight of any type of aircraft. Focus switched to the use of the then emerging technology of the digital computer. This had its own problems. Using delay lines for memory would make the computer too slow to keep up with physical systems. Drum storage would make it far too slow. Williams tubes were the only technology fast enough but tests showed that they were too unreliable to be of use.

Jay Forrester, the leader of the MIT-based research group, known by this stage as Project Whirlwind, had spotted an advert for a nickel/iron alloy with interesting magnetic properties called Deltamax. He and his assistants set about investigating it as a means of storing information. Activity progressed slowly with significant distractions caused by long running budget problems. It took nearly 2 years to get even a prototype working. Complaints about profligacy and over spending were not surprising. The total budget for the analog trainer had started out at $200,000. By the end of the 1940s, this amount was being burnt every 6 to 8 weeks.

In the end, the Whirlwind team chose to form the Deltamax into tiny donut shaped 'cores'. Each tiny donut would have two wires threaded through its center. When a current was passed through one wire not much would happen, the Deltamax would remain in the same state as it had been. When current was passed through both wires simultaneously, the magnetic polarity of the core would flip from north to south, or vice versa. Because of Deltamax's special property of magnetic hysteresis, it would then remain in this state even when the current was switched off. By applying currents in the correct direction, it was possible to flip the magnetic core at will, thus storing one 'bit' of information.

You could arrange a large square grid of cores with one set of wires running horizontally and the second set of wires running vertically. By applying a current to one horizontal and one vertical wire you would affect the polarity of a single core and thus set the value of one 'bit' of information. As a change in state could only be obtained by two wires operating simultaneously, none of the other cores in the grid would be affected.

By 1953 Project Whirlwind, which had long since dropped the requirements to link to an aircraft trainer, equipped its computer with core memory. A single bit of information could be accessed in 9 microseconds making it by far the fastest computer in the world. It was also more reliable than anything using mercury delay lines or Williams-Kilburn tubes. By the late 1950s, few new computers would use anything other than magnetic core memory. Magnetic drums, tubes of mercury and Williams–Kilburn tubes faded into history.

I/O: punched cards, magnetic tape, printer

It should be noted that at this time whilst computers could be said to 'think' it would be stretching the truth to say they could communicate. To pass the computer information, be it the program or the data the program would work on, would probably require the use of punched cards. As today a keyboard would be utilized but this would be part of the card punch used in preparing the punched cards. This activity, which had existed in Hollerith's days, could be performed physically separated from the machine and would not tie up its precious machine cycles.

Once computers started to work at electronic speeds however punched card input was too slow for anything larger than a program. The time that a punched card reader took to shuffle the cards about was time that the expensive central processing unit of the computer sat idle. It was in the late 1940s that UNIVAC, followed by IBM, started to look at using magnetic tape to hold the information that would be manipulated by the program. The only commercially available recording tape at the time was used in recording studios and turned out to be far from suitable. The tape drives couldn't start and stop fast enough and the plastic-based tape itself would stretch and fracture under the intense stresses. A lot of time and effort, which in the early days UNIVAC could ill afford, was expended on coming up with a working industrial tape drive with metal based tape. Whilst it was possible to enter data directly onto tape it would remain likely that data would be punched onto cards first and then written to magnetic tape using a specially built machine.

After the computer had finished munching on the data it had been given, it would want to let the outside world know of its conclusions. Just as punched card input was too slow to keep an electronic device busy, using punched cards to hold output would create a log jam where the computer would have more to say than could be recorded. Output from a computer would thus also require magnetic tape. Of course whilst the computer was happy writing to the magnetic tape, it wasn't the most suitable medium for human beings. In the early days there was a technique where a powder similar to iron fillings could be sprinkled onto the tape which would arrange itself to highlight the arrangement of the magnetic material beneath. A human armed with a magnifying glass could then read the binary pattern arranged on the tape. Normal computer users would be less than happy with this arrangement and took advantage of machines that took data from magnetic tapes and printed it onto paper.

In the early days, computer printers were little more than adapted typewriters and telex machines. These had the advantage that they would produce human friendly output but had the drawback of being slow and unreliable when subjected to hard work. By the mid 1950s, the next generation of high speed printers was available. These used chains with raised letters that could be spun round at high speed to select the relevant letter. A hammer would impact the chosen letter onto the printing surface. Printers were soon available that would print two or more lines simultaneously. The racket created by such a device in full flight meant that it had to be kept in its own soundproofed box. Whilst the technology behind the modern laser printer, that of the office photocopier, had been proposed in the late 1930s, it wasn't until the 1980s that it would be a viable proposition for use with mainstream computers.

Visual display units at this stage were still science fiction. Driving a VDU on its own would require more memory than each computer had access to. It wasn't until the 1970s that they became commonplace. Throughout the 1950s there was no way for humans to interact directly with computers. Not even teleprinter terminals. In the end, all information created by the computer would have to be printed out onto paper either directly or more likely via tape or punched cards.

Vacuum Tubes

Since the Harvard Mark I had been comprehensively shown up as a slow coach by the Moore School ENIAC, electro-magnetic relays pretty much disappeared as a means of implementing logic and arithmetic circuitry in the central processing unit. By the 1950s, vacuum tubes were the order of the day and universally applied to all significant computer designs.

Valves were a distant relative of the common-or-garden electric light bulb. Just as in a light bulb, a filament would be heated by passing an electric current through it. This would release a cloud of electrons into a surrounding vacuum that had been created during manufacture – hence the term vacuum tubes. The electrons could then be induced to flow in the appropriate direction by applying voltages to a nearby 'grid'.

The benefit of the tube over the relay was clear. It was fast. In a tube, to switch from 'on' to 'off' required no more than applying a voltage to the grid. In a relay this required energizing electro-magnets and waiting for a contact to swing from one position to another.

The drawback of the valve was that it was unreliable. Problems centered around the filament which would either crack when repeatedly switched on and off (just like a light bulb) or would lose its ability to release electrons over time as various chemical processes changed its composition. The latter issue was eventually confronted by the manufacture of special 'computer vacuum tubes' with extended life.

Transistor

So the vacuum tube was unreliable, it required a lot of energy to run, it gave off a lot of heat and took up a lot of space. The ENIAC with its 18,000 tubes, gave off 150 kW of heat. That's the equivalent of 150 one-bar electric fires. Fortunately, even before any stored-program computer had run its first program a solution was starting to form at the Bell Laboratory, part of AT&T, in New York state.

At first very few people would understand the possibilities offered by the crude laboratory lash-up on display. It included, amongst other things, a solid piece of the element germanium, some gold foil and a bent paper clip. It was a few days before Christmas 1947 and a handful of relevant managers had been assembled shortly after lunch one Tuesday to view the new device.

The semi-conductor physics team at Bell Labs had tested a large number of devices over the years and these had unfortunately provided an equally large number of failures. The managers would have been hopeful but not optimistic that this item would justify the faith, not to say cash that had been spent, on semiconductor physics over the last decade. This device, to become known as the 'point contact' transistor, was the latest wheeze of the theoretical physicist John Bardeem and the more practically minded, more hands-on, Walter Brattain. Both men worked within the team of one William Shockley, one of the managers who had gathered to watch.

The aim of the demonstration was to show that the new transistor could amplify signals just like the old vacuum tube. Because it was made from semiconductor, there would be no need to carefully create a vacuum in a glass shell like there was in a vacuum tube. Nor would there be a need for the bulky glass shell itself. There would be no need to heat up an element to prepare the device for operation. In short, if the set-up amplified signals, the hot, bulky and unreliable vacuum tube could be replaced by a tiny piece of semi-conductor.

After a short explanation the power was activated and the oscilloscope trace jumped. It could be seen that whilst one voltage was being put into the apparatus, a far greater voltage was coming out. Clearly the device was acting as an amplifier and boosting the signal. As a final demonstration Brattain spoke into a microphone whilst the managers listened, with mild shock, through headphones to his amplified voice. The demo was a clear success. It was a momentous day for Bell Labs. The parent company AT&T used vast quantities of vacuum tubes for boosting phone signals. A reliable semi-conductor amplifier would save time and cost and produce a more reliable service for customers. It was a success worth savoring.

Bardeem and Brattain would indeed savor the success. Shockley, supposedly the more senior member of staff, was on the other hand somewhat frustrated, or to be less polite, somewhat bitter. He had not personally been involved in the research that lead to the discovery. He believed however that some months before he had proposed the underlying principle, known as the field effect, that was used by Bardeem and Brattain in their work. Shockley proposed patenting the device as invented by himself. Unfortunately for him, the Bell Labs patent department chose to see it differently. When the patent department did a search of previous work on the topic it discovered a patent from 1927 that outlined something very similar to his field effect. The concept was not new and any patent based on it would be open to challenge. The patent department chose to create a patent with only Bardeen and Brattain's names on it. Their work was new and could be defended in court.

Shockley was sent into a frenzied solo search for an improved device so that he could show Bardeem and Brattain who was boss. Sure enough, a little over a month later he presented the 'junction transistor'. Physically it was a much simpler device – it required only one piece of semi-conductor and no paper clips – but one that was unfortunately much harder to demonstrate. It was nearly 2 years before Bell Labs could fabricate a working example and years after that before a process to manufacture the device in significant quantities could be developed.

There followed a battle of wits with the mild mannered Bardeem and Brattain being harangued by their boss, Shockley, at regular intervals. By 1951, Brattain had had enough and moved to the University of Illinois whilst Bardeem arranged to be allocated to other work within Bell Labs.

All three members of the team received the Nobel Prize for Physics in 1956. Shockley's belief that he was the most brilliant of the three took a blow in 1972 when Bardeem was awarded a second Nobel Prize for is work at Illinois on superconductivity – the only physicist ever to have received the honor twice.

Shockley's abrasive manner and poor team management skills meant that he would be best sticking to solo research. This was not Shockley's point of view. Before picking up his Nobel Prize, he had quit Bell Labs in disgust because he had not been promoted into management. He obtained funding from the Beckman Instruments company and set up the Shockley Semiconductor Laboratory. He hired a number of promising young physicists and started looking into developing silicon based semiconductors which would have a number of advantages over the germanium devices developed up to this point.

With Shockley's dubious interpersonal skills, it was not long before things got a bit bumpy. When anything went wrong, as happens daily in an experimental environment, Shockley declared that there had been sabotage and assigned blame to an individual. Before long that individual would be banned from working on that area of research. Results were checked with those people at Bell Labs still communicating with him in case his staff were attempting to dupe him. Matters reached a head when he decided the entire staff would have a lie detector test to determine who was to blame for a secretary cutting her finger on an exposed tack. A number of the researchers decided enough was enough and approached the boss of Beckman Instruments to demand that Shockley be removed from management. They would only accept working with him as a technical consultant. The putsch failed and eight workers, labeled 'the traitorous eight' by Shockley, left.

Unsurprisingly, Shockley's venture failed to make any significant breakthroughs and faded into obscurity. The man himself abandoned ship in 1963 and took up an appointment at Stanford University where he, bizarrely and unfortunately, turned his attention to questions of race and genetics. Using the results of crude IQ tests administered by the US Army he decided that African Americans were fundamentally less intelligent than Caucasians. Using his own brand of logic he suggested that certain individuals with IQs below 100 should be paid to be sterilized so that the human race would not enter evolutionary regression. When the Atlanta Constitution accused him of pressing for the return of Nazi Eugenics, he sued for libel claiming $1.25 million in damages. The jury awarded him $1.

Given his extreme views and his interest in genetics, it's not surprising that Shockley was also one of only three Nobel Laureates who donated to the infamous 'Nobel Sperm Bank' (more formally Robert Graham's 'Repository for Germinal Choice'), and the only one to make the fact public. The secretive outfit shut its doors in 1999 and destroyed all its stocks. One of the few facts made public was that no children had been conceived from the 'Nobel' donations.

Whilst Shockley was winding up his young employees in what was to become Silicon Valley, Bell Labs continued to develop transistors for practical use. Bell Labs was however part of the regulated monopoly AT&T which, following 7 years of anti-trust litigation, agreed that it would stick to its core business of telephony. Information on the transistor was made available to other organizations that could make use of it at a minimal cost. Just like vacuum tubes and relays, transistors could be used as a kind of switch and it wasn't long before they were considered for logic circuits in computers. They started to be used in experimental machines in 1954, even before Shockley had left Bell Labs, but it wasn't until 1960 that transistors had made the transition to the switch of choice for new computers, finally displacing vacuum tubes.

55

The leap in performance and the reduction in size of the new breed of computers lead to them becoming known as the second generation. One oft mentioned improvement was the much reduced requirement for air conditioning. The air blowers used to shift the 150 kW worth of hot air created by the ENIAC themselves used 30 kW of power.

Integrated Circuit

Even before the transistor-based second-generation computers were being warmed up for the first time, the next great leap was emerging. As early as 1952, a paper published by G. W. Dummer of Britain's Radar Research Establishment (the new name for the TRE that Wilkes, Williams and Kilburn had worked at during the war) suggested placing more than one component on a single piece of semi-conductor. This would increase speeds and vastly reduce the size of the circuitry. Dummer attempted to fabricate such a device but after initial failures was not given resources to pursue his ideas.

The idea was well known by the late 1950s when a new recruit at Texas Instruments in Dallas, the first company to successfully manufacture a transistor from silicon, made an attempt to get such a device working. Jack Kilby had spent 10 years working for a company that made standardized circuit boards. In the years following the war, this was a very time-consuming process requiring a lot of manual soldering and manipulation of components. Due to the high manual component, it was also one prone to errors. Kilby thought that if many components could be placed on one piece of silicon it would greatly increase reliability, though in the early days with the drawback of considerable additional cost.

Kilby's initial approach was to create a single slab of germanium with several components on it. These would be connected together using normal, though very thin, gold wires soldered to contacts on the semi-conductor. He noted his idea in July 1958, in August he had created the circuit from separate semi-conductor components and in September, on a single crystal of germanium that measured 11 × 1.5 mm, the simple circuit with two transistors and 10 other components sprang into life.

Meanwhile, the 'traitorous eight' had found a backer to let them pursue their work without the manic interference of William Shockley. Fairchild Camera and Instrument, put up venture capital and a new subsidiary, the Fairchild Semiconductor Company, was created.

By early 1959, word had reached Fairchild that somebody in Texas Instruments had achieved something major in the field of miniaturizing circuitry. Fairchild's own special knowledge, which tended to focus more on how to make devices rather than on the devices themselves, could however go one better. Four months after Kilby's device worked for the first time, one of the original eight Shockley refugees, Robert Noyce, set out in his notebook an improved scheme. This would use the Fairchild developed 'planar technique' to create a circuit where not only the components would be on the semi-conductor crystal but also the connections. This would remove the need to solder wires under a microscope which made the Texas Instrument approach less than ideal from a practical standpoint.

Both inventors attempted to patent their approaches and by the 1960s, Fairchild and TI were suing each other for patent infringement. In a very wise move, no doubt discouraged by their lawyers, they agreed to cross-license the inventions and get on with exploiting the work rather than arguing over it.

The major impetus behind the acceptance of integrated circuits was the requirements of missile and spacecraft control systems. These had to be physically small and light and consume as little power as possible. Integrated circuits fitted the bill. Over a period of years, with development bankrolled by the military, the price of a single integrated circuit chip dropped from $1000 to around $25.

Mini Computers

At the same time that Noyce and fellow conspirators were setting up Fairchild Semiconductor in 1957, at the other side of the US, in Maynard, Massachusetts, another type of technology company was taking advantage of venture capital. Digital Equipment Corporation was, very bravely, going to build computers to compete with Snow White and the seven dwarfs.

DEC's first outing was the PDP-1 a mainframe-like transistor-based machine delivered in 1960. It was not a total failure but with only 50 sold, it was clearly not going to take them into the same league as IBM whose 1401 model was released in the same year and eventually sold over 12,000 machines. Even though the machine was not as powerful as an IBM mainframe, it was considerably cheaper, by a factor of 10. DEC did not have any specialist peripherals (printers/tape drives), software or after-sales service such as training. This kept the price down but also made it easy for the likes of IBM salesmen to scare away commercial customers.

The bare form of the DEC computer however was seen as an advantage by a select group of customers: those that wished to 'play' with it. Until an anti-trust agreement in 1956, IBM had refused to sell any equipment to customers, they would only lease items. Being leased meant that although the machines sat at customer premises, the customer was not permitted to adapt or update them in any way. Even after IBM deigned to sell hardware, the salesmen and support staff would make discouraging pained noises when customers suggested making their own adaptations.

DEC made a virtue of necessity and was happy for customers to update or extend their machines, indeed they did everything to encourage it. Detailed descriptions of how the computer worked and how it interfaced with the outside world were documented and openly published, unthinkable under the old regime. With so few PDP-1s installed, this did not make a great deal of difference. It was not until 1965, with the release of the PDP-8, that a whole new way of computing took hold.

Whilst even modern-day toasters have small single-chip computers inside them, in 1965 pretty much the only type of general computer was the mainframe. These sold for at least $200,000. If you could not use a mainframe because of the cost, you could develop specialist electronic circuits to perform the required task. These would be far cheaper but not very flexible. For example, a small manufacturing plant would have to use several small specially built electronic controllers. If that was too much work they could always manage the process manually. The PDP-8 changed that. The machine sold for $20,000 and could be linked to measuring devices and automation equipment to automate tasks where a specialist controller would be too complex or expensive.

The PDP-8 also started the trend for using one company's computer (DEC in this case) as part of a larger machine. They appeared in everything from medical scanners and laboratory controllers to agricultural machinery, which would then be sold on to customers without mention of the controlling computer. This became known as the OEM (original equipment manufacturer) market and helped DEC shift between thirty and forty thousand of the PDP-8 over its lifetime.

The PDP-8, and the other so-called mini computers that soon hit the market, also gave many people their first taste of interacting with a computer, particularly at universities. Previously the user would prepare a deck of punched cards. These would be sent into a data center and sooner or more often later, a printout emerged. The printout would make it clear that the request had not been completed and, if the user was lucky, it would deliver a few cryptic clues as to why. The mainframe was such an expensive beast that its work had to be highly regulated to ensure that it did not lie idle. The jobs to be performed had to be compressed together to ensure that the CPU was never at a loss for something to do. If a user was connected directly to the computer the time taken between keystrokes would be lost and costs would sky-rocket.

By the mid 1960s, the notion of 'time-sharing' on a mainframe had been born and was starting to filter out of the universities. With this, up to several hundred on-line users shared the resources of a single computer with the central machine giving its full attention to each user on request. The operation of time-sharing on a system, however, meant the computer couldn't be used for large-scale number crunching or data processing. Costs were also far from negligible with commercial time-sharing access costing around $10 an hour in the early 1970s. With a PDP-8, it was starting to become economic to allow a single user to monopolize a computer, albeit a far less powerful one.

System/360

With the dawn of the second-generation transistorized computers in the early 1960s, IBM was starting to sink into a morass of incompatible product lines. There were a number of product lines from the most popular basic '1401' to the large '7090' intended for scientific use and several one-off specialist machines such as the Stretch 'super-computer'. There was no saying if equipment built for one machine would work on another and in general it wouldn't. Most troublesome of all, programs written for one computer would generally not work on any other. This meant that if a customer's business expanded and ran up against the performance limits on their current machine, they couldn't buy and use a bigger one without the huge effort and cost of rewriting all the programs.

Within IBM, each of the product lines had their own design team and management who, at the drop of a hat, would heartily engage in battle to defend what they saw as the special features and benefits of their particular model. Resources would be fought over, favors would be called in, deals would be struck to disadvantage mutual competitors. Managing IBM had become a Byzantine exercise in conflict resolution. Any attempt at plotting a future strategy descended into childish bickering.

To get round the impasse, 13 senior managers from across the product ranges were exiled to basic but functional surroundings of a Connecticut motel for 2 months in late 1961. They were told to produce an agreed blueprint for the future of the company by the end of the year and not to come back until they had finished. The resulting document, issued on 28th December 1961, gave birth to what became known as the IBM System/360 and served as the basis for IBM's mainframe products for nearly 30 years.

System/360 was so named because it would encompass '360 degrees' of customer requirements. It would be sold to scientific and business customers alike. It would provide a range of computers, the fastest of which would perform 25 times faster than the slowest, and most importantly the programs written for one model would run on any other allowing customers to upgrade without a major upheaval. Peripherals, like tape drives and printers, would also work across the range.

The underlying ideas were not entirely new. The courage to attempt to overcome the formidable technical hurdles however was. It is now estimated that development of System/360, which first shipped to customers in 1966, cost $5 billion. It did not go smoothly.

In 1961, all new computers used transistors for logic but it was clear that the integrated circuits, where each semiconductor had more than one electronic component on it, were the way forward. System/360 was intended to be the first of the 'third-generation' computers that used integrated circuits to displace transistors. The technology however was immature and IBM ended up using what they called 'Solid Logic Technology', a half-inch think lump of ceramic with components and connections grafted on. It was a pale imitation of the integrated circuits that would soon be available in other computers. In truth, System/360 was more of a 'second-and-half' generation computer.

The biggest debacle of the development of the System/360 was the operating system software known as OS/360. As we will later hear, this stumbled into life late, vastly over-budget and with many holes.

The seven dwarfs reacted differently to these developments. RCA decided to deploy its leadership in electronics and within a year announced System/360 compatible computers that used true integrated circuits and thus had higher performance for the same cost. As a result they could also ride piggy back on IBM's development expenditure. Over time Honeywell, Burroughs and NCR created their own ranges of compatible computers but these would work neither with each other nor with the System/360. General Electric focused on time-sharing which was starting to gain popularity as the System/360 became available yet it was incapable of supporting. UNIVAC, as was becoming its habit, didn't do too much of note but quietly kept producing perfectly acceptable computers.

Supercomputers

CDC decided that it was not worth competing against IBM in the mid-market where it couldn't hope to match IBM's marketing might. CDC had been creating technically superior and cost-effective machines for normal users but had failed to dent IBM's market share. It decided to concentrate instead on one of the gaps in the 360 degree coverage of the System/360, at the top end of computing: the world of the super-computer. Demand for computing power at the heavy end of science and engineering was insatiable. Many of the tasks performed by these machines were somewhat elastic. Customers would buy the biggest computer they could find and then analyze a problem in as much detail as the machine would allow. As soon as a bigger computer became available they could then step up a level, increase the level of detail and produce more accurate results.

One example was weather forecasting. It is customary to simulate the world's climate by splitting the globe into small cells. Each cell has recent weather data loaded against it and then a simulation is run where the interactions of one cell against its neighbors are played out. Having cells 500 miles across with simulation steps every 6 hours would lead to very crude results. Having cells 25 miles across with simulation steps every 15 minutes would lead to far better results but would require vastly more computing power as there are vastly more calculations to be performed.

In the mid 1960s, mathematical problems of this type generally came together with unlimited funding only in the area of nuclear research and many of the most powerful computers of the era were destined for one or other of the atomic research labs in the US.

CDC brought out the model 6600 in 1964. It was designed by the former ERA employee and UNIVAC refugee Seymour Cray. It was up to three times faster than its nearest competitor and was ideal for pure number crunching. At the time, the limiting factor of computing was the speed of the logic circuitry. The computer's memory unit, still using magnetic cores, could send data far faster than the central processor could make use of it. Cray decided that to speed the overall machine up, it would be necessary to make full use of the memory. If the central processor couldn't fully utilize it then it should be given a helping hand. The helping hand took the form of 10 small computing units, essentially small computers themselves, that surrounded the main CPU. The main CPU would issue instructions to each of the 10 units and receive back the results of the work done. In effect there were now 10 mini-CPUs communicating with the memory. The performance of the overall system was startling. The CDC 6600 remained the fastest computer available for 5 years before it was superseded by its own replacement, the CDC 7600, also masterminded by Seymour Cray. Whilst only 50 of them were sold. they went to high profile customers and took with them a large amount of technical cachet.

Having sobriquets such as 'world's fastest computer' applied to someone else's machines was not acceptable to IBM who, almost in a fit of pique, announced a new model in the system/360 range. This was to be the most powerful System/360 yet and a match for the performance of the CDC 6600. Unfortunately for IBM, its raw computing power never went anywhere near that of the CDC 6600 and just over a year after the announcement it was withdrawn from sale. In the 12 months that IBM claimed to have a product, many potential customers for the CDC machine stood back and waited to see if the IBM machine was indeed faster than the CDC machine. This obviously hurt CDC's sales and was to become one of the best known examples in the IT industry of sowing 'FUD': fear, uncertainty, distrust.

William Norris, the chief exec of CDC, had become accustomed to IBM's sales tactics as long ago as the early 1950's while working for Remington Rand. He was the co-founder of ERA, the small start-up that came out of US Navy code breaking. At one point, he was attempting to sell Metropolitan Life, an insurer, its first computer system to replace punched card equipment. Remington Rand was selling the demonstrable UNIVAC, IBM was making claims about a 'paper computer' that had yet to be built. In the end, Metropolitan Life chose the UNIVAC but the episode taught Norris a lesson about the ability of misinformation to confuse and delay customers. CDC launched one of many anti-trust lawsuits against IBM in 1968 and in 1973 IBM settled, handing over its service bureau business to CDC as compensation.

Only 4 years after IBM started shipping the system/360 they announced a new series, the upgraded but technically similar system/370, which this time used true integrated circuits but could still run System/360 programs without amendment. By the mid 1970s, the commercial success of the System/360 and 370 meant IBM had grown to dominate the market to such an extent that the next generational shift in computing, the so-called 'future system' it was planning, had to be abandoned in 1975. This was partially because, after 5 years' development, it just didn't work very well but mainly because it would require too much pain for every customer to migrate to a brand new platform. IBM had become locked to its own highly successful but aging product.

Whilst incremental technological change has kept mainframe performance improving over the years, the basic design of the System/360 served as the basis for large mainframe computers well into the 1990s. It was just a matter of time however before mainframes were forced from center stage by a younger actor.

Microprocessor

In 1968, at the same time that CDC was launching its anti-trust suit against IBM, two of the original refugees from Shockley had grown weary of the increasingly bureaucratic nature of the company they had co-founded, Fairchild Semiconductor. Fairchild was founded on egalitarian principles. There would be no preferment for senior workers: no offices, no reserved parking spaces, no separate canteen for management. There was however the small matter of remuneration. As with all start-ups, the prime motivation is not basic pay, which is often no more than adequate, but the possible growth in share options. Robert Noyce and Gordon Moore, wanted to ensure staff were motivated by awarding them share options. All staff that is, not just the founders and senior staff. This was not the view of Fairchild Semiconductor's backers who rejected the scheme. Noyce and Moore decided to decamp to start up another new company where they would be free to do as they wished. And so Intel was born.

Unsurprisingly given that Noyce had co-invented them, Intel chose to make integrated circuits. In particular, Intel was to take advantage of the growing market for memory chips. The small magnetic donuts of core memory had finally had their day and were by this time just starting to be replaced by electronic chips that were far smaller and required less supporting circuitry. A promising sideline however that could earn some cash whilst the business grew was creating custom chips for use in the new hand-held calculator industry.

The year after it opened its doors, Intel was approached by Busicom a small Japanese manufacturer of calculators to design the chips for use in a new and relatively advanced scientific calculator which included a number of common mathematical functions. The Intel engineer assigned, one Ted Hoff, could have created a special chip which would perform the functions required by Busicom. This would have been the traditional way forward. He chose instead to design one that could be adapted later, on the fly, to perform any number of functions without a physical redesign. As development progressed, it became clear that this was in fact a small programable computer in its own right.

The chip was delivered 2 years later at the start of 1971 but by this time Busicom, along with many other calculator companies, had fallen victim to a calculator price war. In its last months, it negotiated with Intel to reduce the price of the chip in return for allowing Intel to market the device on its own behalf. Intel would have little to lose given that Busicom would shortly not be able to pay for any of their product and having a little income would be better than none at all.

At the end of 1971, Intel advertised the first example of what was to become known as the microprocessor: the Intel 4004.

The 4004 could only operate on 4 bits of data at a time. This could be used, if the user was patient, to power a hand-held calculator but little else. Before long, a more powerful 8 bit version, the 8008, was made available and finally in April 1974, in response to competition from other chip makers who by this time had their own microprocessors on the market, the 8080 was released which would run the same programs as the 8008 but required fewer support chips.

Microcomputer

In the early 1970s, the smallest computers available were still made by the mini-computer manufacturers such as DEC and Data General. The central processing unit of these machines would be made out of lots of individual integrated circuits so physically it would still sit underneath a desk rather than on top on it.

The first computer-like device to make use of microprocessors was the French Micral which used the 8008. Launched in 1973, it focused on industrial applications where the flexibility of a mini-computer would be beneficial but the performance requirements didn't merit a full computer. A few thousand were sold over the next few years before being superseded by more advanced machines.

It was at this point that the hobbyists started to come on the scene and make an impact. Few individuals since Konrad Zuse or Atanasoff had felt able to create their own computer. The desire hadn't gone away, it was just that before the microprocessor there was simply too much physical circuitry for one person to manage.

The way hobbyists communicated and found out about new developments in the days before the Internet was through electronics magazines. One such publication, *Radio Electronics*, announced in its July 1974 issue that readers could 'Build the mark 8: Your personal minicomputer'. Unlike the normal content of an electronics magazine, where full instructions for a simple device were given, this article gave a basic description of the device and had to ask the reader to send off for a booklet. This booklet then gave instructions on how to build the device based on the Intel 8008. The magazine claimed that 'thousands' of booklets were sold but its unlikely that very many purchasers followed through to actually build the device.

As ever in the media, there was a fierce readership war between competing titles and when one magazine had a scoop, its competitors had to respond. The main impact of the *Radio Electronics* project was to goad its competitor *Popular Electronics* into giving its own computer offering. Six months later, in the January 1975 edition, readers were invited to purchase the Altair 8800 from a floundering Albuquerque model shop called MITS, either in kit form for $400 or pre-built for around $500. The

Altair was a basic device. Once assembled the circuits were contained in a rectangular cuboid. There was no keyboard or screen. To enter a program, up to a maximum of 256 bytes, you had to flick needle switches on its front panel. The only obvious output came from the row of LEDs next to them. It did however use Intel's 8080 microprocessor which was the one that required fewer support chips. One of its other design strengths however was that it contained a 'bus' that allowed cards from either MITS or other groups to be slotted in to communicate with the main machine. This meant that it could receive signals from and return output to the outside world in a more meaningful way than just flash LEDs in sequence. Before long hobbyists had managed to attach devices such as teletypes, paper-tape readers and domestic television sets using specially constructed cards slotted into the bus. It was all rather unprepossessing but the microcomputer revolution was starting to gain momentum.

The Personal Computer

Interest grew in creating microcomputers that did not have to be assembled at home but still with the hobbyist in mind. A number of small companies, such as IMSAI, created copies of the Altair and were successful in the market place, often because the small MITS operation had difficulty meeting the flood of orders.

An alternative approach was to create an completely different computer using one of the similar microprocessors available from other suppliers. MOS Technologies 6502 chip was often chosen as it was cheaper than the Intel 8080.

One computer enthusiast, Steve Wozniak, developed a computer based on it: the Apple I. The Apple I, like the Altair, was not a personal computer as we know it: it came in an incomplete wooden case and the purchaser was expected to procure and install the keyboard and display themselves. It did however demonstrate to Wozniak and his fellow travelers Steve Jobs and Ron Wayne that there was a market for such a machine. Wozniak set about designing the follow-up whilst Steve Jobs did what he did best and started to evangelize on the topics of the future and Apple computer, though not necessarily in that order.

Zilog, a company formed by defectors from Intel, launched yet another microprocessor, the Z80. This was used in one of the first fully formed personal computer products: the Radio Shack TRS-80. Launched in 1977, it included the circuitry, a display unit and a keyboard all in one package. There was no need for the purchaser to go near a soldering iron or a screwdriver. Radio Shack did not have the market to itself for long as Commodore launched its PET, which was also usable out of the box, but only if the user was willing to put up with a fiddly 'calculator style' keyboard.

Finally, the Apple II arrived. Based on the same 6502 chip as the Apple I, it was much more customer friendly and was much more polished technically than its predecessor. It came in a plastic case with a proper computer keyboard. Ron Wayne, having lost money in a number of computer ventures in the past, sold up his share in the Apple enterprise when Jobs started talking about borrowing heavily for expansion. This left Wozniak and Jobs to soldier on.

By the end of 1977, it was clear that the personal computer was starting to mature. Gone were the days when to own a computer you had to build it yourself and knowledge of logic circuit design was a prerequisite. Products could be bought from shops with little fuss. From a business user's perspective however these computers were little more than toys. A view that was partially justified given the high proportion of processor time that was taken up playing games.

If one event changed this perception within business, it was the introduction of the original IBM personal computer in 1981. The previous year, seeing that the microcomputer was starting to take off, IBM chose to enter the market in an radical way: radical that is for IBM. They had attempted to sell a small computer built using a microprocessor as far back as 1975 but, unsurprisingly given its price tag of $10,000, few were sold. It was clear that they had to approach the market differently. The PC was too small to be profitably sold by the legendary computer sales force and would thus be sold largely via retail outlets. It normally took IBM around 3 years to develop a product given that it chose to do everything in-house to maximize control and profits. If they had waited 3 years, IBM would have missed the boat. It was decided that, like the rest of the personal computing industry, IBM would source the parts for its new PC from independent component suppliers and merely assemble them before applying an IBM badge to the completed product.

The technology within the IBM PC was thus a rag tag of current technologies. Entering the microcomputer market 4–5 years after the first fully fledged products had appeared did however give IBM an advantage in that it could skip a generation and start by using the newly available 16-bit microprocessors. The Intel 8088 was chosen as it far outperformed the original 8-bit 8080 based systems such as the Altair but, unlike the perfectly suitable Intel 8086, wouldn't challenge IBM's mini-computers (or mid range systems as they liked to called them). Monitors and keyboards were adapted from previously available products and disk drives and printers were bought from outside suppliers. The whole lot was packaged in a chunky non-nonsense case with a prominent IBM logo.

The IBM logo was all that was required to give managers everywhere the confidence to try out the new machines in business. Soon IBM could not keep up with demand even though the cost of a PC was $2,880, over four times the cost of an Apple II. The IBM Personal Computer was seen as a great success.

The shortcomings of IBM's strategy of speed did not take long to become apparent. As IBM did not own or control any of the components of its PC, it was possible for a competitor to purchase quantities on the open market and create an almost identical machine. There was one small area of the architecture, known as the BIOS, were IBM did own the rights. This impediment was soon circumvented. Within a year of the IBM PC becoming available, the 'clone' manufacturers were fully up to speed. They had reverse engineered their own BIOS chips to work identically to IBM's. The most successful at the time, Compaq, did over $100 million in business in its first year.

Just like in mainframes, the success of IBM's PC and its massive installed base meant that there was a huge counterweight to change. Innovation would mean disruption and risk. Companies with large stakes in the status-quo would not attempt to disrupt it. Only incremental changes would be possible in the design and each improvement would have to work with the remnants of the previous product. Companies with a smaller stake would not be risking much by attempting to upset the established order but they had little chance of success.

In the late 1980s and early 1990s, IBM, itself having fallen victim to the clone manufacturers, had little stake in the original PC concept and would attempt to update the PC's design in order to grab control for itself. The resulting so-called 'micro-channel architecture' was however swept aside by the classical-PC juggernaut of its own creating.

Over the years the Intel 8088 was incrementally updated to become the 80286, 80386, 80486 and Pentium chips, with each new generation having more transistors and thus more power and higher performance than the last. Each new generation had to work with the programs developed for the previous generation hampering any attempts to use improved techniques or major new technologies. The fundamental architecture of the PC has changed but in incremental steps and is still basically recognizable 25 years on.

RISC

As the PC was being launched, an alternative approach was already coming to the fore. This was known as RISC or the reduced instruction set computer. The list of instructions the central computer processor would perform would be stripped down to a bare minimum. This meant that for a given size of processor, more processing could be performed. Complex instructions could be simulated using a number of the simplified directives. It also opened the door to the possibility of allowing a single processor to perform more than one task at the same time through a technique known as pipelining (similar to that used in the early supercomputers). It soon became clear that the RISC architecture was superior to the complex instruction set used by the Intel 8086 family but the dead-weight of the installed base of PCs meant the plodding, clunky x86 way of processing instructions prevailed. Only where the users were technically knowledgeable and had a genuine requirement for processing power did RISC processors gain a foothold. This gave birth to the market for high powered workstations based on microprocessor chips other than the Intel x86 series. Suppliers of high-end RISC based workstations included Sun Microsystems, HP, Silicon Graphics (later SGI) and the ever present IBM.

As time wore on, the Intel x86 family started to use the RISC techniques deep inside the microprocessor but presented its old familiar face to the outside world. This meant it started to offer performance close to that of a genuine RISC chip whilst also maintaining compatibility with its forebears. With this and the increase in power of processors in general, more and more of the work that was done by high-end workstations fell within the boundary of what could be achieved by using a high powered PC using the Intel x86 chips. The market for specialist high-end workstations withered and now most desktop computers use some form of microprocessor based on the Intel x86 family.

The Next Steps

The original microprocessors from the early 1970s processed data in chunks of 8 binary bits. The Intel 8086 introduced in 1978 was a 16-bit chip, as was the 8088 used in the first IBM PC. With the release of the Intel 80386 in 1986, personal computers made the leap to the realm of 32-bit computing where they stayed well into the 21st century. It was only ever a matter of time before PCs made the next leap up to 64 bits but the path was not to be smooth.

The first 64-bit processor, a RISC device from a manufacturer known as MIPS Technologies, was used in a SGI UNIX workstation in 1991. It was quickly followed by a chip designed by DEC to replace its venerable but aging VAX computers. The chip was known as the Alpha processor and was moderately successful for a time in the 1990s. The company DEC was first taken over by Compaq and then by HP which decided it was not a semiconductor manufacturer and abandoned the product line. Intel announced that it was preparing to make the leap to 64-bit computing as early as 1994 but it wasn't until 2001 that it finally shipped its Itanium line of processors. Intel's approach to the Itanium was to create a processor that was master of its own destiny without being tied to the aging x86 way of doing things. It also said that it would be in some way compatible with the old x86 programs. Unfortunately, it seems to have fallen victim to the worst of both worlds. There was no base of software that had been written to take advantage of its power and yet the old x86 software ran surprisingly slowly. The repeated delays and the stunning absence of any significant performance improvement meant the word most commonly associated with the launch was 'flop'. Not to be put off, the following year, Intel launched the Itanium 2, the Itanium's successor. Once more, it had no clear advantage over the current generation of processors and the response was lukewarm.

Intel's arch rival, AMD (Advanced Micro Devices), chose a different path. AMD have for years been producing processor chips that work the same as Intel's x86 family and generally offer better performance for the same amount of cash. Their approach to making the leap to 64-bit computing was to make a chip that worked similarly to the x86 but that used 64 bits. Their offering is seen as a commercial success, given that it is only slightly more expensive than the 32-bit equivalent yet still works effortlessly with old programs. Intel has announced that it has also started to design a chip similar to that offered by AMD.

Back in 1965, Gordon Moore, one of Shockley's traitorous eight, and a co-founder of Fairchild Semiconductor and Intel, wrote in a magazine article that he expected the number of transistors that could be squeezed into a given space of semiconductor would double every year. In 1975, he adjusted the time scale for doubling transistor density to once every 2 years. Over the past 40 years, the prediction has been proved broadly true with the time between doubling generally being accepted as once every 18 months. This of course is known as Moore's Law. Unfortunately, it's becoming accepted that the steady pace of progress cannot continue for very much longer. The size of the components and the thickness of the materials that insulate one from another are getting so small that so-called 'quantum' effects will soon start to kick in, reducing the reliability of the device. It will only be a matter of years before the pace of improvement based on miniaturization starts to slow and designers will have to look elsewhere for performance improvements.

Intel, AMD and the other chip makers have started to look at other ploys and have already started to offer processors that use them. So-called multi-core chips offer one way to boost the performance of a single chip. They do so by having two or more processors on a single piece of semiconductor. Each processor core can communicate with the others but without the delay that results from communicating with a distant chip or computer. Intel has produced a version of its Xenon processor for use in Microsoft's Xbox gaming machine. It has three processing cores on one chip. This was a direct response to the news that a consortium led by IBM and Sony were developing a multi-core chip called 'the Cell' to be used in the next generation PlayStation 3. The single physical chip contains a single main processor with no less than eight side processors that together can perform nearly a quarter of a trillion calculations per second.

Clearly, we have not yet reached the limits of what is possible from a single microprocessor.

3 Software

To animate the jumble of wires and semiconductors that we call a computer, you need to tell it what to do. This of course is known as software. Software has been required since the beginning of the computer age. It was even known in Babbage's time. One of his acquaintances, Ada Lovelace, is often referred to as the first computer programmer although she never had a machine on which to test her work. The defense-based programming language of the 1970s, Ada, was named in her honor.

Ada Lovelace

Augusta Ada Byron was born in London on a winter's morning in late 1815 to the wife of the famous poet Lord Byron. Byron was a mercurial character to say the least. He was noted for his uncontrollable lust for women, whether he was related to them or not, and an equally unchecked attraction to adolescent boys. It was he who was originally described by one former lover, Lady Caroline Lamb, as "mad, bad and dangerous to know". Clearly, he had commitment issues. It was surprising that Ada's mother agreed to marry him in the first place and not at all surprising that, a little over a year into the marriage, he abandoned his wife and child. Ada was less than 1 month old at the time. Before summer, he had left the country never to return.

Left on her own to care for the child, Lady Byron ensured that her daughter had a strict, some might say tyrannical, upbringing. There were accusations, including those leveled by letter by a somewhat hypocritical Lord Byron, that the daughter did not spend much time with her mother. It has to be said Lady Byron did ensure that Ada was well educated, by what turned into a string of tutors, ensuring in the process that subject-matter was chosen such that there was no risk of her becoming a poet like her absent father. When she reached the age of 18, Ada was presented at court, as was customary for young ladies of society, and within 2 years had married William King, heir to the earldom of Lovelace.

It was around this time that Ada was introduced to Charles Babbage. Babbage was well known in London society in his younger days and would frequently hold dinner parties to lobby on behalf of his various causes. Within weeks of making his acquaintance, she had visited his house to view the small demonstration Difference Engine. The two corresponded and visited each other regularly for a number of years and, after the birth of her third child, Ada chose to take up a structured study of mathematics.

She set about translating into English a paper that had been written by a Turin-based mathematician called Menabrea on the topic of Babbage's Analytical Engine. Babbage had visited Menabrea in the early 1840s and had told him about the concepts behind the device. Menabrea had gathered these thoughts together and published them in French. Ada's translation added copious 'notes' which ended up being three times the length of the original article. She included a list of instructions that could be used by the Analytical Engine for calculating various mathematical functions. The whole lot was published in 1843 with the author specified only as AAL. Whilst only her friends and acquaintances knew who AAL was, Ada was delighted to have had her first scientific publication and wrote in excitement about what she intended to work on next. Unfortunately, the paper was to become the high point of her scientific career.

The marriage to King does not appear to have been a happy one. She had a number of paramours and became embroiled in a number of minor scandals. Her husband took pains to intercept her letters to suitors on many occasions. Clearly there was some Byron left in her that her mother couldn't eradicate. Her drinking became troublesome and over time she racked up considerable debts from gambling on horse racing. A woman married in the upper echelons of Victorian society would be permitted very few outlets for her energies. Her studies were clearly meant to give her such a release but she didn't receive the support she needed. Originally, Babbage had guided her work but as the 1840s wore on, his interest in it drifted, as did his interest in most other activities. Ada was left to her own devices to do what she could to alleviate the stultifying boredom.

Shortly after the publication of her article on the Analytical Engine her health began to fade leaving little energy for mathematical work. After a long and painful illness she died from cancer at the age 37.

Assembly Language

The relay computers of the late 1930s and early 1940s were similar in many ways to Babbage's analytical engine. According to the plans, Babbage's machine would accept instructions from a stream of punched cards similar to that used to control the early automated Jacquard looms. The early relay computing devices would get their instructions from reading punched paper tape, or in the case of Zuse Z3, used celluloid film. The instructions would be at a very low level. These would instruct the machine to move numbers between holding areas and to add, subtract, multiply or divide but little else. More complex activities would have to be built up from multiple actions of a simple nature. Programming, preparing the list of instructions, would require an intimate knowledge of how the particular machine worked and, when calculations were necessary, of binary arithmetic.

The first electronic machines, ENIAC and Colossus, had their instructions set using plug-in cables as seen in early telephone switchboards. In effect, their processing was wired into the machine. The use of the plug board just made it easy to change the wiring. There was however an acknowledged skill in preparing the instructions for the machine which was seen as separate from the expertise required to develop the electronics.

It was with the arrival of the first true 'stored-program' computers that the journey to software as we know it began.

The first stored-program computer to function, the Manchester 'Baby', had its instructions entered by flicking switches and peering at blobs on the screen of a Williams–Kilburn tube. With a machine so basic, there was no need to worry about software, especially given that the machine was only intended as a test harness for the Williams–Kilburn tube.

The team working on the Cambridge EDSAC, a fully functioning computer, took the issue of programming far more seriously and did a considerable amount of work which today seems obvious but at the time was ground breaking. Their first task was to define a language they could use to communicate with the computer.

The Harvard Mark I and ENIAC both worked using the decimal system. This meant that the inner workings of the machine were easy for humans to understand but meant the circuitry was considerably more complex than necessary. In the days of vacuum tubes, more circuitry meant more electrical failures. Thus before the ENIAC was complete, the Moore School team had already determined that decimal arithmetic was a clumsy way to do computing and chose the binary system for their follow-up EDVAC computer. The Moore School Lectures demonstrated the superiority of the binary system and so the Cambridge EDSAC also used binary.

This meant that both the program and the data being worked on would be held inside the machine as strings of binary numbers. These collections of 0 and 1 would be unintelligible to the human operating the machine. They would become known as 'machine code'. As the workers on the Manchester Baby had discovered, dealing with a computer in its own binary language was tedious in the extreme and prone to errors. An example of a machine code instruction would be '0001000101110101'. The Cambridge group, again following the lead from the Moore School, defined a language more comprehensible than raw binary machine code. Over the coming years, this would become known as assembly language. The instruction to store a value of 78 in the 'A register' might look something like 'STR 78 A'. It is not obvious to the uninitiated what this means but as a programmer it is far easier to deal with than a string of binary.

Whilst it is easier for humans to deal with, it still cannot be understood by the computer in this form. Uncompromisingly the machine will only understand raw binary. Somehow the assembly language instructions must be converted into the binary machine code. The Moore School, at the time of the lectures, had put little thought into the process of conversion and assumed that it would be performed by a human. The Cambridge team, as the arrival of a working computer became more imminent, wrote a computer program to perform the conversion which they called 'initial orders'. It was in effect the world's first 'assembler' program. An assembler takes instructions in a form that is acceptable to skilled humans and converts it into the raw binary that the machine is able to work with.

Once they had starting using the assembler, the Cambridge team were struck by a far more intractable problem that they had not foreseen. Whenever they created a new program and ran it on the computer for the first time, it never worked. It must be remembered that at the time no-one on the project had ever done complex programming and it was considered a similar process to solving an equation or writing an essay. These tasks could be performed with pencil and paper and if a mistake was made it was straightforward to detect and correct. Programming at the time was also initially performed using paper and pencil but when the program was transferred into the computer and converted to machine code it would either run amok or do nothing at all. The process of working out what went wrong and fixing it, to become known as debugging, has blighted computer technology ever since. It has to be said that the situation had been encountered by the early relay computers but the ability of the stored-program computer to bounce about the computer's memory made the problem far worse.

One way to cut down on the amount of debugging that was required, and the loss in machine time and increased cost that resulted, was to prepare standard 'sub-routines' which performed common tasks. These would be prepared once in advance and converted to machine code. When some new task was to be performed a new master program would be written to link together a number of sub-routines and supervise the operation. Because the sub-routines were prepared in advanced and were used in a number of programs, they could be trusted to a far higher degree than a newly crafted master program.

One of the most popular applications of the first computers was a mathematical technique called numerical integration. This repeatedly performed the same operations over and over again in order to work out the required value. If the operation had to be performed 1000 times, it was possible to create a huge program with the same instructions repeated 1000 times or it was possible to create a small master program that repeatedly called a small subset of instructions 1000 times. Given the limited program memory of the first computers the later approach, repeatedly calling sub-routines, was far more practical.

At the time what is now called a program was known as a 'routine'. A repeated set of instructions within the 'routine' was logically called a sub-routine. Whilst the term routine would fade from use, the term sub-routine has stuck and is still used today.

Compilers

As computers became more powerful and computer memories increased in size, the size of programs that could practically be executed became larger. Unfortunately, the effort required to get an assembly language program working is not directly proportional to its size. To get a program 10,000 lines long working will almost certainly take much more than 10 times the effort of a program 1000 lines long. At the same time, computer resources remained precious and processor time could not be wasted on frivolous schemes to help programmers.

One of the first people to push the notion of 'natural language' programming was Grace Hopper. She had joined Howard Aiken at Harvard shortly after the US had entered World War II to work on the programming of the Mark I relay computer. She moved to UNIVAC in the late 1940s focusing on the programming activity. By the early 1950s, her group had written the 'A-0 compiler'. The instructions that the compiler would read were far more comprehensible to humans than assembly language which was basically a shorthand for the computer's machine code. Programming languages such as A-0 describe the operation of a program in a manner that is closer to the way humans see the world using normal words like 'Move' and 'Add'. It is the job of the compiler to convert the program, as written in 'human' form, into machine code. This was a far more demanding task than that performed by an assembler and the initial attempts showed it. The A-0 compiler would take an hour just to convert the program into machine code. The freshly minted machine code would then, to use modern technical parlance, run like a dog.

As was the case across the board in the early 1950s, UNIVAC had a head start over IBM but it was not long before they started to return fire. In late 1953, John Backus, who worked on IBM's first 701 'defense calculator', which had been installed behind the ground floor windows of the Madison Avenue Office in New York, persuaded the management to fund work on a compiler for scientific use. It was expected to take 6 months to complete but in the end it took 12 programmers two and a half years. The result, FORTRAN, for FORmula TRANslation, quickly became popular with scientific users because it was easy to program, compiled into machine code without undue delay and produced machine code that ran almost as fast as that hand crafted by a human using an assembler.

There were alternative languages and compilers provided for other platforms such as the Math-Matic, an improvement on A-0 provided by UNIVAC but, with the increasing prevalence of IBM machines, FORTRAN led the way.

FORTRAN was designed as a scientific tool, and was not well suited to commercial processing. It was more worried about handling long numbers accurately than going anywhere near the strings of characters used in names and addresses. Like the scientific market, the business market had a morass of different languages and compilers, at least one from each of the manufacturers. This meant that it was difficult to switch from one computer supplier to another as all the software would have to be re-written in the language provided by the new manufacturer. The US government quickly lost patience with the muddle and invited CODASYL (Committee on Data Systems and Languages) to come up with a single across-the-board standard that could run on all different manufacturers' computers. By 1960, they had defined what was to become the standard business language: COBOL (COmmercial and Business Oriented Language). It was announced that the government would not lease or purchase any computer without a COBOL compiler. Unsurprisingly, the manufacturers swiftly fell into line and made sure they had one available.

Neither FORTRAN nor COBOL are considered perfect for their respective tasks. They did not evolve after considered debate amongst the cognoscenti. FORTRAN was created by John Backus's team in such a way that the compiler would create efficient machine code. Flexibility and ease of use were secondary considerations. COBOL was clearly the creation of a committee and, whilst effective, has never been considered an elegant or ideal language.

The benefit for the organizations that owned computers was that there were now de-facto standards for scientific and commercial programming languages. It would be far easier to find staff trained and experienced in these languages, given that virtually everyone was using them, than in the soup of small specializations that existed before. They could also move their FORTRAN or COBOL programs onto a machine from an alternative manufacturer and get them working with minimal effort. A number of the alternative languages persisted and many more have been created since. These survived not by competing with FORTRAN and COBOL head-on but by concentrating on some need that they did not serve well.

One language that was created to fill one of the gaps in their coverage was BASIC: The Beginners All-purpose Symbolic Instruction Code. It was developed on a computer at Dartmouth College, New Hampshire, in 1964. The college wanted a system that any of their students, including those in non-technical subjects, could use to learn the concepts of computing. FORTRAN and COBOL, along with virtually all other languages at the time, were compiled languages. Compiled languages take a program and convert it into machine code in one fell swoop. This allows the compiler to take everything into consideration during the conversion and produces the best results. Unfortunately, it also means a lot of processing time is taken up when a compilation is attempted. In a 1960s commercial environment, a program would be compiled a few times to eradicate errors and would then probably run once every day for years without amendment. Full compilation was wise because the commercial user received the benefit of efficient machine code. In a learning environment, the program would probably be 'compiled' more times than it ever ran and would be riddled with fundamental errors because the programmer was only learning. The key for a learning language was that the language itself should be easily understandable and that the compiler should favor fast, efficient preparation over fast, efficient execution. A program written in BASIC would be simple to write and would take up few machine resources to prepare but the speed of the program when you ran it would be far from exciting.

Because of its ease of use, BASIC spread widely as a learning language and was the natural choice as the first programming language available on the microprocessor-based computers of the mid 1970s.

Batch vs Interactive

In the early days of electronic computing, a computer would only be able to work on one activity at a time. Generally, a program would be fed in at one end using punched cards and a print-out would emerge at the other. As there were no computer terminals with impatient users, there was no need to worry about sharing out the scarce processor time between different competing tasks. When one program had finished, the next set of punched cards would be loaded and so on.

For scientific computing, the central processor would be given a problem to solve and would be able to munch its way through the necessary calculations before spitting out the answer. The acts of reading in data and outputting answers were insignificant compared to the amount of processing that went on inside the machine.

In commercial 'data processing', the central processor would perform far simpler tasks but many, many of them. The key to a successful data processing computer was to match the computer's ability to process data internally with its ability to read it in and print it out. The input and output tasks were at the time both limited by physical movements. Input from punch cards could only go as fast as a punched card could fly. Output to a print could only go as fast as the printer could hammer out its characters. Special hardware devices known as channels were created to manage the input and output functions of the computer so that the expensive central processing equipment would not be left waiting for physical input or output.

Into the early 1960s, computers would not need special programs to help the machine coordinate all this activity. They were simple-minded beasts that would only perform one activity at a time. This became known as batch processing where one batch of data was processed at a time. The entire machine's resources were devoted to a single problem for as long as necessary. The ability to talk to the computer's various resources, input and output channels, tape drives and printers would be separated into 'sub-routines' and called, carefully, when required. There was no need to worry about the resource being asked to do two different things at the same time.

As usual, the first group to demand more advanced processing was the US military. A number of large military projects were started in the late 1950s where the computer's inputs and outputs were not punched card or tape. The largest of these military systems was called SAGE (for Semi Automatic Ground Environment). It was intended to remedy the slow, confused manual system for responding to incursions into US airspace, potentially by nuclear-armed Soviet bombers. It would accept all the information arriving from ground stations and radar outposts and present it to users who could make decisions quickly and cleanly. One of many innovations introduced was real-time human–computer interaction. This didn't take the now familiar form of keyboard and VDU but a large circular 'radar screen' and a light pen. When the light pen was pointed at a image on the radar screen the details of the selected object were displayed to the operator in text. The human could then take the appropriate action. It was the human's involvement that made the system 'semi-automatic'.

SAGE was a gigantic project which included upgrading radar facilities and the development of improved interceptor aircraft. In the end, it cost $8 billion to fully implement and by the time it was complete it would be obsolete. The threat of Soviet bombers had changed to that of inter-continental ballistic missiles which scrambled fighter aircraft could do little about.

At the time the SAGE project was kicked off, no commercial computers could operate fast enough to support these tasks. The only computer that could operate at the speeds required to produce a system that could interact with humans in 'real-time' was the Whirlwind computer, the MIT-based experimental system originally intended as an aircraft trainer. This meant that throughout the 1950s the development of human–computer interaction was impossible in the commercial and academic arenas. This had started to change when the concepts behind the military systems started to filter into academia in the early 1960s at the same time as transistorized computers.

Time Sharing

The notion of bringing humans closer to the computer was discussed widely. It was still going to be far from economic to allow a single user to monopolize a large half-million dollar mainframe. That was why batch processing was so popular. The notion of time-sharing was born. Time-sharing splits the time available on the computer's central processor into small chunks that would be allocated in turn to waiting users. An experimental time-sharing system was written at MIT, the home of Whirlwind, and to an extent SAGE, in 1961. It was limited to three simultaneous users but the compatible time-sharing system CTSS had proved the point that time-sharing was possible.

The first major commercial system to allow multiple users to request information directly from a central computer and receive answers back immediately was the American Airlines SABRE system for reserving seats on its flights. It was rolled-out by IBM between 1962 and 1965. This linked a central mainframe with 800 MB of hard disk storage with over 1000 terminals, each one a souped-up IBM typewriter costing $16,000. Whilst SABRE was an interactive system, it was not a time-sharing system. The entire system's software had to be written by IBM from the ground up at great expense. A user of the SABRE system could only do one thing – book seats on flights. The user of a true time-sharing system (like CTSS) had full access to the computer and could edit and run their own programs as well as those of fellow users.

A following for time-sharing started to build. In 1964, Dartmouth College had built their Basic system which sat on a multi-user time-sharing operating system developed in-house by a group of undergraduates. MIT moved on from CTSS (1961) to Project MAC (1963). Within a couple of years, the project MAC computer was overstretched and they started to work on a more demanding general operating system known as MULTICS. MULTICS was to use the same GE computers as the Dartmouth College system but would require a significant amount of new software to be written because the BASIC system focused on ease of use and not performance. Bell Labs, AT&T's research arm that had come up with the transistor, was hired to help develop the software. There followed a classic software fiasco where the perception of the amount of work required to finish the job steadily ballooned until in 1969, Bell Labs gave up and walked away from the project. This was the trigger for GE to leave the mainframe computer business.

Whilst MULTICS is rarely talked about these days, it did lead to a more long-lasting legacy. Two programmers from Bell Labs that had been working on MULTICS took advantage of the relatively free-wheeling atmosphere of the research organization to develop a more basic, and thus more achievable, system. They called it UNIX, a pun on MULTICS. It was initially developed on an ancient underpowered DEC PDP-7 mini-computer that could support one user but, once they had found a potential business application as an excuse for further development, a shiny new PDP-11 was procured. The programmers, Ken Thompson and Dennis Ritchie, developed their own programming language known as 'C' and set about rewriting the operating system using it. The benefit of using 'C' meant that once a 'C' Compiler was available for a certain computer, the UNIX operating system could, with a bit of effort, be 'ported' and made to function on its new platform. This was revolutionary. At the time, few if any operating systems would work on more than one type of hardware.

UNIX, developed by knowledgeable enthusiasts that were not in a great rush, has become the archetypal 'operating system'. Its design is minimalist and elegant. It did not attempt to do everything that a user could wish; it just provides a stable and reliable platform for others to build on.

Having been developed by a government regulated monopoly, UNIX was sold to customers by Bell Labs at a nominal price. Whilst it may have been cheap to acquire there was no after-sales support to speak off and so it was only suitable for a user community with more expertise than money – colleges and universities. Through the 1970s and 1980s, UNIX spread from one university to another to become the main computer operating system of academia.

As we will hear later, from the late 1970s, it was also appropriated and improved by a number of third parties. These included commercial organizations such as the Santa Cruz Organization and Sun Microsystems as well the main academic update performed at University of California at Berkeley. This unfortunately had the effect of triggering a diaspora of UNIX look-a-likes that were all reliable and elegant but sadly incompatible.

The 'C' language, intended purely for the development of 'system software', that is the fundamental programs that control the operation of the computer, took on a life of its own to become a general programming language. To this day, it occupies the ground between the high-level, human-readable languages like COBOL and FORTRAN and the machine-speak of assembly language.

Object Orientation

In the early 1980s, the 'C' language was extended by a Bell Labs employee, Bjarne Stroustrup, to include the concepts of so-called object-oriented programming. Object-oriented programming offers several advantages over the previous generation of so-called procedural languages like COBOL and FORTRAN.

As an analogy, imagine it became necessary to stage a drama at an avant-garde arts festival. It would be possible to follow the traditional approach of creating a single large script where each actor was told exactly what words to say and in what order. This would be equivalent to traditional procedural programming where the set of instructions are considered as a whole. The execution of the script or program starts at the top and ends at the bottom. With object-oriented programming, each actor would be given a description of the character they were to play and the rules of how to interact with the other players. A simple plot line would be developed and the actors would be left to their own devices. They would use the rules they had been given to decide themselves how to interact. As long as they stuck to their own rules, they could do what they liked. This is equivalent to object-oriented programming where each object (actor) has its behavior defined and is then left to interact with the other objects (actors) as it is programmed.

The primary benefit of object-oriented programming is that it is easy to reuse program code. This is similar to reusing a character for several plays. The same character description can be used for any number of plays. For example, once a philandering popinjay or a redoubtable matron has been defined, there is no need to write their descriptions again. With the traditional approach, the whole play, or program, would have to be written from scratch.

This extended version of C, known as C++, is widely used, especially in developing applications that work with a graphical user interface. Each item on screen, such as a button or a spreadsheet cell, is defined as an object. The objects can interact as necessary depending on their own particular behavioral script. There are other programming languages that can perform such tasks but because C++ is based on the low level 'C' language, it can interact with the computer at its lowest level. This means it is fast to run. Users can click on a menu option or button and expect a quick response. Using other languages that don't have such detailed access to the computer's recesses means that they would be slower to perform the same task. This also leads to the main drawback of C++ as a language: because it is tied so closely to the computer's workings, programs can't be easily moved to work on another type of computer.

It was this 'portability' issue, the difficulty in getting C++ programs to work on more than one type of computer, that led to the popularization of the Java programming language. Java had originally been developed as part of an exercise at Sun Microsystems to develop the next generation of set top boxes for cable TV providers. The system proposed would allow customers to interact with the device. Options for the customer to select would be presented using multimedia. Images would move and dance about to brighten up the user's day. It was 1993 however and the cable TV providers weren't quite ready for all that yet. The software that drove the set top box had been design in two layers. The first layer was known as a 'virtual machine'. This had to be written once for each type of device the system was to run on. It would know how to perform a predefined set of actions such as accept input or format the display but would do nothing useful itself. The second layer was the program, written in the programming language that was to become known as Java, that would instruct the virtual machine what to do. The Java language could only ask the virtual machine to perform actions on its predefined list. It didn't have access to the underlying computer. This did however mean that once a program had been written in Java, it would work on any computer that had a suitable virtual machine available. The problems that arose in C++ programs where an individual computer's functions would be called directly were not relevant. This separation from the foibles of the underlying computer and the fact that the language itself was simple and elegant meant that it was an obvious choice when application developers were looking for a programming language that wasn't tied to any one computer platform or software company.

Java has not, and will not, replace C++. The two languages are complimentary. Because of its two-layer approach, Java will always be slower than C++ and it is not good at dealing with the detail of low-level computer operations. On the other hand, it is far easier to program and, once a program has been written, it can be moved from one computer to another with relative ease. Both languages of course offer the benefits of object orientation.

Hard Disks / DOS

Before electronic computers came along, data were stored the same way they were processed – on punched cards. With the advent of the very first UNIVAC, retrieving data from punched cards was far too slow and all the original computer manufacturers developed tape drives of one form or another. The technology now known as hard discs did not see its first outing until 1956 when IBM introduced the RAMAC. A RAMAC unit held 6 Megabytes of data on 50 magnetic discs of 2 feet diameter. A single unit would cost $200,000, about the same as a low-powered computer, and so the device would not gain widespread popularity for some time.

To keep costs manageable, business data would be held on magnetic tape and the way the computer worked would have to be designed around its particular way of working. The prime consideration of any computer installation was to avoid leaving the processor idle. This cost money. Shuffling around a tape trying to find the data of interest while the central processor waited was not acceptable. The data on tapes would thus be sorted in some fashion such that the data were presented to the processor in the right order.

Let us consider the example, 1960s style, of updating a computer's stock records to take account of items that have recently been received in a warehouse. Input data, that is the list of received goods, could arrive in any order and would have to be sorted into sequence, say by product code, before the main event could commence. The master files, in this example stock balances, would be held on a separate tape drive also sequenced by product code. The processor would start working through the sorted input data one receipt at a time. It would only ever have to go forward through the stock master tape as this was in the same sequence as the input data (product code). When the relevant master stock record was found on the tape the stock count would be increased. If a brand new product had been received that was not in the master file, this would have to be written to a third tape drive: a new record could not be created immediately as this would obliterate some other stock information on the master file. At the end of the process all the new products on the third tape would be added to the end of the stock master file and the whole lot sorted back into product code order. Twenty years after the introduction of the first UNIVAC, it was estimated that 25% of all computer time was spent sorting.

Tremendous effort was applied to avoid sorting data. In a commercial operation, all the daily updates to the master files would be scheduled carefully with due weight put on the order that updates and sorts would have to be performed. This was known as the 'batch schedule' and formed the core of daily activity in a computer center. This was the norm for computers in the 1960s and 1970s. A user wanting information would submit a request one day, this would go into the batch schedule that night and hopefully a printed report with the requested details would be available the following morning. The report producing program would be set to run at the end of the batch schedule after all the day's updates had hit the master files.

This well ordered and computer centric mode of operation would have to change with the arrival of reasonably priced hard drives. Data would be available to the computer throughout the day and not stuck out of reach on a tape rack.

Reading and writing data to the hard drive however presented new problems. Writing data on the first free space available would be quick but would mean you would never find it again. Clearly similar data had to be kept together in 'files'. There had to be some way of allowing multiple files to co-exist on the hard drive without trampling over one another. There had to be a naming convention that allowed a process to retrieve a file of data when it needed it.

A new class of software, called the disk operating system, was created to take on these tasks. Each program that needed access to data on the disk would have to route its requests via the disk operating system.

The most famous, or more appropriately infamous, early disk operation system was IBM's OS/360. This was the disk operating system for the System/360 mainframes and was a key part of IBM's attempt to create a single range of mainframe computers that would all run each other's programs. Without a common operating system base, there would be little chance of getting programs to run on many different types of computers.

Writing an operating system is complex at the best of times but the IBM team tasked with delivering it had a huge range of issues to face: the computers had not yet been built, there were no less than seven different types of computers, the designs of each one changed constantly, there were tight deadlines. As with all projects, work would slip behind schedule. In order to recover the lost time, more people were drafted onto the project. These people would take weeks and months to get up to speed before doing anything useful whilst simultaneously taking up the time of those already on the project. Within a couple of years, the programming team had exploded to 1000 confused and angry people.

OS/360 limped into customer premises in 1967, a year late, having cost $50 million to write. Even then it barely functioned and performance improved by a factor of 10 in later releases. There were accusations that IBM had created a slow operating system to force customers to lease larger computers than were strictly necessary. Unfortunately IBM didn't have any great choice in the matter.

Databases

A company's first step into the world of disk operating systems would be to move their tape-based batch schedule onto a hard disk computer. This would at least allow them to stop loading and unloading tapes. To get full advantage of the ability to read and write data throughout the day, they would eventually have to change the way their programs worked. This would require a leap to what is known as 'on-line' systems, and yet more software would be required.

While an operating system will happily look after files of data, it rarely goes so far as to look after the data within the files. Let us say a user wants to read a customer's address from a file of data. A program can get the operating system to open the file but it has no way to request a specific customer's record. The program has to search through the entire file for itself.

The software that looks after such filing data on a hard disk is known as a database. It must allow for fast retrieval of specific information on demand and allow the same information to be stored immediately so that others can see it. It must allow for many people to view data and write data at the same time and to keep everyone's view consistent. This is well beyond the capabilities of operating systems.

One of the first major database product was IBM's IMS (information management system). Launched in 1969 it remains on sale today. It holds the raw information but it also holds an index, like a old-style library card index, which allows fast access to that information. The benefits of IMS over other databases is that is can handle immense volumes of transactions (millions per day) and hold vast quantities of data (terabytes). The drawback is that the data can only be accessed in very specific ways.

IMS is an example of what is known as a hierarchical database. This means that the only way to get at the data is through the index. Unfortunately, the index is not friendly. If you know all the information the index needs, known as key fields, you can expect fast efficient service. If you can't supply all the key fields you have a long wait ahead of you.

At the time IMS was introduced, an IBM researcher, Edgar Codd, was developing a scheme for allowing more flexible access to data. This became known as the relational database. A team at IBM's San Jose Research Laboratories built a demonstration of the concepts known as System/R which was put in the public domain but not for sale as a product. The computing power required to run a relational database was far greater than the equivalent old-style product so the concept was left to rest whilst the power of hardware caught up with the demands of the software.

An academic, Michael Stonebraker, at nearby University of California at Berkeley developed a similar product, christened Ingres, which was widely distributed. Most of those in Northern California that had an interest in such matters would be aware of the concepts.

By the mid 1980s, a number of small companies had sprung up to provide relational databases. Stonebraker had left academe to set up what was to become Ingres Corporation. Oracle had shipped its Version 3 relational database in 1984. Sybase, set up in 1984, shipped its first database in 1988. IBM meanwhile, sensing that the moment had come to leave hibernation, had been at work on System/R and renamed its offering DB/2.

Over the years, the products were improved and extended but perform generally the same task as they did in the late 1980s but with somewhat improved reliability and performance. The market leader is Oracle with IBM's DB2 hot on its heals. Together they take about 70% of the revenues from relational databases worldwide. Microsoft with its SQL Server product, which started out as a licensed variant of Sybase's SQL Server, is slowly gaining share at the less demanding end of the market, restricted as it is to operating on Microsoft Windows operating systems.

Middleware

So an operating system looks after hard disks along with devices like keyboards, displays and networks. A database looks after large quantities of data held on hard disks. There is an additional layer of software, often described by the rather opaque term of transactional middleware, which sits between the database and a program that interacts with a user. Middleware is used in the most demanding of applications where several processes or users want access to the same piece data at the same time. Without some form of co-ordination and management, such simultaneous processes can trample over one another and leave the data they are working on in a corrupt muddle.

The classic use of middleware is the booking of flights with an airline. Suppose a flight has just been canceled and the unfortunate would-be passengers have made it hot-foot to the airline ticket desk to book themselves onto the next available flight. The booking agents deal with passengers in order until the time comes when there is only one seat left on the next flight but two remaining passengers. Both passengers gain the attention of a booking agent at the same time. The agents look up the availability of seat. Both agents see that one seat is left unreserved and take the passenger's name and contact details. Both booking agents hit the 'save' button to record their respective bookings at around the same time. It is the middleware's job to see that only the first passenger gets the seat and that the second is clearly told that they'll have to walk. It should also ensure that no trace of the second booking, the one that was dropped, is left on the system. Leaving the contact details on the relevant database without a flight booked would mean that the airline's databases would be inconsistent. Inconsistent databases make any kind of operation impossible and must be avoided at all costs. It basically means that there would be two versions of the truth which is a situation only politicians and lawyers can cope with – not computers.

The grandaddy of the family of middleware is IBM's CICS. This was released in the late 1960s to allow utilities companies to maintain their customers records on-line: hence the name Customer Information Control System. It was soon used well beyond its original remit to coordinate transactions that involved data distributed across several databases and where many simultaneous transactions can be performed on the same piece of data. Today, it is still used widely by airlines, banks, energy utilities, credit card companies and those bodies with a need to handle vast numbers of coordinated transactions. Any time you use a bank ATM, book a flight or make a purchase using a credit card, it's likely that you are using CICS.

There were other brands of transactional middleware in the 20th century but they always tended to be in CICS shadow. Recent years have, however, seen the emergence of what are known as 'web application servers' which undertake much the same coordinating and managing role when serving up web pages. They come under two broad groupings. The first group is the J2EE engines which are all built around an open defined industry standard which uses Java as the common programing language. Programs written for any brand of J2EE engine should work on any other J2EE engine without many changes. Available J2EE application servers include IBM's Websphere, BEA's Weblogics, SUN's One, SAP's Netweaver and Oracle's Fusion. Competing with the industry-wide standard of J2EE is Microsoft's .NET platform where the necessary functions can be found somewhere in the depths of the 'server' editions of the Windows operating system. Programs written using .NET will only run on Microsoft Windows servers.

And so it came to pass that, whilst there are myriad different ways to configure a corporate computer system, in the near future they will tend to fall into one of three camps. First there is the big-iron old-style 'IBM' approach which would use a mainframe sized machine (IBM now calls them zSeries servers) with the latest descendant of the OS/360 operating system known as z/OS. This would use the classic IMS database with CICS co-ordinating. This kind of set-up is still necessary for the very largest and most demanding of applications such as large-scale banking, insurance, travel and financial operations. Typically, such systems would be capable of handling millions of transactions each day and managing thousands of gigabytes of data. Given the specialist nature of the hardware and software, it does not come cheap and it is far from straightforward to use. Specialist staff will have to be found to tend the temperamental mammoth and to try and reduce the likelihood of a destructive tantrum.

The next camp is the Java application server approach. The computer tends to be a commodity server bought off the shelf from any one of a number of hardware suppliers. The operating system will probably be some version of UNIX. The database will probably be bought from Oracle and any one of the previously mentioned J2EE engines used to coordinate activity. This will mean that all the processing logic will have to be written in the Java programming language. All of the components, even the Oracle database, could be changed with a competing product without too much difficulty so prices of the components tend to be far more reasonable than when using a big-iron approach. Likewise staff who can handle the technologies are relatively easy to find.

Finally there is the Microsoft approach. Like the Java approach, the hardware is bought off the shelf from any suitable supplier. Unlike the Java approach, the operating system has to be Microsoft Windows. The database will probably be Microsoft SQL Server (or possibly Oracle) with the .NET framework co-ordinating activity. The programming logic could be written in any .NET compatible programming language such as Visual C++, Visual Basic or C# (Microsoft's attempt at creating a competitor to Java), all of which must be bought from Microsoft. Apart from the hardware and, with difficulty, the database, there is no option to replace any component with those from any other supplier. The costs however are similar to the Java approach and there is a large pool of capable people available to look after the system.

There is a fourth approach that is growing in popularity, known as open source, but we'll hear more about that later. So that's how the large computers that live in secure temperature-controlled computer center's work. Let us turn instead to look at the software that drives their smaller cousin's, the computers that sit on our desks.

The Early Micros

Just like the Manchester 'Baby' in 1948, the first programs for the early microcomputers of the 1970s were entered in raw binary by flicking switches. The results of the tiny program would be viewed by looking for a pattern on a panel of lights on the front of the machine. In the age of minicomputers, UNIX and time-sharing systems, this would not last long.

The first software offered for the Altair from Albuquerque, the first popular microcomputer, was a version of Basic. This, as has become a matter of legend, was written in the winter of 1975 by a young Bill Gates, then studying in his second year at Harvard, and his friend from pre-university days, Paul Allen. They formed a partnership, Micro-Soft (the hyphen was later dropped), and persuaded MITS, the Altair 'manufacturer', to resell the BASIC program. MITS gladly did so as it envisaged selling a considerable number of memory upgrades on the back of the demand for a programming language. Micro-Soft received around $30 for each copy of BASIC sold which was to provide much of their income for the remainder of the 1970s.

As with all microcomputers, the machine code and BASIC programs written on the Altair would be lost forever when it was switched off. The process of getting the machine back on its feet when the power came back on was fiddly and time consuming, generally involving much flicking of switches and the feeding of a paper tape through a tape reader. This was suitable for hobbyists but precluded the Altair from doing any serious work.

At the time, this 'boot' problem was relatively new even to the mainframe world. Core memory, the tiny magnetic donuts used in the IBM System/360 and its competitors in the late 1960s, could hold its data while the power was off. The boot routine, or kick start, of the computer could thus be read from the main store when the machine was powered up.

At the start of the 1970s, the mainframes being introduced used integrated circuits for memory instead of magnetic core which meant they were as forgetful as the Altair when they lost power. It was as a mechanism for loading the initial instructions into the IBM System/370 that the floppy disc drive was introduced. Initially 8 inch diameter magnetic discs covered in a square of black plastic, these could hold 160k of data, more than enough to get the computer up and running.

It would be ideal if floppy drives could also be harnessed to a microcomputer. This was not a straightforward task. First of all the disc drive would need controlling circuitry to communicate with the computer. Then the computer would need software to look after its interactions with the disc. Just as with mainframes, this is known as the operating system.

The first successful operating system for microcomputers was developed by Gary Kildall, a computer science PhD who taught at the US Naval Postgraduate College in California. Kildall acted as a part-time consultant to Intel who had asked him to come up with and then implement a programming language, based on IBM's PL/I language, for their new micro-processors. The resulting language and compiler would then be packaged by Intel and sold in development kits to their customers.

Kildall procured one of the 'new' 8 inch floppy disc drives and arranged for a colleague, John Torode, to develop the controlling circuitry. With the assistance of his students, Kildall wrote a program that would store and retrieve data from the disk drive. The program would make the micro act and behave like the DEC PDP-10 computer Kildall was most familiar with. The commands, such as those to list and copy files, were very much taken from DEC's repertoire which had the benefit that they were widely known in computer circles, even if it was not clear to anyone else what they meant.

After Intel showed no inclination to purchase his disc drive work, Kindall chose to attempt to market it himself as CP/M (Control Program/Microcomputer). He created his own company under the preposterous name of Intergalactic Digital Research and orders trickled in. Later it was adjudged wise to drop the 'Intergalactic'. (Science fiction was clearly to the front of 1970s computer pioneers' minds as the Altair is alleged to have been named after the destination for the Starship Enterprise in one episode of Star Trek.)

MITS was the leading supplier of Intel-based microcomputers but had asked another group to produce a similar operating system. Unfortunately, it turned out to have 'uneven' reliability at best yet MITS still refused to license it to anyone else. IMSAI, the maker of MITS clones, started to ship computers to customers with floppy drives with the promise that an operating system would soon follow. This was a bit naughty because they did not have an operating system and the floppy drives were close to useless without one. In desperation, given MITS intransigence, they purchased copies of CP/M from Kindall and passed it on to their customers.

CP/M had to be adapted to work with the IMSAI set up. Instead of making bespoke changes to the overall product, Kindall sent all the communications with external devices through a separate 'Basic Input Output System' or BIOS. This had the effect of isolating the bulk of CP/Ms operations from the individual hardware that it was expected to work on. Later, Digital Research would reap the benefit of this work as it was simple to port the CP/M program to hundreds of different types of computers with changes only to the BIOS. For example, the popular Tandy TRS-80 and the Commodore Pet would both run CP/M within a few years. Apple meanwhile chose to go their own way.

QDOS

By 1980, the crash program to build the IBM Personal Computer was getting under way. Virtually all personal computers used the CP/M operating system, except Apple of course, and even theirs could be made to use CP/M if you purchased the 'Soft Card' from Microsoft (a rare piece of Microsoft hardware). All these computers were based on 8-bit microprocessors and CP/M was 8-bit software. The IBM PC would be based on a 16-bit microprocessor and could not use the standard version of CP/M.

IBM's first choice as supplier for an operating system was still Digital Research: the clear leaders in microcomputer operating systems. Kildall had been working on a 16-bit version for the newer Intel chips, known as CP/M-86, but it was in abeyance whilst he worked on other products. IBM visited Digital Research to discuss using CP/M-86 in their new computer. Digital Research however wouldn't talk.

The stumbling block was IBM's notorious non-disclosure agreement which, to paraphrase, says IBM could broadcast anything that Digital Research told them but that Digital Research could not so much as whisper anything that IBM said. That is if IBM chose to say anything at all. Digital Research wouldn't sign. The meeting broke up without IBM even saying what the purpose of the visit was.

IBM moved on to Microsoft in Seattle who were much more accommodating. The non-disclosure agreement was signed by Gates and Allen. As was their right under the agreement, they chose to say very little of substance and yet managed to create an impression of being able to do business. The Gates family were much more on IBM's wavelength. Bill Gates' father was a leading Seattle lawyer and his mother served on the organizing committee of the 'United Way' movement alongside John Opel, then president of IBM.

IBM discussed the purchase of Microsoft BASIC for the new PC and as an aside mentioned the problems they were having obtaining an operating system. Gates and Allen indicated that they might be able to help IBM there.

Gates knew of a local company, Seattle Computer Products, that was trying to sell a 16-bit kit microcomputer. Unfortunately, Digital Research had not yet been able to supply the 16-bit CP/M-86 operating system to make it work. The company had asked one of their programmers, Tim Paterson, to build one instead. It didn't have to be too good. It just had to allow them to get some kits out the door. He built a CP/M look-alike 16-bit program which was known internally as the QDOS: quick and dirty operating system.

Microsoft bought the rights to use the software for $15,000 and after some swift repackaging presented it to IBM as PC-DOS. The IBM personal computer shipped with PC-DOS, which could be sold independently by Microsoft as MS-DOS. Later, IBM would provide the option to replace PC-DOS with CP/M-86 or a system known as UCSD p-code but neither of the alternatives proved popular.

As everyone now knows, the IBM PC with the MS-DOS operating system was a runaway success and within a few years most of the alternative microcomputer set-ups were in trouble and one by one exited the market. One in particular was more stubborn. The Apple II would take some dislodging. It had been launched 4 years before the IBM PC and still used an 8-bit processor which would clearly come off worse in a drag race with a 16-bit machine. Its days were numbered but Apple had a trick up its sleeve.

XEROX PARC

The next generation of Apples was to be heavily influenced by the work of XEROX PARC. XEROX was the company that held the rights to many of the patents on the process of photocopying and the company had reached the position where its name was often used as a generic – 'to Xerox a document'. In the early 1970s, there was a concern that the company did not have a path mapped out beyond copiers. The Palo Alto Research Center (PARC) was created to perform basic research in the area of office tools that could supplant the photocopier in the future. PARC was most certainly not to pursue the commercially relevant activity of R&D; XEROX had a R&D center at Rochester in New York that did that. PARC was intended to think about the future, 10 or more years ahead.

Xerox hired a manager for the new center who had been heavily involved in the Pentagon's Advanced Research Programs Agency (ARPA) but had left government employment after the Vietnam war had changed the nature of his job both directly, through missions to the war zone, and indirectly, through budget cuts. Bob Taylor was interested in taking computers beyond the then recent technology of time-sharing. Time sharing had been revolutionary in that it allowed humans to interact with computers directly. He believed that by taking this further, computers could aid and expand human abilities rather than replace them as was the main thrust of research at the time. He saw XEROX PARC as an opportunity to move forward his vision of making computers easier for mortals to work with.

At Taylor's insistence, PARC had no hierarchy. Everyone worked directly for Taylor. This meant that the size of the team was limited to 50 people which in turn meant that the team had to be of extremely high caliber and of a certain 'self-confident' disposition. Recruitment for positions was brutal and involved potential recruits proposing ideas in front of a group of the current researchers who would then take pot shots at their proposals. The atmosphere was intense and this showed in the results.

PARC created many of the technologies in use in computers today. This included the laser printer, the pixelated monitor, software where the printed output looks like that present on screen (what you see is what you get – WYSIWYG), and the concepts of windows and icons. It's often forgotten that it had quite a body of work to build from. The 'mouse' for example had been demonstrated many years before by Doug Englebart at Stanford Research Institute.

By 1979, the work done at PARC was coming together as a product that could be sold, the XEROX Star, when Steve Jobs, the co-founder of Apple, paid a visit. Jobs was bowled over by what he saw and almost instantly became possessed by the need to create a computer like the Star. It was clear to Jobs that no-one would want to deal with an old-style character-based computer, like the Apple II, given the option of working with the 'graphical user interface' (GUI) of the Star.

Apple

On return to Apple, Jobs persuaded the company leadership (Jobs by this time only held around 10% of the company's shares) to institute a project to create a computer like the Star. This was to become known as the Lisa. The Lisa was similar in many ways to the Xerox Star. It had a bit-mapped screen, a mouse, used a GUI and was far easier to use than traditional computers. Unfortunately, it was also similar in that it ran very slowly and cost a fortune (well over $10,000 each). Unlike the Star which had been introduced to rave reviews but poor sales in 1981, the Lisa did not have any networking capability. It also failed to make a mark commercially.

This pleased Jobs. Not because he had changed his mind about GUIs, but because the management, whom he had persuaded to start the Lisa project, had seen fit to install someone else at its head. Incensed, Jobs mounted a coup on an already running project to create another Apple computer and declared himself leader. The project had been started before Job's visit to PARC, by an ex-PARC researcher called Jeff Raskin that had subsequently moved to Apple. It was intended to develop the next generation computer to replace the Apple II. Unlike the Lisa this included making it affordable. It was named after Raskin's favorite apple: the Macintosh.

Once in charge, Jobs took eight of the most talented and iconoclastic young engineers and set them to work in an office far from the main corporate center. The team grew as time wore on, on many occasions plundering the software written for the Lisa project, but taking care to ensure that the computer was designed in a more cost effective manner. By 1984, the Macintosh was ready to launch.

The launch itself was notable. The high point was to be a 45 second TV advert shown during the Superbowl. It showed a sea of pallid-gray men in a large hall listening, stupefied, to the words of a Orwelian Big Brother character whose image was being shown on a large screen. A young woman, the only human not dressed in gray, sprints into the hall pursued by guards. She thrusts a long handled hammer into the screen bearing the image of Big Brother. The scene is flushed with light and the voice-over intones:

On January 24th Apple computer will announce Macintosh. And you will see why 1984 won't be like 1984.

The advert, directed by Ridley Scott (of *Aliens*, *Bladerunner* and *Gladiator* fame), cost $1.6m to produce and was shown by Apple only once (the one slot cost $500,000). It was however shown repeatedly over the following months as the media debated the impact of both the commercial and the computer. Ten years later, it even topped one advertising industry poll for the best advertisement of the previous 50 years.

Marketing, however powerful, could not make the Macintosh a runaway success. The machine itself appeared a little slow and, as it was both ground-breaking and very idiosyncratic, there was not much software available for customers to buy when it was first launched. Compared to the IBM PC and its clones, that were by this time taking the market by storm, it was a backwater that only ever achieved 10% of the market. At $2,400 it was too expensive for the domestic market and, as it did not have an IBM badge or a large sales force supporting it, it was not destined to make it in the business market. It did however become popular in the media and publishing industries where the aesthetics and ease-of-use were fully appreciated.

Personal Computer GUIs

Whilst the Macintosh gave the computer-buying public their first sight of GUIs and mice, industry insiders had already seen this as the way forward. There were a number of attempts to bring the same concept to fruition on IBM-compatible PCs, but without exception all attempts failed, at least initially. Just like the Macintosh, all required applications, such as spreadsheets and word processors, to be re-written from scratch. Something the application developers were unsurprisingly reluctant to do given that they were at the same time fighting for market share on the old MS-DOS platform.

The first attempt came from VisiCorp. Their offering, VisiOn, was released in January 1984 around the same time as the Mac but was visually not as appealing. It was fairly rudimentary, there were no icons, it worked only in black and white and could be seen as a halfway house between the old character operating systems and the XEROX PARC concept. Despite drastic price cutting to try to generate sales, and get some return on the rumored $10 million development cost, it sold very poorly.

Digital Research, the CP/M people, shipped GEM. First for the Atari ST and then, in April 1985, for the PC. It was much closer to the spirit of PARC and the Mac, so much so that Apple apparently sued. It suffered from a lack of applications and was never widely adopted.

On launching the PC/AT, which used the next generation microprocessor – the Intel 80286, IBM launched 'TopView'. This was a 'character-based' system that allowed users to switch between two applications, both of which appeared to be running at the same time: an innovation. This was done because the new processor used in the PC/AT was capable of handling multiple processes but the MS-DOS available at the time was not. It turned out customers didn't yet care, and the product disappeared.

The most significant of the pretenders was, of course, Microsoft. Bill Gates allegedly stood transfixed through three full cycles of the VisiOn Demo at the COMDEX computer show in 1982 and was determined to offer a repost. One year later in November 1983, Microsoft Windows was announced, with product availability in Spring 84. Spring 84 became May 84, August 84, January 85 and finally November 85. A full 2 years after its announcement and long after its competitors had been and gone, Microsoft Windows shipped to a rather lukewarm response. The system had crude icons and used a mouse but that was about it. The 'Windows' couldn't even overlap or be resized.

Unlike its GUI competitors, Microsoft had a steady stream of income from MS-DOS and could continue to develop their product. A much improved but still barely usable Windows Version 2.0 shipped in 1987 and the first serviceable, but still unreliable, version Windows 3.0 arrived in May 1990. Windows 3.0 still required a 16-bit MS-DOS as a foundation thus ensuring Microsoft's ongoing hegemony.

In the mid 1980s, IBM became uncomfortable that Microsoft was more in control of the PC platform than it was. It was also becoming clear that MS-DOS had a limited shelf life and that within a few years a new generation of hardware would require a new generation of operating systems. IBM and Microsoft agreed to start work jointly on that next generation. IBM decided to attempt to wrest control of 'its' PC platform back from the market in the same stroke by planning a new line of personal computers, to become known as PS/2, using its own proprietary architecture that could not be legally cloned.

The first product to come out of that partnership was OS/2 version 1.0. Released at the end of 1987, it was a text-based operating system, like MS-DOS, but it allowed more than one process to run inside the computer at the same time, which MS-DOS could not.

Work continued at Microsoft on the upgrades to OS/2 which grew to include a PARC style GUI by 1989. The following year however IBM had become increasingly dissatisfied with the pace of progress at Redmond (Microsoft's base). It appeared that Microsoft was placing more resources on the parallel development of the competing Windows for

DOS. In truth, this may have had as much to do with the panic surrounding an unstable new release as it did in Microsoft's wish to look after its own commercial interests. IBM decided to take on the delivery of OS/2 itself without the help of Microsoft.

By 1992, OS/2 version 2 would be shipped. This would be the first mainstream operating system to make full use of 32-bit microprocessors (available since 1986). This would be a grand claim but few people were listening. OS/2 by this stage had a reputation for having few applications available and being unable to talk to many printers, displays or sound cards. Once IBM took charge of development, these issues were largely rectified but the label had stuck. Over the coming years, OS/2 would be improved and upgraded many times and would generally be declared superior to Microsoft Windows by those who took the time to look at it. Unfortunately for IBM, Microsoft Windows had such a grip on the market that they finally threw in the towel in 2005 and withdrew the product from sale.

When IBM and Microsoft parted ways in 1990, the long-range product that had just started development, previously expected to become OS/2 version 3.0, was retained by Microsoft. This was always intended to be an operating system for 'file servers', that is the central computers that store files for groups of workers. Before long, this became known as Microsoft Windows NT (New Technology).

Windows NT was introduced by Microsoft in early 1994. It would be available to work in parallel with the old 'desktop' versions of Windows intended to run on the PCs that sit on users' desks. The market that Windows NT was entering was dominated by a company called Novell. Their NetWare operating system had a 70% share of the market. Unfortunately for them, in order for a desktop PC to talk to their central server, Novell Software had to be installed on every individual PC. This was a great hassle for corporate IT departments. Because Microsoft owned the desktop version of Windows, it could link to Windows NT without any additional software. Corporate IT departments found it far simpler to avoid the hassle of installing Novell software and switched to use Microsoft software at both ends. By the end of the 1990s, Windows NT had become reliable enough to supplant the Netware Operating system. It is rare today to find a company that runs its file-servers using anything other than Microsoft software.

Over the years, Windows NT was renamed Windows 'Server' and the desktop versions that run on PCs were renamed Windows 'professional' and 'home' (which is largely the same as 'professional' but with its wings clipped). Periodically, new versions of each are released which offer a steady stream of income to Microsoft but few meaningful new features for users.

Productivity Applications

An operating system, such as Microsoft Windows, is little use without an application. As the name implies an application is a piece of software that does something useful. System software, such as operating systems, just look after the administration.

Spreadsheets

The first major example of the so-called productivity applications was written by a student on the famous Harvard MBA course. Dan Bricklin had been a programmer for DEC, amongst other companies, but had become convinced that he was not guaranteed a job in the future because programming was becoming so much easier. Life in financial services beckoned.

During his course, one of his lecturers described the analysis performed by production planners for scheduling manufacturing. The calculations were carried out on large blackboards divided into cells, each of which were interrelated: when the production of Item X went up, the supply of parts Y and Z had to be increased proportionally. Not only did this take up a lot of space and manpower but it was prone to errors where the analyst neglected to update linked cells.

Bricklin got together with a friend from programming days, Bob Frankston, and formed a company, Software Arts, to develop a computer-based version of the blackboards: the spreadsheet. At the same time, a recent Harvard MBA graduate, Dan Fylstra, was in the process of starting up a new type of company, the software publisher. His company, Personal Software would market software developed by others, much like a book publisher markets books written by others. Fylstra lent Bricklin and Frankston an Apple II and the pair set about developing their program. Initially, it was expected to take about a month to complete but, as had been the case so many times before, the development process dragged on for almost a year.

The finished product, VisiCalc, hit the shops in October 1979. Take up was initially slow. Frankston would demonstrate it at local computer stores but most punters left nonplussed, perhaps after buying another computer game. A few hardy souls purchased a copy to play with and eventually, over a period of 12 months, slowly but surely it percolated its way into the corporate market.

Initially VisiCalc, the only spreadsheet on the market, would only work on the Apple II. This was a boon to the sales of Apples and catapulted them into the business market. For a time, Apple was the leading microcomputer in the business market, largely on the back of VisiCalc. This was not to last long with the IBM PC waiting in the wings.

Given that Personal Software's hit product was called 'VisiCalc' the company was rebranded VisiCorp (well they were Harvard MBAs after all) and other packages were commissioned to join the 'Visi' stable.

One such minor product was VisiPlot/VisiTrend written by Mitch Kapor based on earlier work he had done whilst at MIT's Sloan Management School. After a period being sold on the same commission basis as VisiCalc, VisiCorp decided to buy out Kapor. They paid him a large lump sum so that they could keep all the profits from the software sales without having to pay a royalty for every copy sold.

Kapor took half the money he received and bet it on the newly emerging IBM PC. He arranged for a spreadsheet, written in assembly language to avoid any loss of performance, to be developed specifically to take advantage of the configuration of the IBM PC with its new PC-DOS operating system. He set up the Lotus Development Corporation and obtained additional venture funding.

This still being business-school territory, the consultancy McKinsey and Co was engaged to advise on the launch. Unsurprisingly, a multi million dollar general marketing blitz was chosen alongside the creation of a direct sales staff to sell straight to businesses. Gone were the days of bamboozling demos in computer shops and organic growth that had served VisiCalc so well.

Lotus 1-2-3 went to market in January 1983, a little under 18 months after the IBM PC's introduction. In its first year, it sold nearly 20 times its original projection of $4 million worth of software. Whilst VisiCalc was eventually ported (adapted) to the IBM PC platform it was never as comfortable with it as it was on the original Apple II and sales didn't take off. Lotus had become top dog.

A couple of years after the launch of Lotus 1-2-3, Kapor bumped into Dan Bricklin, the progenitor of VisiCalc, on a flight. Software Arts, Bricklin's company that owned the rights to VisiCalc, was in interminable discussions with the publisher, VisiCorp. VisiCorp wanted to buy out Bricklin, just like they had Kapor, so that they would not need to pay royalties but the two sides couldn't agree terms. Kapor did a deal. Lotus bought out Software Arts and shortly after discontinued VisiCalc, by this time a fading force in the market.

VisiCorp meanwhile imploded after the protracted and disastrous development effort to produce the disappointing VisiOn windowing environment. It ended up being bought by a tiny competitor to avoid going bankrupt.

Shortly after putting VisiCalc out of its misery, Kapor parachuted out of Lotus which was being led by one of the original McKinsey consultants, Jim Manzi. It led the market for spreadsheets on the PC platform until it stumbled whilst making the leap to Windows in the early 1990s.

Word Processors

The first popular word processor was WordStar from a small outfit called MicroPro. MicroPro was set up by Seymour Rubenstein, the former marketing director of the company that made the IMSAI Altair Clone. IMSAI was the company that started the CP/M bandwagon on 8-bit microcomputers and when he left to start up a software company, it was natural for Rubenstein to make sure his product worked on the CP/M system. Working on one CP/M machine meant that it worked on all. WordStar was popular but it was not a runaway success. By the time the IBM PC was introduced, under 10,000 copies has been sold but for the relatively expensive price of $495 each.

The product was completely rewritten for the IBM PC and in the early days took about a quarter of all word processor sales on the platform. WordStar had successfully made the transition to the PC but in 1984, introduced WordStar 2000 with a radically new look-and-feel. Users of the old system would essentially have to relearn how to use it. Many didn't bother and chose to learn something else instead, with WordPerfect being a popular choice.

Like Lotus 1-2-3, WordPerfect lead the word processing market throughout the 1980s only to botch the transition to Microsoft Windows in the early 1990s.

Databases

The most famous database application of the early PC days was Ashton-Tate's dBase series. It was originally written by a lone programmer, Wayne Ratcliffe, in his spare time after work at the NASA Jet Propulsion Laboratory. It was originally known as the Vulcan database. Ratcliffe made a stab at marketing his creation in the late 1970s but quickly tired of the hassle of order fulfillment.

A software publisher, Software Plus, run by one George Tate heard of the product's demise and negotiated to sell the software on a royalty basis. In the kind of marketing effort not taught at business school, Tate renamed both the company, to Ashton-Tate, and the product, to dBase II. There had never been a Mr Ashton nor had there been a dBase I. The names just sounded good and the use of the II signature gave the impression that the product was more mature than it truly was. The chutzpah paid off and the product sold well both on early microcomputers and on the IBM PC platform.

The wheels came off the cart however during the development of the upgrade to dBase IV in 1986. After the all too familiar sad story of frayed tempers and schedule slippage, a bug-ridden product limped out to the market often causing upset and mayhem – unacceptable in the database market. Ashton-Tate's customers remained loyal for a time but there was to be no more growth. The company was bought by Borland in the early 1990s.

Microsoft Office

The PC software market was of course not as simple as these tales suggest. There were many contenders for all three types of software. In the early day, the barriers to entry were low and any two or three person outfit could launch an adequate product. As time wore on however it took more and more effort and know-how to compete with the big software organizations.

One also-ran in the 1980s market for work processors and spreadsheets was Microsoft. Bill Gates had lured Charles Simonyi, the PARC researcher that helped develop the first WYSIWYG editor for the XEROX Alto, to Microsoft back in 1979 to look after applications development. As far back as 1982, the Microsoft Multiplan Spreadsheet was released. The following year, Microsoft Word followed but neither were well received and both made little impact, failing to dislodge the independent products provided by Lotus and WordStar/WordPerfect. Things started to look brighter in 1985 when Microsoft released Microsoft Word and Excel for the Apple Macintosh.

Because it was much more difficult to write programs for a GUI, and because the Mac was a relatively small market, there were far fewer competitors. The Microsoft products quickly shot to the top of the pile and by 1987, the Mac applications were providing half of Microsoft's revenues.

Word and Excel for the Mac proved to be the making of Microsoft. Not only did they produce profits to bankroll the rest of the operation, including the refinement of Windows, but far more importantly in the long run they introduced Microsoft to the art of writing programs for GUIs.

When a passable version of Windows did hit the streets in 1990, Microsoft was amongst the few companies able to deliver workable, if still a bit flaky, productivity applications for the platform. Lotus 1-2-3 and WordPerfect were late to market with working and reliable Windows versions and were never seen again. Shortly after, Microsoft started to bundle the headlining applications, like Word and Excel, with lesser applications, such as PowerPoint, as a single offering called Microsoft Office and the rest of the industry was on the run. By 1995, it was believed that Microsoft had well over 90% of the market for such software.

Spreadsheets and word processors are all very useful and have become indispensable in many ways to the users of PCs but they sit at the edge of the ecosystem of computers. Electricity and water companies don't use spreadsheets to keep track of their customer's bills. Manufacturing companies don't manage their operations using word processors. Let us turn to look at how computers are used in business: the world of information technology.

4 Computers in Business

LEO

J Lyons & Company were unlikely pioneers. Their primary business was the provision of revitalizing refreshments, most commonly tea and a slice of cake, to tired shoppers across the UK. They had grander establishments in cities, including the legendary Lyons corner houses in London that could each feed 5000 diners at a sitting, but their mainstay was a chain of provincial teashops. In the inter-war years, their name was synonymous with good value, high quality and polite and efficient service provided by the uniformed waitresses known as 'nippies'.

The operation was rigidly controlled from the central site, Cadby Hall in West London. Waste, efficiency, costs and profits were all heavily analyzed as a matter of course. In order to keep their offering competitive, costs were kept down and profit margins were wafer thin. By the late 1930s, the central office had become a heavy user of punched card tabulating machinery to keep track of the operation and ensure costs did not get out of control.

In 1947, a couple of young managers where sent on a tour of the USA to find out what they could about advances in management techniques that had evolved during the war. These could then be applied to the central bureaucracy at Lyons to help keep them competitive. They had read press reports about the ENIAC at the Moore School before leaving and thought that it would be worthwhile to look into the use of a similar device for repetitive business calculations. During their trip, they met up with Herman Goldstine, part of the original ENIAC team. By this time, he had left the Moore School and moved to Princeton's Institute of Advanced Study to work with Von Neumann on their new computer. The IAS was intended to be a theoretical establishment and Von Neumann had to battle to be allowed to build a computer at all. Other members of the staff, including Albert Einstein, thought it was overly practical and should be done elsewhere. The IAS team were certainly not going to worry about commercial applications of computers. On their initial visit, Goldstine was happy to tell the visitors all he knew about computers but suggested talking to the other computer groups about how they might be used by business. He pointed them to the Eckert-Mauchly Computer Corporation in Philadelphia and, to the visitors' great surprise, a team at Cambridge University working under Maurice Wilkes, the gentleman who had such difficulty getting to the Moore School lectures in 1946.

Several weeks later, once back at Cadby Hall, the Lyons team wrote up a proposal outlining how an electronic computer could be used within the central office. They suggested financially assisting the Cambridge team to complete their computer and then arranging to copy it. In October 1947, the Lyons board approved the donation of £3,000 (around £50,000 or $75,000 in today's money) to the Mathematical Laboratory of Cambridge University.

It would seem odd for a tea shop company to attempt to build its own computer but Lyons was an odd company. In today's business speak, it would be described as heavily vertically integrated. When the need arose to clean table cloths and uniforms for example, the company set up in the laundry business. It was one of the UK's largest employers, employing over 35,000 at peak in its various lines of business. They had identified the need for a business computer. The fact the only company in the world interested in supplying business computers did not yet have a product and was on the other side of the Atlantic did not put them off. They merely decided to build their own.

After their brisk development efforts, and the free gifts of surplus vacuum tubes from the Ministry of Supply, the Cambridge team ran their first program in anger in May 1949. Lyons by this time had already hired a chief engineer to look after the technical side of their new machine and preparations were well advanced. It became clear that an exact copy of the Cambridge machine would be too small to perform useful business applications. The scientific applications that Cambridge were interested in had very few inputs but required a lot of repetitive work within the central processor. In business there was generally a large number of inputs, each of which required a small amount of work in the central processor. They also tended to need a lot of shifting and sorting. This meant that the Lyons Electronic Office, or LEO as the computer would be known, needed twice the memory of the Cambridge machine. It would also need more advanced equipment for input than the basic paper tape reader in use at Cambridge. This would be far too slow to keep the main processor busy and was woefully unsuitable for large quantities of data. Lyons hired an outside company, Standard Telephones and Cables, to prepare magnetic tape drives to speed up the input and output.

The contract with STC did not run smoothly. The rest of the LEO computer was ready in mid 1951 but it had no serious input capabilities. The experimental tape drives STC were working on proved unable to start and stop fast enough to be effective, just like UNIVAC's early efforts. In order to get the rest of the computer doing useful work a traditional paper tape reader was attached. A job known as 'bakery valuations' comparing the income and expenditure associated with bakery produce was lined up as the first task LEO would undertake. The first trial run was in September 1951 with the computer generated numbers replacing the manually calculated figures in the reports sent to management on 29th November 1951. Computers had arrived in business.

Given the limited input capabilities of the machine, the work undertaken was also initially limited. It was however one of only three electronic computers in the UK so its spare time was rented out to organizations that needed a computer for scientific calculations. The military used it for ballistics calculations, placing a red ribbon round the machine to indicate a security cordon. The meteorological office used it for weather forecasting and the Institute of Actuaries used it to calculate insurance tables. By mid 1953, the STC tape drives were finally abandoned. A much faster tape reader was procured that used light to detect holes rather than metal contacts and the green light was given to start moving the more demanding business applications from manual processing onto the computer. In February 1954, the pay packets of selected workers were calculated electronically for the first time.

GE Appliance Park

Around this time, similar activities were starting to stir on the other side of the Atlantic. A scene was forming that would become familiar over the next half century. The management of the large engineering conglomerate GE had decided that their traditional factories were too set in their ways. Investment was needed to prepare for the future but the local managements were inactive and the unionized workforces were resistant to change. In a bold move, they invested around $300m in a vast new manufacturing complex at Appliance Park, Louisville, Kentucky to replace several plants dotted around the east coast of the USA. By 1953, six new factories were sitting next to one another knocking out everything from domestic washing machines to refrigerators.

To create these goods, the facilities employed the latest factory automation techniques. Echoing the thoughts of Charles Babbage, one manager, Roddy Osborn, thought that the time had come to apply technology to office work as well as manufacturing. There was considerable skepticism within GE but he managed to arrange for the funding of a study by external consultants from Arthur Andersen. During the spring of 1953, they compared the computers that were then 'available': the UNIVAC and a prototype of IBM's 702. After 3 months, Andersen alighted on the UNIVAC largely on the basis that the IBM machine had not yet been shown to work. The recommendation was accepted by Osborn. This did not please IBM who arranged for pressure to be applied by GE management in Schenectady for the decision to be reversed. Osborn stood firm and the eighth UNIVAC, the first to a commercial customer, was installed at Appliance Park in January 1954. Then the fun really began.

The first application to be performed on the computer was payroll. The time recording period in the factories ended on a Sunday evening with the cash earned being handed to the worker on the Tuesday of the following week. A total of 9 days lag. Before the project kicked off,

Osborn initially envisaged that the time and work records could be converted into payslips in around 20 minutes. It was supposed to take around four GE staff programmers, one or two from Andersen and one or two from UNIVAC to write the programs required.

It didn't take long for things to deviate from plan. In the middle of 1954, there were around 30 programmers working on the payroll application alone. In October, the first production run took place with a limited number of employees. Instead of the 20 minutes originally predicted it took 44 hours of machine time. This did not include the time taken to find and fix blown vacuum tubes and debug malfunctioning programs. This ran to many more hours. Often one week's payroll would just be going out the door as the next week's arrived. On a number of occasions, when the machine was being truly recalcitrant, operators would have to pack up the data on punched cards and journey to another UNIVAC customer or the UNIVAC service bureau in New York to complete the job in time. As one of the project leaders said 'every week was an adventure'.

Each week, following program tweaks and re-writes, the GE payroll would run a little faster until it was only taking 20 hours to process over 10,000 employees pay. As the payroll stabilized, GE moved on to using the computer to plan the usage of materials in the factory. The aim was to reduce the level of stocks in the factory whilst making sure that the production lines never halted for lack of parts. Having excess stock literally lying around, tied up working capital which could be put to better use elsewhere. In the first year of operation, the raw material stocks were reduced by $1m and a planned warehouse expansion was canceled. This was when GE management, outside the computer group that is, started to take computing seriously.

Osborn had by his time left GE. He, along with many others, had been downgraded in a large internal reorganization. He was apparently fired when he arranged for the parking area outside the computer building to be paved over without the authority of a higher manager.

The GE implementation had been a trailblazer for UNIVAC. They had undergone a significant amount of pain to get the system working. There was unfortunately little that could be done to reduce the pain for later customers. The first business customers of computers needed to have the same level of pioneer spirit that the computer manufacturers had. Once a computer arrived on site it was up to the customer to do something with it. They couldn't expect much support from the manufacturer. Of the early manufacturers, the one that gave by far and away the most help was IBM, but even they only had a small number of staff that were part of the marketing function. UNIVAC in the early days were far too concerned with delivering hardware to be able to spare any significant resources to help the client after delivery.

USE and SHARE

Once the machine had been delivered, it was software that was the big problem. Customers had to write it themselves. All of it. In binary machine code. Whilst of a different nature, the technical demands of programming in those days were of the same order as designing the computer itself. This was clearly going to strain the resources of a teashop or washing machine manufacturer. And so it had proved. It must also be remembered that very few of the workers on the GE project would have worked with a computer before let alone programmed. They would have been sent on a programming course and then thrown in at the deep end with a team of others like themselves.

The set of software tools created on the GE implementation was distributed to all the other UNIVAC customers that could make use of them. This was considered an act of kindness to other souls in the same predicament as yourself and not as a commercial act of profit.

The arrangement of sharing computer code and experience was soon formalized in the notion of a computer user group. The concept of users groups, where a number of users of a particular firms equipment would gather to exchange war stories, was not new. They had been many user groups of punched card equipment. Both UNIVAC and IBM facilitated the set up of user groups for their computer customers known as USE and SHARE respectively.

SHARE grew out of an organizations set up in 1952 on the West Coast of the USA where a number of aerospace companies had bought the first of IBM's computers, the 701 'defense calculator'. IBM's resources were spread pretty thinly at the time given that they were working on getting the 701 operational whilst also completing the development of the business-oriented 702 and the 'mid-range' 650. One of the area's salesmen, Blair Smith, decided to get the customers talking to one another to see if they would help each other out. The meeting did not get off to a good start:

I do remember that some of the 701 customers were pretty upset with each other over the former pirating of personnel, and it seems to me I had to buy about three rounds of drinks before we became friendly. In fact, I believe it was the largest single expense account I've ever filed in all of my years with the IBM Corporation.

The 'pirating of personnel' was a significant concern. The only place that customers could send staff to learn the ways of the 701 was at IBM's Madison Avenue Office in New York. For many trainees, their extended visit to the Big Apple was quickly followed by a job offer on increased pay by another IBM customer eager to obtain their skills.

Software Contractors

By the end of the 1950s, there was a universal shortage of programming staff. It was the large military projects with the most complicated systems that suffered the most. In 1954, SAGE, the $8 billion system to manage air-defense against Soviet bombers, had been given the go-ahead. This was the first system to use any form of visual display unit with the operator using light pens to interact with the display rather than a keyboard. The system worked in real-time, that is to say it had to process information very quickly. Getting this kind of system working was far more complicated than commercial programming for businesses. If there was difficulty finding people to staff a business computer project, staffing SAGE would be impossible. IBM, who were sub-contracted to build the mammoth SAGE computers, Bell Labs and MIT were all invited to look after the programming effort but declined. In the end, the hot potato was dropped on the RAND Corporation.

The RAND (Research ANd Development) corporation had been set up following the war to maintain a center of excellence for operational research. It was a government-owned non-profit making organization focusing exclusively on military research, generally for the US Air Force. It had nothing at all to do with Remington Rand.

RAND was the spiritual home of the doctrine of Mutually Assured Destruction (MAD). MAD propounded that the best way of ensuring that your enemy does not even attempt to attack you is to ensure that they know you have the capability to destroy them even after their most fierce assault. This grew out of its application of the mathematical discipline of 'Game Theory', sometimes more prosaically known as the 'theory of bluffing', which was originally popularized by John Von Neumann (of 'first draft' fame). Von Neumann himself had a more worrying view when he became a consultant to RAND in 1948. He believed that the US should perform a pre-emptive strike against Moscow to stop the Soviet Union developing into a nuclear power. Thankfully no-one took him too seriously.

By the end of 1956, there were more people involved in programming efforts than in the rest of RAND combined and so the programming group was split off into a separate non-profit entity, the Systems Development Corporation or SDC. By 1960, there were 3,500 programmers and support staff working there. It was reckoned at one time that SDC had over half the programmers in the USA working for them but like their business-based brethren, the SDC staff where not immune to offers of higher salaries and annual staff turnover sat at a rate of around 20%.

At the same time, there were stirrings to create similar software companies in the private sector. The first successful programming services firm was formed in 1955 by two refugees from the IBM technical computing bureau. The firm, the 'Computer Usage Company' or CUC, initially worked out of a founder's New York apartment and employed four programmers and a secretary. The outfit was an instant success and at the end of its first year, it had charged $200,000 to clients. In 1962, they had 240 staff and revenues of $2m.

Four years after CUC started up, in 1959, three leading lights of the west coast computer establishment, including one of the founders of SHARE, formed their own company. They called it Computer Sciences Corporation, CSC, and their first major job was to develop a compiler for business use for the computer manufacturer Honeywell. The compiler, FACT, ended up being completed by Honeywell themselves after the initial 18 month contract with CSC had expired. Given the ascendancy of COBOL, it was largely ignored by the market but this was not before CSC had been paid $300,000 for their part in its creation. The company grew phenomenally and 10 years later its annual revenues broke through the $100m mark. It remains in the list of the world's top ten IT services companies today.

By staying around this long, CSC was one of the few exceptions. Many hundreds of small outfits sprang into life in the 1950s and 1960s to provide programming for the confused customers of the computer manufacturers. Few grew to any appreciable extent and most fizzled out within a few years without leaving much trace.

Go-Go

The lucky ones grew enough to be floated on the stock market with an initial public offering. CSC for example floated in 1963. Others followed and by 1968, an investment frenzy was building driven by the release of the IBM system/360 mainframes a couple of years previously. Up until this point, the more conservative businesses were just as likely to renew their punch card tabulating machines as they were to move onto computer technology. With the offer of an entire range of computers, a clear standard, supported and sold by IBM, many business finally took the leap into the digital age.

The later half of the 1960s are often referred to as the go-go years. The prices of shares in the new breed of technology companies doubled and doubled again, driven by, amongst other things, hype about the emergence of the 'computer utility'. The computer utility of the late 1960s was very similar in concept to the application service provider (ASP) model that was being pushed at the end of the 1990s. It stated that corporations would cease to own and operate their own computers. They would instead lease their computer time from a utility-like organization that would also rent them software. The utility would be better placed to provide the skills and disciplines required to manage large hardware and software installations. Spare capacity and back-up facilities could then be rotated between several companies rather than having to be bought for the use of a single operation.

The 'computer utility' was distinct from 'outsourcing', the leading exponent of which was Ross Perot's EDS. In the early 1960s, Henry Ross Perot was an IBM salesman and, so the story goes, an extremely effective one. One year he had sold his annual quota of computers by the third week of January. This meant that he would earn no more commission for the remaining 11 months of the year and so left IBM to do something more challenging. His chosen field was to take over a company's computer function, rip out the inefficiencies and run the more streamlined operation on behalf of the original company. His fees would be based on the cost of the function before outsourcing. The more chaotic and inefficient the computer center was initially, the more profit he would make. EDS was founded in 1962 and floated in 1968. By the end of that year, Perot was worth over $1 billion on paper.

Just like application service providers 30 years later, the computer utility did not take off. Neither the necessary infrastructure nor software existed. This had not stopped a number of software contracting firms from buying a large number of mainframes to support the anticipated flood of business. When the US economy slid into recession in late 1969, the fortunes of the companies that had bought into the computer utility vision slid also. The entire computer industry was tarred with the same brush and share prices dived. It was essentially the deflation of a stock market bubble: irrational exuberance over a technology which was supposed to change the paradigm of business but did nothing of the kind. Does that sound familiar? The hangover from the go-go years would last well into the 1970s and beyond.

Unbundling

The end of the go-go years signaled the start of a new era in computing for different reasons. Ever since the first commercial installations by LEO and UNIVAC, software had been freely distributed. Each manufacturer had a library of programs that could be given to customers to help them get a return on their investment in hardware. A number of these programs would have been written by the manufacturer for this purpose. Many would have been written, and effectively paid for, by other customers as part of their installations. At the end of the 1960s there were only a handful of software products that could be paid for. Virtually everything would be made available for free.

This also meant that the largest computer companies had the largest catalog of useful software. A new customer looking for a new computer would tend towards buying from a larger manufacturer as it was more likely that they would have useful software. Given the huge commercial success of the System/360, IBM was once more coming under pressure from the anti-trust authorities. At the end of 1968, it was announced that it would be charging separately for the provision of software. From within IBM, this would be seen as a reasonably harmless sop to those who wanted it to reduce its market power.

This so-called 'unbundling' decision was a key point in the development of the software industry. Before unbundling, it was virtually impossible for a company to sell a software product because customers would probably try to get by with a similar item that had been made available for 'free'. After unbundling, it was possible to compare a manufacturer's offering with that prepared by third parties and choose the most appropriate based on price.

Gradually, as IBM started to put a price on its already existing software, the artifacts previously created by the software contractors were also priced. Few brand new products would be created in the 1970s due to the dearth of capital created by the stock market collapse of 1969. It became clear that it took at least 2 to 3 years from kicking off the development of a software product to the point at which a regular revenue would be earned. That was enough to put off jittery investors on its own. Add to this the amount of money that had to be pumped into marketing to make the product visible to customers and few would be brave enough to chance their arm on building new software for sale. In truth the development of the actual product was relatively insignificant compared with marketing costs. In the early days, the software contractors like CUC or CSC needed little in the way of marketing. Finding work was done by exploiting the founder's network of contacts. For a small company, marketing would normally cost well below 5% of revenues. Larger companies could spend up to 15% of their income on maintaining sales forces, sponsoring conferences and general advertising. When they switched from providing programmers to supplying finished products, the marketing expenditure sky-rocketed to around 50% of revenues. The proportion of income spent on the various forms of 'sales support' has remained at this level ever since.

We have already encountered the types of software products that were used to keep the computer happy: the system software that includes operating systems, databases and transactional middleware. These are necessary for smooth operation and are highly complex but computers and not bought to run them alone. Let's take a look instead at the activities that business computerize and the software products that can be bought to satisfy their needs.

Common Software Tasks

Financial Software

The aim of any business is to make money. Investors wouldn't put money into a businesses if there was little chance of getting it back and with a little extra on top. Managers have to be able to show that they are indeed making money. Any sign that they are losing money and eating into the investors' cash will have swift and irreversible consequences for their careers. In order to convince doubting investors that they are indeed worthy of their mountainous share options, managers have to keep track of what is going on financially in such a way that it is beyond reproach. This is known as financial accounting and involves keeping an up-to-date 'general ledger'.

When money arrives in a business is must be logged in what are known as revenue accounts. When money leaves the business it must be logged in what are known as expense accounts. The value of assets, the extent of future liabilities and the capital (in effect what the business is worth to the investors) should also be monitored by updating the other relevant accounts.

At the end of each accounting period, the end of the month for most large businesses, the accounts are closed off. The overall total value on each revenue and expense account is accumulated and transferred to a single master account known as the 'profit and loss account'. If the total revenue exceeds total expenses, it will show a profit. If expenses exceeds revenue, it will show a loss.

It is the monthly nature of the closing of accounts that leads to the controlled frenzy that is 'month end processing'. All information that is relevant to the month must be with the accountants before they start closing the accounts. Anything that arrives afterwards will lead to a restatement. The management will be breathing down the necks of the accountants to get the monthly results as soon as possible and become uncomfortable and suspicious of foul play if there is a delay. Month end is a fraught time for all concerned: the accounts want to avoid annoying the managers, the managers want to avoid annoying the investors.

It is the information in the general ledger that is used to prepare the financial statements that are presented to investors and shareholders at the end of the year. Summary information is also published every quarter by companies that trade their shares on public exchanges. Without a reliable general ledger, companies wouldn't be able to tell their investors if they were making a profit or loss.

The general ledger doesn't record where cash has come from or gone to. It only records the fact that it has arrived or left. More detailed records of the provenance and destination of money are held within what are known as the accounts receivable and accounts payable functions. Accounts receivable looks after the money that the business expects to receive from customers. Accounts payable looks after the money that the business expects to pay to suppliers. Every customer or supplier has their own account showing the value of product that has been sent or received and the related payments. It is in the interest of the business to keep the difference between the two as low as possible in accounts receivable (i.e. get the cash off their customers fast) and as high as possible for accounts payable (pay their suppliers as late as possible).

The general ledger and accounts receivable and payable functions are all required, in one form or another, to allow the business to keep track of its affairs. This is true of all businesses. Without them the business will probably be operating illegally, if for no other reason than they won't have a clue what taxes they should pay. Together, it is these processes that are known as financial accounting.

Basic financial accounting doesn't however give a detailed view of the company's effectiveness. It may be that of all the sites where a business operates, half are fabulously profitable whilst the other half make eye watering losses. To get information at an additional level of detail requires the discipline known as management accounting, sometimes also called cost accounting.

Management accounting provides the business' management with far more detailed information regarding the internal operation of the business. This can be used to change the way the company operates to improve profitability. Normally, each appropriate transaction that is posted to the general ledger has additional 'cost objects' tagged onto it which can later be separated and analyzed. There are many types of cost objects, the most popular being cost centers (applied to expenses), profit centers (applied to revenues) and project codes.

Financial accounting must be applied by all businesses big or small. Management accounting is applied, to a greater or lesser degree, by all large businesses.

Sales Order Processing

In order to make money, it is necessary for most business to sell a product or service. The remaining businesses, those that provide no products or service but still receive income, are known as rackets and are subject to criminal proceedings. Once a customer has decided to make a purchase from a legitimate company, this is normally recorded in document known as a sales order. A sales order lists the items to be delivered along with the quantity of each. At this point the price of the goods will be calculated and agreed. Those who think this is a trivial uncomplicated process have not been involved with the sales order process in a large organization. It often turns into a confused morass of conflicting deals and special offers. After all do the price breaks (5% discount if you buy 10, 10% if you buy 100) override the seasonal discount? Do they both apply at the same time? Salespeople can also agree special price lists with each of their large customers meaning that there are often more price permutations than there are customers or products.

Additional documents are created as the sales order progresses through to delivery and billing. The last of which is sent to the accounts receivable function who can start the all important process of chasing payment.

Procurement

The purchasing function tends to be tightly controlled as this is where cash leaves the business leaving plenty of opportunities for skullduggery. When something needs to be bought in, the first step is to raise a purchase requisition. This is a vague statement that something is needed. It does not mean that it is permitted to buy the items. The approval for this is given once the purchase requisition has been reviewed by a manager with suitable spending authority who assents for it to be converted into a purchase order. It is the creation and approval of a purchase order that gives the clear message that the goods can be bought. Once a purchase order has been created and approved, someone or something communicates with the supplier to let them know that goods are required. The supplier will then create their own sales order, normally referencing the purchase order in case there is a problem later on.

A record is kept when the ordered goods finally arrive so that when the supplier asks for payment there is some paper trail of what has arrived, and should therefore be paid for, and what has not yet turned up.

Inventory

Having an accurate count of the items of stock on hand is imperative if the correct purchasing and manufacturing decisions are to be made. Each time goods are received or issued, the amount arriving or leaving must be recorded and added or subtracted from the stock count for that item. The stock count should be held for each separate location. That is to say that a warehouse and factory that sit next to each other should have two separate stock counts for each item. Stock counts are not only used in the planning of the physical operations but they are also used to determine the value of the assets on hand for recording in the general ledger.

Warehouse management

Inventory stock counts are useful for planning and accounting but they are at far too high a level for managing large fast-moving areas like warehouses. For example, when presented with a delivery request for 10 pallets of soap powder, a stock count of 10 pallets is a good start but it would be nice to know where in the warehouse the 10 pallets are. Knowing they are in there 'somewhere' is not good enough. Warehouse management takes inventory management to another level. It splits the warehouse into a series of 'bins' and remembers what quantity of what product is stored in each. Warehouse management systems also help manage the warehouse by working out what steps workers should take and then telling them exactly what to do in the correct order.

Production control

Often the goods that are sold are not in the same state as they were when they were purchased. This is the situation in manufacturing companies where raw materials and sub-assemblies are purchased and completed goods are dispatched. The means of getting the goods from one state to the other must also be managed. The control of production revolves around the production order. This states how much of the finished item is to be made and what its components or ingredients are. Often it includes details such as a list of the operations to be performed, what items of plant are required and how long each step will take.

MRP

Before LEO at Lyons and the UNIVAC at GE, all of the above processes were performed manually. Given the mountain of paper that resulted, there was little opportunity to closely match production volumes to sales volumes, purchase volumes to production volumes and so on. The glue that held everything together was stock. A significant buffer stock of components would be kept on the production line so that it would not stop if purchasing accidentally missed an order. An equally significant buffer stock of finished goods would be held so that peaks in sales could be fulfilled without upsetting customers.

Holding stock has a number of drawbacks. In the case of Lyons, stock would go stale. It would have to be carefully rotated and even then waste could not be avoided. The main problem though is that stock costs money. If all the unnecessary stock was sold to customers, the resulting cash that was freed up, known as working capital, could be invested back in the business perhaps by buying additional manufacturing capacity. Stock basically acted as an anchor on the business, holding it back from what it could achieve.

Shortly after they got their payroll systems working, both Lyons and GE moved on to look at ways of reducing stock. They worked on the so-called material control applications where purchasing orders were closely matched to stock levels and production schedules. This was an early form of material requirements planning (MRP) which by the 1970s had become widespread.

MRP required several items of information: production order schedule, the stock available, the minimum order quantities that suppliers would accept, the lead time before the supplier could deliver the goods and the absolute minimum level of stocks permitted. It would then stir it all up and produce a list of any additional purchases or production that was required.

After MRP came MRP II, manufacturing requirements planning. This took account of more variables than MRP such as production capacity (how may production lines were available and what was their capacity) and sales trends. MRP II could reschedule production if it found a combination that better suited the availability of production capacity, purchases and stock.

Beyond MRP II came ERP, enterprise resource planning. An ERP system held all the sales orders for a company, all the production control information, all the stocks and all the procurement information. It holds all the information necessary to allow it to work out when to make items, when to buy items, how many of them to make or buy and even, if there was more than one plant or supplier, where to get them from. In sales order processing, it could look after the delivery requirements and billing. In inventory control, it could record all the goods receipts and goods issues. Of course everything would be fully integrated with the financial and management accounts so that financial performance could be easily monitored.

SAP

The pre-eminent ERP software supplier is known as SAP. SAP was formed in 1972 by five programmers who had left IBM with the conviction that the world needed a set of standard applications that could be dropped into a company's operations without the fuss of large-scale program development. They saw the possibilities of the then new concept of time sharing systems and chose to make their new system interact directly with the user. This was a novel concept at a time when virtually all business computing was performed in a batch mode, often still using punched cards in some way. It should be remembered that this was only 2 years after IBM shipped its first computer capable of dealing with multiple users without extensive hardware modifications and that VDUs were still not widespread.

Their initial work was completed as software contractors. They would build an application program for one customer and then take this program and drop it into another customer as the starting point for their application. Over time and through working with a number of customers, the application grow in scope and reliability. The first contract was at the manufacturing plant of the chemical company ICI in Ostragen, Germany followed by a cigarette manufacturer and a pharmaceutical company. First came the financial accounting module then the material management module, which included the purchasing and inventory processes, followed by the asset accounting module. By 1978, the business was well and truly on its feet and the decision was taken to prepare for the leap to the next generation.

R/2 as it was to become known, 'R' standing for real-time, was created with a view to servicing an international customer base. The original applications had been written exclusively in German but R/2 was to work with several languages and currencies at the same time. It had to work in Italy for example where sales of over a billion lire were not uncommon. Figures that large would be too big for many less comprehensive packages. It was introduced to the market in 1981 and by the end of the following year was at work in over 250 sites in Germany. The rest of the decade was given over to international expansion from the strong home base. By the end of the decade, SAP was a major player in the market for mainframe business software. It didn't have the market to itself though. Dun & Bradstreet, with a long list of applications acquired over the years from various sources, was the market leader. This was particularly true in the USA where SAP had fewer than a hundred installations.

In the development of R/2, SAP had come up with its own technical platform intended to allow the applications to run on many different types of computer. This separated the business logic, written in a high-level COBOL-like language called ABAP, from the underlying computer hardware by putting an 'abstraction layer' known as BASIS in between. This made it far easier to move R/2 onto new types of hardware when the need arose. To get the applications working on a new type of computer, all that would be required would be to fiddle with the BASIS layer. The old ABAP programs would work just as they did on the original system.

This trick came in very handy when, in the early 1990s, SAP made the leap to 'client-server' computing. At the time, client-server was a radical departure and it spelled the relegation of the mainframe computer to specialist niches. As the 1980s progressed, a single large UNIX server could handle an increasing number of users simultaneously. By the end of the 1980s, they could comfortably handle 50 to 100 users at the same time which was as many as a small mainframe. A UNIX server meanwhile was a commodity item that was available for a fraction of the cost. In more demanding circumstances, it was possible to link a number of UNIX servers together. One server would be left to look after the database whilst others handled the requests from users. It was even possible to offload some of the processing load onto the recently popularized PC.

SAP was one of the first companies to offer serious business applications using the client server model. Its R/3 product, first released in 1992, moved the business applications from the mainframe onto UNIX servers and interacted with the user using a specially written GUI program on the then recently stabilized Microsoft Windows version 3.1. R/3 was a single large application that covered virtually every area that a business needed to administer from accounting (financial and cost) and logistics (purchasing, inventory management, sales and distribution, production management, project management, quality control, plant maintenance) to human resources (recording personal details, calculating payroll, managing training and employee expenses). It held all the information required to perform detailed ERP processing. The only drawbacks were that it was indescribably complex, belligerently inflexible and cost a fortune to get working.

SAP did not have the market to itself. PeopleSoft was a strong competitor but its lack of international focus early on dented its take up outside the USA. JD Edwards sold a far more basic ERP package called 'Worlds' but until the late 1990s, this was only available on IBM's AS/400 platform which once again restricted its application. For example, one of the world's largest oil companies would use SAP in large markets, where the size of the business would justify the cost, and use JD Edwards in smaller markets that did not need all of the functions provided by SAP R/3. In 2005, both PeopleSoft and JD Edwards were bought by Oracle which already had its own in-house ERP software known as 'E-Business Suite'.

Supply Chain Management

The step beyond ERP has become known as supply chain optimization or supply chain management (SCM) but unlike ERP, which completely replaced the systems that performed MRP and MRP II, SCM must sit on top of an ERP system. SCM products are generally split into three sections: demand planning, supply planning and transportation planning. Demand planning looks at historical sales data, works out the trends and then extrapolates these into the future. Unlike traditional ERP, this would take account of Christmas peaks or summer troughs in customer orders. The demand planning sales forecasts could then be used along with the stock levels from the ERP system to plan how to manufacture or purchase goods in the months ahead. This is supply planning. The resulting plans could then be returned to the ERP system for execution at a detailed level using its production control functions. Transport planning is used to optimize how an organization distributes products both within its own network of plants and warehouses and also with those of its customers.

Another more specialist area of SCM is known as CPFR (collaborative planning forecasting and replenishment). Certain types of business, notably large retailers like Wal-Mart, Tesco and Carrefour, have started to demand that their suppliers provide stock for their warehouses without being paid for it. The retailers only pay for the items when they have been sold to the end consumers. This allows the retailers to use the cash that would be tied up in stock for other purposes. There is a strong incentive on the suppliers to leave only the minimum of stock in the retailer's warehouse but should the store run out, they would have to cough up penalty payments to the retailer. The balancing act between keeping larger stocks at retailers (to make sure the retailer never runs out) and sending smaller stocks (to keep inventory costs low) is managed by specialist CPFR software.

If you were to ask an analyst in the late 1990s which companies were the leaders in supply chain optimization software, the answer would probably be Manugistics and i2. The years have not been kind to them unfortunately as the traditional ERP vendors have fought back with rival products of their own.

Customer Relationship Management

An ERP system takes care of the process of sales order fulfillment which starts whenever the customer has given a firm order. Many customers however take many months to get to the stage where they will make up their minds. This is particularly true of large high value orders such as airlines buying aircraft or corporations buying computer equipment. An ERP system doesn't really help during that period as it just sits waiting for the firm sales order.

A new breed of software originally known as sales force automation software was introduced to fill this gap. It would keep track of which salesman said what to which customer and on what day. It would distribute this information within a sales team so that everyone who needed access could have it, even when they were away from the corporate network. This should stop the customer being asked the same question twice (unless that is the sales team wanted to get a different answer from last time). The software would assign new sales prospects to a sales territory and thus to an individual sales manager. It would schedule sales calls and allow salesmen to configure products and create sales quotes without having to fiddle with product guides or price lists.

Given that the software could hold contact details for customers and could schedule sales calls, it was only a matter of time before it would be used in call centers. The call center version of the software would even display a step-by-step sales script which could be adapted depending on the responses given by the customer.

Before long, the term sales force automation sounded a bit specific so the class of software became known by the far more nebulous title of customer relationship management or CRM.

One of the first providers of such software, and certainly the most successful at the turn of the century was Siebel Systems. Tom Siebel had worked as a salesman for Oracle from 1984 to 1990 but left just before the company had a temporary fit of financial embarrassment in 1991. In 1993, he got together with another former Oracle sales executive, Patricia House, and formed a company to provide software to help co-ordinate sales forces. It went public in 1996, largely cornering the early market in CRM.

Supplier Relationship Management

Not to be outdone, the procurement people got their own version of CRM. Unsurprisingly, this became known as supplier relationship management or SRM. Like CRM, this performs tasks on the procurement side of the organization that are not done by the ERP system. Typically this will include simplifying and managing the purchases performed outside the MRP process. A catalog of approved products would be presented to users who could select what they require. The resulting requisition would then be presented to the appropriate manger for approval before being converted into a confirmed purchase order on the ERP system. It is the intention of an SRM solution to speed the process up and to push the users to use lower cost options selected from a list of preferred suppliers.

An early entry into the SRM market was by Ariba. Unfortunately, their original concept was closely bound to the notion of all business being conducted via an Internet exchange and the product didn't take off. Its popularity started to build once the discredited universal exchange aspect received less emphasis.

Data warehouses

Want to know who your best customers are? Want to know your most profitable products? The impatient would be unwise to ask their ERP systems. The ERP systems were designed for what is known as online transaction processing (OLTP). That is to say dealing with individual transactions, such as sales orders or purchase orders, one at a time. The underlying database is not technically optimized to take large numbers of these transactions and look at them as a group. This requires a different kind of set up intended for online analytical processing (OLAP).

OLAP systems extract raw transactional data from the likes of ERP systems and hold them in special data formats that make it far easier to analyze. Typically they also hold the data for a long time to allow trends over a period of months and years to be viewed and dissected. OLAP systems are also known as data warehouses given that they hold very large quantities of data collected over many years.

The database products used to hold data for data warehousing are provided by the same companies that supply the databases for OLTP systems. That is to say Oracle, IBM's DB2 and at the lower end Microsoft's SQL Server. The most popular tools used for preparing and viewing the data are provided by the likes of Cognos and Business Objects.

HR Software

When the management of sales, procurement and finance functions moved from paper to electronic form, it was only a matter of time before the human resource function followed. The HR function performs many distinct tasks: recruitment, storing personal details, looking after the organization structure, managing training, travel expenses and, most important of all, payroll. The problem with HR is that each company has their own take on how to perform each of these functions and each country, and in some cases state or region, has their own set of laws governing the process.

The original leader in HR systems was PeopleSoft although they originally had a clear focus on the North American Market.

Good Enough

The 1990s proved to be times of astronomical growth in all the software segments that have just been mentioned. The 21st century has not been so bounteous. Most companies that would benefit from ERP now have an ERP system so the market is commonly seen as saturated. In order to keep growing, SAP and Oracle have chosen to start encroaching on areas beyond their traditional strengths. Oracle has bought PeopleSoft, and with it JD Edwards, to cement its position as the number two ERP vendor. Both it and SAP launched CRM and SRM offerings to compete with the likes of Siebel, i2 and Manugistics (Oracle even bought Siebel in 2005). The so-called 'pure play' vendors, that focus on one area of specialty, have been hurting. Whilst few would say that Oracle and SAP have better products, customers have been switching to their software not because it is the best but because it is 'good enough' and is often significantly cheaper. It won't be long before most companies use Oracle or SAP products with only customers with special requirements selecting niche software.

Software Crisis

At the outset of commercial computing in the early 1950s, it was acknowledged that programming was not for the man in the street. The use of binary machine code or assembly language meant the programmer had to deal with the machine on its terms. Throughout the 1950s, there was a shortage of programming talent able to fit this rigid frame of thought – hence the creation of the likes of the SDC offshoot from RAND to provide a supply of suitably pliant minds. The load became a bit more tolerable with the advent of computer languages and compilers towards the end of the decade which meant the machines were starting to give some leeway to the programmers humanity. In the early 1960s however the situation slipped back into what became known as the 'software crisis'. Improving technology, such as the arrival of the transistor, meant that computers were becoming much faster. They were capable of doing much more than the old computers or the old programs that had been written to run on them. Writing programs to take full advantage of their capabilities started to stretch the capabilities of the programming fraternity. We have already encountered two of the most notable debacles: the creation of the OS/360 for the IBM system/360 and the creation of MULTICS by GE, MIT and Bell Labs. The OS/360 did eventually see the light of day but was an embarrassment to all concerned and received frequent major improvements. MULTICs was abandoned by Bell Labs before it was complete and led to GE giving up on computer manufacturing.

It was towards the end of the 1960s that effort was applied to change the preparation of software from a black art practiced by a priesthood of bearded programmers to something more akin to a traditional profession. The term 'software engineering', now known as the structured discipline of software development, was first coined as the title to an academic conference in Gamisch-Partenkirchen in Germany in October 1968.

Waterfall

Over the years, many approaches to software engineering have been proposed but rarely are they applied with any level of enthusiasm or rigor. One of the earliest methodologies was the so-called waterfall model published by one Winston Royce in 1970. It remains the predominant model of software development but in truth it is only the name that is used. The principles behind it are pretty simple. First you work out what you are trying to do: the Requirements. Then you document how the computer will meet these requirements: the Design. Then you implement the design: Programming or Coding. You check that everything you have built works together: Testing. Your software is now ready to go. The idea is that the output of one step of the process cascades to form the input to the next step just like a multi-step waterfall.

The first step of any software project is to gather requirements. Requirements documents should not include technical specifics but be a high-level statement of what processing is required from a business perspective. Indeed they don't even need to mention the computer at all. They are normally prepared by a project team working with representatives of the group of users who will fall victim to the system once it is complete.

The requirements are used by the project team to create the design. The design documents should state in detail how the requirements will be implemented technically. This is done by experienced analysts working in the project team. This step is often split into two separate steps: the functional design and the technical design. The functional design can be considered to be a more detailed definition of the requirements. The functional design document will generally be around five to ten times the size of the requirements they relate to. The technical design states where data will be held, how it will be accessed and what technical components need to be written.

Once complete, the technical design is handed to the programmers who, as the job title implies, write the programs using whatever tools are available to them. The programmers should test the completed program code against the technical design document. This is normally known as a unit test.

Once a number of related items have been programmed, an analyst will check that these work together as detailed in the functional design document. This is known as a string or integration testing. Once all the programs have be written and have passed an integration test, the whole system is put together and tested by the project team. This is known as the system test. Finally, the victims are called back to check that the system performs as specified in the original requirements documents. This is known as user acceptance testing.

The Flash Flood

That is how the process is supposed to work. Without exception it never does. Those that have been involved in a number of software development projects know the drill and can sense by about halfway through the design step how late and ineffective the final system will be. A more typical project would go something like this.

The IT project team ask the user group for some time to help draw up the requirements documents. The user's management declines the request because his or her team is very busy and can't spare the time. After all why worry about a computer system that is nearly a year from completion? The IT project starts to get behind schedule. The IT project team starts to write the requirements documents based on what they think is done by the user group. This may be correct. It may also be complete fantasy. Some of the more junior, inexperienced staff from the user's department may be sent occasionally to the IT project to keep up appearances.

One way or another, the requirements documents are completed in draft. Under intense pressure from senior management, the user's management 'signs-off' the requirements documents. This is done without reading them in depth. They proclaim that they have not had enough time to give the task justice. They make it clear that any errors are the fault of the IT project team and that they may have to make changes to the requirements later.

As the requirements documents are late, the IT project had to start writing the design documents before the requirements had stabilized. The more experienced analysts draft solid design documents but have to go back and revise them when the final requirements have been signed off. Mistakes are made. A number of the less gifted analysts are confused by the lack of clarity and end up largely copying the requirements documents into the design as the deadline for their completion approaches. These design documents barely mention the computer at all.

As the schedule has slipped even further because the analysts had to rework their documents based on the changing requirements, the programmers had to make a start converting the incomplete design documents into program code. Computers don't like uncertainly and incompleteness and only the most experienced programmers make progress. When presented with design documents prepared by one of the less gifted analysts, the junior programmers become confused and stall. They need a detailed design not high-level requirements. The programmers' manager enters into interminable philosophical discussions with the analysts' manager about what makes up an acceptable design specification.

The original project plan had the experienced, and thus more expensive, analysts leaving the project after the designs were completed. As time goes on, in order to keep to budget, the more experienced analysts are rc-allocatcd to other projects. This is done to the original schedule not according to the true state of the project.

One of the design specifications created by the less gifted analysts is sent to an offshore provider of programming services. After a week, the design document returns from the offshore development 'center of excellence' with a status of 'program code complete'. The program code accompanying it appears to have been written for a different project using a different type of computer. The unsuitability of the program is pointed out to the offshore provider who in reply states that it meets the vague and incomplete design specification. There are lengthy discussions. The IT project team seeks out a technical analyst who used to be a programmer and asks him to 'update' the design document. Following the 'update', the design document has a striking resemblance to program code. This document is sent to the offshore 'center of excellence' and a week later an arrestingly familiar program is sent back.

The project moves forward very slowly and is dropping significantly behind schedule. At this time, the manager of the end-users department takes up her prerogative to adapt the requirement documents. The IT project manager objects saying that this will adversely affect the already shaky schedule. The user manager has an informal chat with the company management who make it clear to the IT project manager that the project should be 'business driven'. The update to the requirement document is accepted and analysts are found to update the design documents. Changes to the design document mean changes to the program code. Mistakes are made.

When they have written a program, most of the experienced programmers give it a good thrashing to ensure it works adequately. They know that any problems or bugs left in the program will come back to haunt them later. The junior programmers, having not yet learned this, run their programs once and, should they not affect the stability of the system, move on to their next task.

As time moves on, the analysts that have not been reassigned prepare and execute integration tests where a number of programs are tested together. The less gifted analysts choose to focus on getting a single set of data through the string of programs. Once this has been achieved under a single set of conditions, the programs are declared fully operational.

Several weeks or months behind schedule, the project gathers to perform the system test. Normally a large system requires a set of widely used 'master data', such as product codes or customer numbers, to be in place before anything can happen. Everyone assumes that someone else will prepare the master data and they wait for the announcement of its availability. Little is tested in the first few weeks. As the deadline for the completion of the system test approaches, the IT project manager starts to apply pressure on the analysts to declare the system working so that he can keep to his updated schedule. Tests are skipped and bugs are reclassified until there are no known 'major' problems. This is very different, of course, from there being no problems. The system is 'signed off' by the IT project as ready for the users.

A number of things can happen next. The users can once again decline to get involved saying they are too busy. They can wholeheartedly join in user acceptance testing and then find that the system does not do what they want and demand major changes. More probably, a number of users will turn up and start poking holes in the system. The holes have to be patched up but each fix can in turn introduce new problems. The crescendo of testing and fixing builds until the IT manager, the user manager and the company management start putting pressure on the users to sign off the system. Under duress, they put pen to paper and systems development is officially complete. Cut-over may begin.

Cut-over

Cut-over is the process of getting a new system into a productive 'live' state. In order to avoid a regrettable fiasco, it is wise to come up with a formal cut-over plan. These are similar to the countdowns used during the launch of space vehicles with go/no go decisions at key points. The tasks or checks to be performed should be documented along with the time that they should take place. For a large complicated system, the cut-over plan will probably list tasks every hour for a period of 4 or 5 days over the go-live period with more vague guides for tasks being performed in the weeks either side.

One of the major tasks that can take many weeks in a large system is the migration of data from the old to the new computer. This includes the static or master data like product codes, customer details or suppliers' details. It also includes so-called transactional information such as the sales orders or purchase orders that were in the middle of being processed at the time of the go-live. When switching between systems that include stock or accounting information, there are many financial checks that need to be carried out to ensure the data are migrated correctly and do not leave the cut-over process open to fraud. All these should be documented and scheduled into the cut-over plan.

Botched cut-overs have caused many systems' catastrophes over the years but given the myriad things that can go wrong, it's hardly surprising that they do: it's only a question of how many. Cut-over management, like the whole of the systems development cycle, is a high-stress activity that managers are often keen to relieve themselves of. This opens up tremendous opportunities for third parties who are willing to shoulder the burden of dealing with IT systems for a large fee. Enter the computer consultants.

Consultancy and IT Services

The profession of computer consultant is almost as old as the stored-program computer itself. Around 1950, two of the brahmins of Chicago were in conversation. One was Willis Gale, the chairman of Commonwealth Edison (the Chicago electric utility), the other was Leonard Spacek, the managing partner of the Arthur Andersen accounting company. Gale asked Spacek about his opinions on the use of the computer in business and is reported to have received the reply, "What's a computer?" Spacek, whilst he wasn't aware of the computer, was a great believer in the power of punched card equipment to automate business and, once enlightened, set up a working group to look into the new computing devices. They visited the UNIVAC group in Philadelphia and presented their findings to the Arthur Andersen board in early 1951. When GE wanted someone independent to advise on their adventure into computing at Appliance Park in 1953, Arthur Andersen was a natural choice. They ended up also providing manpower for implementing the system they had recommended. Even in these early days though, the job did not run smoothly. They had trouble in persuading their client that they had completed the agreed work and didn't finally leave until 1956, some time after GE had stopped paying for their services. It has to be said in their defense that this was because no-one at the time fully appreciated that a full time support staff would be required for a computer installation. They thought that, as with the construction of a building, once a computer system had been built, you could leave it to its own devices. Both Arthur Andersen and GE were setting out on a voyage of discovery.

The computing and consulting activities of Arthur Andersen grew swiftly and by the late 1980s the consulting business was highly profitable and a large revenue earner. In 1989, the computer side of the business was split into a separate entity called Andersen Consulting whilst the original Arthur Andersen continued to concentrate on accounting. Both firms remained as partnerships. This means they had no shareholders and that the senior staff, the all-powerful partners, owned the business. It was clear at the time of the split that the two businesses would not earn exactly the same amount of money per partner. One or the other would be more profitable. In order to stop the partners in the less profitable arm of the organization losing out, and thus blocking the deal, it was agreed that a proportion of the profits of the most profitable firm would be paid to the other. In the early 1990s, it became clear that the consulting business was the more profitable per partner, partly because there were far more junior staff earning income for each senior partner. It is indicative of the atmosphere of greed that was building in the firm that the deal had started to unwind within months. The accountants, spotting an opportunity to increase their income, started their own consulting business. This competed directly with the Andersen Consulting unit for the same long-standing Andersen clients. The Andersen Consulting partners meanwhile started to feel aggrieved that they were paying a proportion of their profits to what was increasingly becoming a competitor. At the end of 1997, Andersen Consulting sued its Swiss-based parent company and, after a lengthy process of arbitration, split off to become Accenture, currently notionally based in the tax haven of Bermuda.

The accounting firm Arthur Andersen famously imploded after its questionable behavior with regard to its audit of the fraud-wracked Enron. After the Enron debacle, it became necessary for the other large global accounting firms to separate their consulting businesses from the auditors to ensure that there were no conflicts of interest. PriceWaterhouseCoopers sold their consulting arm to IBM. KPMG floated the majority of theirs off to form BearingPoint and sold their UK and Dutch IT consulting business to Atos Origin. Ernst & Young

Consulting was bought by Cap Gemini. These, along with the likes of EDS and CSC and the consulting divisions of the former hardware companies like HP and Fujitsu, form the basis of the IT services industry.

The concept behind IT services consultancy is to persuade client companies that they need help in dealing with their internal computing and IT operations. To do this, the IT services company must appear to know more about business and technology than the client. Tremendous effort is put into projecting this image. No opportunity to appear in front of potential clients can be missed: conferences must be attended, events must be sponsored, adverts must be placed. The superiority of the consultancy must be demonstrated time and again. The simplest and most common way of doing this is to cloud the comprehension of anyone listening by nonchalantly deploying buzzword laden clichés. Often communications with senior consulting staff sound something like this:

By partnering with industry leading, stakeholder-focused enterprises, we drive out business transformation programs to deliver high performance. Our unique and award winning methodology is cross-functional, cross-process and interdisciplinary. We exploit our unrivaled thought leadership and business process insights to drive value creation and deliver business success right across a newly invigorated enterprise. We tirelessly seek synergies between the performance driving techniques of rightsizing, benchmarking, strategic realignment and initiative engineering. We offer speed to value and delivery excellence by focusing on the adaptive transformation of optimized, scalable infrastructure. Practically speaking, we put the spotlight on breaking down operational silos, balancing leadership trade-offs, and ensuring stakeholder buy-in. In short our clients become committed to realizing our shared vision of maximizing their resource effectiveness through value chain excellence. Often we find this delivers an unquestionable step-change in innovation and nothing less than customer delight.

This kind of bluster is extremely vague and non-specific. Such a sermon can be delivered safely whilst knowing absolutely nothing about the client's business. It applies equally well to potato farming as it does space exploration. Given that senior managers in client organizations have little detailed understanding of the operation of their business, and even less understanding of the technology it uses, it is unlikely that they will enter into discussions with seemingly clued-up consultants. The sales pitch from consultancies is also delivered in the tone of voice that implies the benefits of the work being proposed is already fully understood by the manager. It would risk embarrassment to the manager if they were to challenge the seemingly sound reasoning. Their self-confidence kicks in and they become fully committed to the shared 'vision'.

When attempting to sell to clients, the way that the IT service industry hunts in packs is also helpful. At any one time, there is normally a single stratagem that is popular across the whole industry. A client manager will be subjected to similar sales pitches from any number of IT service providers for the same seemingly important service. In recent years, common themes have included year 2000 audits, shared service centers and e-enablement. With this wall of concurring advice, the poor manager won't be able to believe that their business will be able to survive without the service offering even if no-one within their organization has mentioned it even once.

Consultancies and IT service companies are similar in many respects to investment banks and lawyers firms. The reason for their existence is to make money. The world would probably get by perfectly well without them. If the companies that sell computer hardware or software disappeared, we would be in trouble. If consultancies disappeared, life would continue much as it did before. As a result, the aim of the highly incentivized managers in consulting practices is to make money for themselves: doing good for their clients comes in as a relatively low priority. They do pay lip service to the notion of achieving a high quality in order to gain repeat business from valued clients but any genuine concern normally evaporates as the end of an accounting period approaches. Once a client has signed up to buy IT services from a consultancy, they often find it surprising how quickly their best interest diverges from that of the consultancy. Any items under dispute always seem to be resolved to the benefit of the consultancy. They might have thought that they were in some kind of partnership but it doesn't normally take long for them to be disabused of the notion.

To those who have never worked for, or closely with, a consultancy, this characterization may seem a little cynical. This is not surprising given how much effort the consultancies put into cultivating their external image. To those who have been at the receiving end of consultancy services from one of the large global groups, it will seem all too close to the truth.

IT Management

The people that employ consultants, that is senior business people, are special. There are certain traits that mark an individual out for service at the top of an organization. Unfortunately, these tend not to be of the type that are mentioned in business books or job descriptions. Let's look at a few of them:

Self Interest. To make it to the top of an organization your own interests must take priority over all others. From a senior person's perspective, there is little point in doing anything if it does not serve to earn promotion, an increase in salary or an increase in power. Expending energy on any task which does not serve your own interests should be avoided, preferably delegated. People who spend their days actively toiling at tasks related to their job description will not make it to a senior level. Aligning the interests of managers with those of the business is fundamentally a good thing but most schemes, such as profit-related pay or share options, will be subverted before long to place more emphasis on the interest of managers.

Self Confidence. Senior people have complete faith in the own fundamental and inalienable superiority. In many cases, this may not be entirely justified. Senior people have learned from an early age that since their response to any problem is always unquestionably the correct one, there is no need to stand aside for others with more experience, knowledge, talent or understanding.

Slogans. Senior people generally have no recent experience of actually undertaking the task that they are overseeing. Their decisions are thus informed by easily understood slogans, often passed to them by sales people. Genuine understanding at a deeper level is unnecessary (see self-confidence above).

Consensus. When there is a decision to be made and there is a clear consensus for an obvious choice, the selection must be announced by them in a bold manner. When there is no clear consensus, meetings should be held until one emerges.

Concern for appearances. Anarchy, blight and failure are perfectly acceptable as long as nobody important notices. All public statements should be positive and can be issued freely without any knowledge of the underlying situation. There is no benefit in issuing negative statements even if they are true. Focusing on the positive improves your standing with those who are appraising your performance (see self-interest).

Eliminate the negative. To the ears of a senior manager, all negative news is overblown. The person relaying it clearly misunderstands the real issue or the wider picture. They should be tasked with clarifying the situation, in order to improve their own comprehension that is, until the negative reports stop. Should this not do the trick, the individual should be actioned with resolving the issue themselves and then their progress (and not that of the underlying problem) monitored.

Management is clearly more complicated than this but the six traits can be observed in action everyday in virtually all large organizations. The behaviors are more in evidence the higher up an organization you go.

The person on the board with responsibility for IT is normally the finance director or chief financial officer. It's unsurprising that the CFO is normally an accountant and does not care to hear about problems within the IT department. He or she will want to remain focused on the accounting function and leave someone else to look after IT. The individual who is delegated to look after IT is often known as the chief information officer or CIO. All senior executives must fit culturally with the colleagues they deal with everyday in order to gain acceptance. Put another way, this means the CIO will not be very interested in technology. They will see their role as trying to get the IT group to do things that are useful to the business. Or at least appear to be doing things that are useful to the business. Technology matters are further delegated to a chief technology officer or CTO although in some cases, the role is taken by a 'chief technical architect'.

Selecting a new CTO is troublesome. Who after all is going to conduct the interview? None of the more senior company officers have a clue about technology beyond the slogans fed to them by software providers and the media. The result is that the role is often occupied by the most self-confident individual that applied for the job on the basis that they 'appeared to know what they were talking about'. It's not unknown for the CTO to be a self-opinionated, bombastic charlatan who shouts down any dissent. In other cases, they can be a big-budget gadget freak that will buy any unworkable half-finished items of equipment or software that is put in front of them by suppliers. More often than not they are just another career-driven individual attempting to work their way up the corporate ladder. Unfortunately, this means they will have no passion for, or deep understanding of, technology and will do anything to avoid rocking the boat.

The unfortunate corollary is that the senior staff making large investments in hardware, software or IT services often do so on the basis of thin understanding formed from the slogans provided by sales people. Should their choice be questionable, no negative input from those below them in the organization will have any effect. In order to sell technology products, suppliers are well aware that all they need to do is to create an atmosphere where their chosen offering is seen as the way forward by the few people at the top. That is to say, that it will serve their self interest by earning a bigger bonus. The fundamental quality, efficacy or value of the product on offer is of little concern if the salesmen can only mesmerize the leaders with a 'compelling vision'.

It is for this reason that, in the corporate market, technologies often follow unexpected trajectories. It is a market where turkeys fly and rising stars fall to earth. The underlying quality of a technology is of minor importance compared to the ability of leading vendors to market it successfully to senior customer staff.

Why Do IT Projects Go Wrong So Often?

IT service organizations are normally called in to a client company either to assist with the development of a particular project or for the outsourcing of an entire function, such as accounting or IT. They're not engaged solely on the basis of manipulative sales techniques. Clients know that they have trouble getting large IT projects to work and genuinely want to be helped. They want to believe that hiring a supposedly skilled consultancy will help them to successfully deliver key projects. Sadly the reasons behind failed projects are well known and understood and involving a consultancy often makes matters worse rather than better. Let's look at some of the common reasons and how they affect an IT project.

Incomplete Requirements

First of all, it is vital to have a clearly defined set of requirements. What exactly is the project trying to achieve? How will everyone know that the project can be judged a success? As we've already heard, the user group may not be very committed to, or indeed very interested in, the project. Attempting to build a system without getting them to agree to a list of requirements will clearly lead to an unwanted system that will fail to be accepted by its supposed customers. The requirements must also be to a sufficient level of detail. Saying to a house builder that you want him to build you a 'place to live up on the north side of town' leaves open the opportunity for some serious misinterpretation. You could end up with anything from a wooden tool-shed to a concrete bomb-shelter.

The same goes for IT projects, unless you make it abundantly clear what is wanted, everyone should expect the unexpected. The process of trying to generate interest in the user community so that requirements can be accurately divined at an early stage is known as getting 'user buy-in'. Once a user has 'bought-in', they understand the reason behind the project or at the very least, accept its inevitability. Without user buy-in, the project will be able build something but what they build may not be of much use.

Scope management

Assuming user buy-in has been obtained, it is possible to define the system's requirements. It is then necessary to stick to them. Countless computer projects have been blown off course by changes in the requirements. It is not just the large one-off changes that cause problems but the accumulation of small incremental changes over time. The process of managing scope is known as change control. Each deviation from the original requirements must be documented in a change request and get past the individual or committee in charge of change control.

The change control manager for a project is normally regarded with the level of opprobrium normally reserved for traffic wardens. It's their job to enforce the rules to ensure the project doesn't go off the rails but these same rules are often viewed by workers on the project as an unjustified impediment to their hard work that should be removed. The change control managers have to dance along a delicate line of keeping the project stable whilst allowing enough changes and corrections through to keep the project relevant.

All too often, the change control manager is brow beaten into letting through inappropriate changes. Frequently, they will simply be overruled by more senior managers eager to please a vested interest. The extra work of adding, replacing and removing functions from a system all adds to costs and causes delays.

Optimistic Project Planning

Many IT projects are accused of being delivered late or over budget. This of course must be viewed in relation to the originally published timings and budget which may, in the first place, have been implausible or indeed absurd. There is no law against being optimistic. There is no need for proposed project timings and budgets to give a fair and balanced view. This leads naturally to **Ludo's first law of project management:**

> The initial timescales and budget of a project are set at the level that would allow the project to be approved, not necessarily the level required to successfully complete it.

This is a restatement of an accepted rule that has been widely known for decades and has been particularly widely applied in the realm of defense procurement. Here the prices bid by defense contractors for projects have little relation to the actual cost of delivering a particular piece of equipment. The bid-figure is arrived at by second-guessing what level the other bidders will pitch at. Bidding realistic prices based on detailed analysis is rather pointless and will lead inexorably to losing business. Far better to put in a winning bid initially and then claim poverty later once you've won the contract and 'had the opportunity to conduct a more detailed analysis'. The project's original backers can be sure to raise a chorus of support and arrange for the supply of additional funds.

The same process of optimistic planning and pricing is regularly deployed when large IT projects are being planned. This is true of projects being delivered both within an organization and using external service companies. Definitions are tweaked, assumptions are made, 'innovative techniques' are promised and a project plan is formed that clearly demonstrates the unquestionable value of undertaking the project.

It is only later, once the project is under way, that the definitions need to be reinterpreted back to their old meaning, the assumptions turn out to be groundless and the all-new innovative techniques start to appear very similar to the old ones.

When the project has been running for some time, it will almost certainly feel like there are not enough people to do the necessary work. This is because of **Ludo's second law of project management:**

> Resources will be removed from projects until they are on the edge of failure.

Let us say for argument's sake that there are 60 people working on an IT project which is progressing satisfactorily. A manager, eager to show his commitment, will suggest that the project can get by with only 55 people. Gradually, the number of workers will be reduced. Management rationalize this by saying that, because it is only a time-limited project, any extra effort required from the remaining staff will only be needed for a short time. When the workers increase their effort, a manager suggests that the project can succeed with only 51 people. Again the changes will only affect the workers for a limited time. The process goes on until the number of workers is genuinely below the level that will be able to complete the project. Deadlines slip and deliverables are missed. A few additional staff are brought in to stabilize the situation and all is well, even if the project staff are overworked, until another manager suggests that the project is 'over the worst' and that it would be possible to continue with fewer staff. Communications are never perfect and in the end, the steady-state level of resourcing may well be below that which is genuinely needed.

Incompetence

Another reason for projects not going to plan is plain old-fashioned incompetence. The main reason for its presence on IT projects is cost consciousness. Everyone managing a project would prefer to have dynamic experienced workers toiling away beneath them. Experienced workers know the pitfalls and shortcuts because they have seen it all before. They are unfortunately more expensive than inexperienced staff. All projects thus have to make do with a mix of experienced and not-so-experienced workers. The balance between the two can be pivotal. The inexperienced staff are incompetent in the strict sense of the word. That is, they are not yet fully competent to fulfill the required role and can wreak havoc with vague and misleading specifications, inefficient and inoperable program code or deficient and incomplete testing. A number of the IT consultancies in particular have a reputation for sending in 'yellow school buses' filled with recently graduated neophytes to staff client projects. A number of the inexperienced individuals will discover, once they have been on a real systems project, that their talents lie elsewhere and do not return to technical work. These individuals are a dead loss to the project whilst they are still around. They do little useful work and can get in the way of others attempting to make process. If they work for a consultancy there is little chance of them being moved on because they are so profitable to their employers where they are.

The major difficulty in dealing with incompetence however is spotting it. Those who are responsible for staffing projects generally can't tell the difference between good and bad specifications and program code. They normally give people the benefit of the doubt and leave those without strong skills to stumble on.

Bad Testing

The projects that fall victim to the problems just outlined will, at the very worst, dent the profits of their parent company. They won't actually stop the main operation going about its business. The projects that cause the most misery are those that are inflicted on the organization's main operation before they are ready. The key to halting a destructively incomplete computer system going into live operation is to halt its progress during the user acceptance testing. This is when the user community tests the system against the originally defined requirements.

A user acceptance test can however be rendered useless for a number of reasons. The users can remain aloof and refuse to get involved. This is of a particular concern where a system project has already gained a bad reputation. The user staff will believe that they will be blamed for the system's state when it goes live. By staying out of the way, they can't be blamed. They will also see testing computer systems as a job for the IT department and will be reluctant to do what they see as other people's work. It's far more relaxing just to remain where they are and blame the IT group for any problems that are found later.

Those who have done the task before will have another reason to avoid it. The management end up putting pressure on users to lie. The user acceptance test occurs at the end of a long, expensive and possibly painful project which often costs well over $1 million a month to keep going. When users show an inclination to pick holes in the system, it is not unknown for management to make it clear that they expect the system to be accepted quickly to avoid incurring any more costs. Any problems uncovered by the users, genuine as they may be, are thus seen as an act of treachery. By the end of the process, all the management wants to hear is that the system has been accepted and that the project will stop hemorrhaging cash. Serious problems are reclassified as minor. Minor bugs disappear off the radar altogether. Anyone refusing to keep quiet will be taken into a room and repeatedly asked subtly evolving questions until a form of words is found where it is possible to construe that they have given the all clear.

All this can be done as a background to testing which is far from rigorous. An experienced tester understands that they are not trying to show that the system works. They are trying to break it. The most convoluted and obscure scenarios should be dreamed up to test the furthest recesses of the new system. Getting a system to handle the simple scenarios is relatively straightforward but will only simulate 90% of the transactions. It's necessary to get well over 99% of transactions through the system without failing before it can be declared ready for use. Systems that have gone live and subsequently caused mayhem have either had their testing subverted by management or have not been rigorously tested.

Organizational politics

There is a common thread linking many of these potential problems: wishful thinking by management. It's usually obvious to experienced staff when user requirements are unsuitably vague. If this is the case, the project should be stopped until they crystallize. Normally, management will not accept that there is a problem and demand that the project continues anyway. The dangers of fiddling with project scope are well understood but it is management who overrules change control procedures in order to move the goalposts. Project aims and time lines can be wantonly undeliverable to those who are experienced in the art but there is no way to persuade management of this. There is no way to force management to be firm when it comes to removing less able staff from the front line. There is no way to stop management opportunistically ignoring test results they do not want to hear. Unfortunately, none of this can be stopped without changing human nature. It's the character traits of management that drive these behaviors. Large IT projects will continue to go off the rails until we change human nature in some way and that is not going to happen any time soon.

5 Networking

Survivable networks

The year was 1949. The Eckert-Mauchly Computer Corporation had found itself in financial straights after Harry Strauss, the VP of the American Totaliser Board, had died in a plane crash. Round the table one lunchtime at the plant in Philadelphia sat the 23-year-old Paul Baran and a number of his elders-and-betters.

> I was quietly munching on a … sandwich taking it all in as the older and wiser engineers discussed the company and its future. I think it was Jerry Smollier 'the power supply guy' who thought that the company had orders for three machines. 'Okay', someone said, 'let's assume we get orders for another three–six computers. Okay, let's double it again. What sort of business is it if your market is only a dozen machines?'

Things looked grim and desperate times called for desperate measures. On one occasion, when potential saviors came to visit the site, the electronics specialists like Baran were asked to dress-up in overalls and make their way to the workshops. During the tour, the visitors were thus treated to scenes of diligent industry as teams of workmen, in reality the play-acting electronics engineers, pressed holes in metal sheets.

This did nothing to boost the confidence of the Polish born Baran who had only recently graduated from a local college and had taken the job out of expediency rather than any great dedication to Eckert and Mauchly's vision of the future. As a matter of fact, he had little understanding of computing. He abortively signed up for a computing course at the University of Pennsylvania but, having missed the first lecture, abandoned it completely when the lecturer started off the second session by writing the boolean expression '1+1=0' on the board without further comment.

Without any deep commitment to computers and with little faith in the stability of Eckert-Mauchley, Baran decided it was wise to move on. After a period working on telemetry systems for rockets he moved to the home state of his new wife, California. His new job was once more aerospace electronics but this time for Hughes Aircraft. The year being 1955, transistor technology was starting to be applied but having been out of education for a whole 6 years, he had no idea how they worked. He took another run at learning a new discipline, this time at UCLA, and was much more successful, earning his masters degree before making a start on a PhD. His commitment however was clearly not all that high because he abandoned his studies one night after he 'couldn't find a single parking spot in the whole of UCLA and the entire adjacent town of Westwood'.

By this time, he had left Hughes and had moved to work for the RAND corporation. He joined the computer science department in 1959 and started to look at long standing issues surrounding 'command and control' and in particular the ability of a command network to continue functioning whilst under sustained attack. This was not just about the ability to give the command to 'fire' but also the ability to issue the command to 'ceasefire'. As Baran put it, this meant that

> Not only would the US be safer with a survivable command and control system, the US would be even safer if the USSR also had a survivable command and control system as well!

As a result, very little of the work that followed over the next 5 years would be classified.

His initial proposal for a survivable network, expanding on an early idea by the RAND president, examined the possibility of using the AM radio stations dotted across the US to relay messages. FM stations couldn't be used due to the effect of a nuclear blast on the ionosphere. The initial idea was based on the assumption that the network would be used for very short messages, sent only by the most senior officers. It quickly became clear that this was not acceptable to the top brass who anticipated being a bit more loquacious. More capacity was needed.

Baran went back to the drawing board and came up with a number of fundamental principles his network would have to follow. There should be no central controlling entity that could be blown up. The approach should be 'distributed', that is no one point should be more important than any other. There must be a significant level of redundancy to allow for multiple failures.

This mandated a network of 'nodes' passing messages between each other. There would be no star or hub-and-spoke formations that would allow central nodes to be taken-out thus crippling communications for an entire area. After a simulation study it turned out that linking each node to three or four others would create robustness close to the theoretical maximum.

The messages that passed through the network would be in a 'digital' format not 'analog'. Analog signals were prone to distortion when sent over a long distance and the problem increased the more repeating stations were added between sender and receiver. For example, with analog transmission, a signal of 12.2 volts at the sender could turn into 12.35 volts at the receiver. With digital transmission, the 12.2 volts is converted by the sender to binary and then transmitted using ones and zeros. If a low voltage is detected at the receiver, this is a zero. If a high voltage is detected at the receiver, this is a one. If a voltage in between is detected then you know something is going wrong. At the receiving end, the ones and zeros are reconstituted and a perfectly replicated signal of 12.2 volts emerges. In the early 1960s, digital communication was not unheard-of but virtually all run-of-the-mill communication was still performed using the old analog techniques.

Another principle was that messages would be split into manageable bite-sized snippets, known as 'message-blocks'. It was always accepted that things would go wrong: messages would go missing or arrive corrupt. If the whole message was sent in its entirety and something went wrong, the entire message would have to be re-transmitted and would probably fail again. If a message-block went missing, only that small piece of data would need to be sent once more. This did however mean the network would need to have intelligence to determine which message-blocks had successfully arrived at their destination.

Message-blocks would be sent between nodes on the basis of 'hot potato routing'. When a message arrived at a node, it would reflexively be passed on to another node. Processes were suggested that would send the message-block in the general direction of its final target. By bouncing between many nodes, generally being given a push in the right direction with each hop, the message would eventually arrive at the right target.

A physical system was designed to implement these principles. A small computer-like device, based on transistorized electronics and around the size of shoe box, would be attached to a microwave transmitter/receiver. A network of such base stations would be scattered around the US to provide the required node profile.

The concepts behind the system were complete in 1962 but it took a further 3 years of discussion and refinement before the survivable network was formally recommended to the Air Force in 1965. A RAND-like software company called MITRE conducted a 3-month review at the request of the Air Force and concluded that the scheme was complete and practicable. They recommended implementation.

The individual with spending authority was one Frank Elldridge Jr. His job title of 'Special Assistant, Command Control and Communications, Office of the Assistant Secretary of Defense, Controller (Systems Analysis)' gave some idea of the bureaucracy inherent in military activity. He was an ex-RAND employee and long-time associate of Paul Baran. He was strongly in favor of the proposed network but like Baran he had reservations. The reservations were not technical but political and bureaucratic. If the go-ahead was given, the work would be completed by the Defense Communications Agency. Baran's opinion was that the organization was hidebound and had a strong aversion to anything that was not traditional analog communication. As he put it himself:

> If you were to talk about digital operation, they would probably think it had something to do with using your fingers to press buttons.

154

After some discussion, Baran and Elldridge decided to put the project on hold rather than see the Defense Communications Agency fail and then turn around and claim that this was because the design principles were unsound. If this were to happen, it would be very difficult to get the political will together to restart the project at a later date. When Baran left RAND 18 months later, work still had not started on the network.

When Baran was dealing with it, the Defense Communications Agency had only recently been formed from the separate signals operations of the three armed services. Since 1949, politicians in the US had been trying to reduce the lost productivity caused by fractious inter-service rivalry. When any of the services started looking at a new type of toy, the other services decided that they had to look at it also. It was against their competitive nature to select a single design and move forward, each would go its own way as a means of demonstrating its superiority over the others. The creation of a single DCA was one of many attempts to stop the jostling and make the services work together. Whilst the aim was laudable, it proved in the end to be a little optimistic.

Space exploration in the early 1950s was another example of counter-productive inter-service competition. Both the US Navy and Army had competing rocket programs. In 1955, the US Navy was selected as the main US Government backed space program with its proposed Vanguard rocket. The launch of Sputnik by the Soviets in October 1957 however forced their hands and they made a rushed attempt to launch a satellite into orbit just 2 months later. The rocket exploded in front of the world's media just two seconds after lift off. It hadn't even cleared the tower. As a result of this dramatic failure, the US Army rocket group, with design team led by ex-Nazi Werner Von Braun, was given the go-ahead to attempt a launch of their competing Redstone rocket. At the end of January 1958, the Explorer I satellite was successfully sent into orbit that, unlike Sputnik, could at least claim to have performed useful work. The Explorer I team it has to be noted were as much in competition with the US Navy as they were with the Soviets.

ARPA

As a result of the Sputnik debacle, advanced military research was regrouped under the auspices of a single organization known as the Advanced Research Projects Agency: ARPA. Within months, it had a sister organization for space exploration: NASA.

155

By the early 1960s, ARPA had a group looking into command and control in addition to the team at RAND that Paul Baran had worked for which was, of course, funded directly by the US Air Force. The area of behavioral psychology was becoming seen as an area for blue sky research and a new manager was hired to look after the area. It's unclear if psychologist J C R Licklider was hired to look after command and control and behavioral psychology or just the latter but before long he was the director of a combined group. It was renamed the 'Information Processing Techniques Office', IPTO, to make it clear that it wasn't just focused on old-style command and control.

Licklider had a vision. He had worked on the massive SAGE air defense system and in particular the human factors surrounding the display units with their light guns. He believed that the future could be found in computers working in tandem with humans interactively. At the time, given the state of computing technology, this meant working on time-sharing systems.

When he arrived, APRA tended to disperse its grants to the research arms of commercial companies. This did not suit Licklider as he 'was interested in a new way of doing things, they were studying how to make improvements in the way things were done already.' After his arrival, more money was directed to universities who were more likely than industrial outfits to engage in blue sky thinking. Licklider only stayed at ARPA for a couple of years before returning to MIT but he had managed to set a direction for the IPTO which was maintained by his successors.

Licklider's immediate successor only remained in Washington for around a year before in turn being succeeded by Bob Taylor who had spent that year as deputy director. This is the Bob Taylor who we have already met and who would go on to be the manager of Xerox Parc. Taylor had been chosen mainly because he was a disciple of the interactive computing concept expounded by Licklider and, as a true believer, continued the focus on time-sharing systems that had been started some years before.

ARPANET

One day, he looked around his office, so the story goes, and his eyes alighted on the three terminals that allowed him to log in to the ARPA-funded time-sharing computers at MIT, SDC and the University of California at Berkeley. To log in to the MIT time-sharing system, he had to use the MIT terminal. To log in to the SDC time-sharing system he had to use the SDC terminal. The same for Berkeley. None of the researchers at any of the institutions could log on to a machine at any other center. Taylor saw this not only as a waste of space in his office but a barrier to communication and a waste of computer resources. Why not set about linking the systems so that they could operate together?

After a '15-minute conversation' with his boss, the Director of ARPA, in February 1966, he was given the go-ahead to proceed with a $1 million project to look into linking the systems. Taylor started the search for a program manager to look after his new networking budget. His prime candidate was one Larry Roberts who worked at the Lincoln Laboratory near MIT but Roberts did not want to become a Pentagon bureaucrat, preferring hands-on research. He turned Taylor down flat.

Taylor was not a man to give in lightly. He pestered Roberts over the coming months but received the same reply. In the end, Taylor went to the director of ARPA once more and asked him to call the head of the Lincoln Laboratory. The conversation concentrated on how the Lincoln Lab was 51% funded by ARPA and how much it was in 'everyone's best interest' that Larry Roberts chose to take up the position at ARPA. Within 2 weeks, with his arm firmly up his back, Roberts had accepted the generous offer and by early 1967 had set to work. He soon found that he needed Taylor's persistence and also to use his forms of 'persuasion'.

The IPTO was funding time-sharing computers not batch processing. This was just as well because traditional batch processing systems could not handle being interrupted by randomly arriving requests from other computers and were thus unsuitable for networking.

Time-sharing computers were very much at the leading edge of research in the late 1960s and processing capacity was precious. Each research group had their own computer which was guarded jealously and carefully managed within the group. Outsiders were kept well away. None of the groups would contemplate letting anyone else stray onto their machine to take up precious processing time. Unfortunately, in order to get the computers talking, some kind of networking software would be needed to run on all of them which itself would take up system resources. All the research groups declined to get involved.

As a way of focusing minds, Roberts made it clear that he would not be funding any more computers for any research group until the total capacity of all current computers was utilized. This of course would require a network to exist to allow jobs to be shifted between computers.

One of Roberts' former research colleagues, Wes Clark, suggested a way to remove the main stumbling block: the presence of networking software on the main time-sharing 'host' computers. He put forward the idea that instead of relying on the host computers to perform the networking tasks, why not off-load the responsibility onto one of the new breed of mini-computers. ARPA could install a mini-computer at each point on the network. The mini-computer would do all the hard work of networking and leave the host unencumbered. Not only would the main 'hosts' be largely unaffected by networking problems but also the network hardware would be kept under central ARPA control. Roberts assented and a paper was prepared outlining the intention to build a digital data network between time-sharing systems with mini-computers located at each site looking after transmission. The mini-computers become known as 'intermediate message processors' or IMPs and would be linked by normal telephone lines.

The paper, basically a high-level statement of intent, was presented at a conference at Gatlinburg, Tennessee in October 1967. Also being presented at Gatlinburg was the paper design of Britain's first attempt at a general purpose computer network.

NPLNet

The UK's National Physical Laboratory was set up in 1900 in reply to the state funding of science in the rapidly militarizing Germany. Over its life, its most widely known role was to look after the national standards for weights and measures in the UK though it did get involved in scientific research. As a government body however its approach to research was more bureaucratic than academic. It was pervaded by the stultifying air of the civil service. In the late 1940s, Britain had three computer projects under way: two at the Universities of Cambridge and Manchester and one, the automatic computing engine or 'ACE', at the NPL. The NPL's management made attempts to merge the three and operate the remaining project under their own direction. The universities resisted as they were making good progress on their own and the NPL team contained personalities that were known to be difficult to work with. As the universities' work was not funded directly by government, the NPL had little option but to leave them alone.

The universities did ground breaking work. The Cambridge team was the first in the world to get a 'von Neumann' style computer fully functioning. Manchester University was the first to get the CRT based 'Williams-Kilburn' tubes, a common form of memory in early computers, working and produced a working electronic computer long before IBM (partially because IBM's 701 used Williams-Kilburn tubes). The NPL's efforts followed an independent design which, whilst being perceived as having an elegant hardware architecture, meant it was almost impossible to program. The computer finally stumbled into life in 1950, functioned adequately but was eventually abandoned in the technological cul-de-sac down which it had been constructed.

Many of the individuals at work within the NPL had tremendous energy and vision but, as with all large government organizations, these tend to be more than outweighed by the effect of unimaginative, risk-averse management operating under a different agenda.

One individual who ended up working for the NPL all his life and, as he made it into management, would probably disagree with the previous statement was Donald W Davies. He joined the NPL in 1947, around the time that the chief designer of the ACE, Alan Turing, was about to up sticks and move elsewhere in frustration at the lack of progress. By 1965, Davies was a senior member of the NPL's computing division. After a tour of the key sites in the US, he arranged a discussion on time-sharing to be held in the UK.

Time-sharing was clearly going to be the next-big-thing but one problem that struck Davies was the means of linking a terminal, generally in those days, a teleprinter style device, to the computer. Each terminal would have to be connected by a continuous wire all the way to the computer. If the terminal was not in the same building a dedicated phone line would be required. If there was more than one terminal, a phone line would be required for each device. Given that a typical user would only use around 1% of the line's capacity, this was clearly wasteful. It would be beneficial to link a number of devices to the computer using a single piece of cable. If a number of terminals were required in a remote location, one cable or phone line would be far more efficient.

At the time, a well-known approach for passing data was known as message-switching. The classic early example of which was the telegraph. Hand-written telegrams would be sent by messenger to a local telegraph office. Here they would be converted to Morse code and sent to a telegraph office near the destination point. This office would dispatch a second messenger who would run, or more likely walk, to the destination. If the original telegraph office did not have a direct connection to the final office, the message would be sent to an intermediate office for relay onwards.

Message-switching had a competing approach: circuit-switching. This was used in the early phone systems and gives a clear and uninterrupted electrical connection all the way from source to destination. In general however it is possible to serve many more customers down a single wire using message-switching than through circuit-switching. Essentially, this is done by taking the pauses out of conversations.

Message-switching has its drawbacks. Should a long message need to be sent, it will monopolize a line for some time, forcing everyone to wait. If an error is detected during transmission, the whole long message has to be sent again, doubling the frustration. There is also the phenomenon of lock-up. As more and more messages are passed, they may arrive faster than they can be relayed onwards. Once the rate of arrival increases beyond the rate of departure, they must be held in a queue until capacity is found. Once the queue gets beyond a certain size, the system from a customer's perspective appears to have stopped functioning.

Davies solution was to split large messages into standard size chunks, or 'packets'. These would be sent through a network of relay stations. The stations would continually resend data until they had a confirmation that it had been received correctly. As the packets were small this would not involve retransmitting the whole original message. The relay stations would be intelligent so that once a particular path became either unserviceable or log-jammed, the packets would be sent via a different route.

This may sound very familiar. When Davies presented his 'packet-switched' approach in March 1966 at a lecture in London, it also sounded familiar to a gentlemen in the audience named Arthur Llewellyn who at the time worked for the Ministry of Defense. After the lecture, Llewellyn took Davies aside and told him that very similar ideas had been circulated in the States a couple of years before by a man called Paul

Baran working for RAND. It was the first that Davies had heard of the work on survivable networks. The two approaches were very similar even though they had been developed in isolation. When Davies met Baran some years later, he would admit as much, saying: 'you may have got there first, but I got the name first.' The term used to describe these networks from this point on would be Davies' 'packet switching' rather than Baran's original clumsy name of 'Distributed Adaptive Message Block Switching'.

Davies' input was not restricted to just the name. His 'packet-switched' network system was documented and one of his colleagues, Roger Scantlebury, was chosen to present it at the October 1967 conference in Gatlinburg where ARPA presented their original IMP design for the ARPANET. ARPA had come up with a framework for their network using IMPs but had not worked out the detail of how to link the IMPs. Packet switching was an ideal solution. Scantlebury was able to point the ARPA participants in the direction of Baran's extensive reports which had been gathering dust back in ARPA's offices in the Pentagon.

ARPANET II

In the months following the Gatlinburg conference, the ARPANET started to take shape. It was now known that there would be a small IMP computer at each site that would talk to the main time-sharing 'host'. This would be linked by phone lines and use the packet-switching approach set out by Baran at RAND and independently by Davies' group.

The contract to design and build the IMPs was awarded in January 1969 to a Boston consultancy known as BBN that was generally peopled by academics that had drifted away from the nearby institutions of MIT or Harvard. The initial work was for the first four IMPs to be shipped by the end of the year: one each to University of California at Los Angeles, University of California at Santa Barbara, Stanford Research Institute and the University of Utah.

Meetings were held in 1969 between BBN and graduate students from each of the target institutions to discuss what to do with the new network once it had been built. It quickly became clear that BBN were very focused on the single goal of getting a binary stream of bits from one IMP to another quickly and reliably. They did not see their role as including anything to do with making the network useful or worrying about getting a message from one of the main hosts all the way to another.

The graduate students decided that there must be another group somewhere that had been engaged to look after the key task of designing the network protocol, or the set of rules, used to make the main computers talk. As the months went by, they were still waiting for this group of experts to 'announce itself' and decided they had better make a start themselves. The participant from UCLA, Stephen Crocker remembers 'having great fear that we would offend whomever the official protocol designers were.' The group of students, who ended up calling themselves the 'Network Working Group', documented their ideas in such a way that they would not affront the mythical protocol gods should they one day turn up. The tone of the documents were subdued and ideas were outlined as proposals rather than fixed edicts. The documents themselves were thus called 'Requests For Comments' or RFCs. To this day, the Internet working groups publish ideas as 'Requests For Comments' even though now there is little possibility of a major change once the document has been published.

The 'official protocol designers' never did turn up and a few ad-hoc protocols were knocked together in time for BBNs delivery of the first IMPs. At the beginning of October 1969, a little over 2 months after man first stepped onto the moon, two IMPs were in place: one at UCLA and one at SRI. The phone links were in place and the teams stood by to perform the first test. Letters were to be typed into the source machine at UCLA and sent, one by one as they were typed, to the responding machine at SRI. When the computer thought it recognized a word, the word was automatically completed, in the manner of predictive text on mobile phones today. UCLA typed the letters 'l', 'o' and 'g'. These zipped across the network to the SRI machine. It recognized the start of the word 'login'. The machine went off to perform the login procedure and promptly crashed. The ARPANET was live, but there was still a lot of work to do.

By the end of 1969, all the four initially ordered nodes were in place and operational, soon to be joined by a cross-country link to BBN back in Boston so that they could monitor the network. The physical links were all in place and working. The hosts were communicating using the ragbag of protocols knocked together by the Network Working Group. Larry Roberts however was not entirely happy. At a meeting in Utah in

December 1969, he made it clear that he thought the group's 'first step was not big enough'. The group thus went 'back to the drawing board' to come up with a new more robust and generally applicable set of protocols.

To get the hosts talking to one another, the Network Control Protocol (NCP) was defined. This would ensure that data got from one host machine to another but would not do anything useful itself. Another layer of protocols was defined to sit on top of the foundation provided by the NCP. One which is still very much in use today is the file transfer protocol or FTP which is used to move files between computers. Another, TELNET, allowed users of one machine to log on and issue commands on another and is still used on virtually all UNIX systems.

Email was also taking on a new, more mobile, form. Many systems of the 1960s had mailbox systems where users could send messages to one another. They were however very shy and didn't talk to similar systems on other computers. This was unsurprising because there was no network to link them. Full email became possible by linking these traditional message mailbox systems to the new FTP style protocols which could transfer data between computers. It took a bit of time however before a single standard would become accepted with the issue of RFC 680 in 1975.

The next batch of IMPs was delivered in early 1970 to the next four institutions, MIT, RAND, SDC and Harvard after which the roll-out continued. By the end of 1971, there were 15 network nodes linking 23 host computers.

Those who used the system were aware that the ARPANET was a great success. The powers that be however were not really aware of the ARPANET at all. It was decided to mount an academic charm offensive. The event selected to be the focus of the effort was the International Conference on Computer Communication to be held at the Washington DC Hilton in October 1972. This was the point where the communications establishment stopped thinking of the packet-switching network as a curiosity and started thinking of it as a possibility.

Inter Networking

Shortly after the Washington conference, Larry Roberts decided to move into the private sector to have a go at creating a market for packet-switched networks. Control was passed to a gentleman called Robert

163

Kahn who had been one of the leading lights of the ARPANET work within BBN. Kahn moved to work for ARPA itself and, with the network bedding down nicely, his thoughts naturally turned to connecting the ARPANET to packet-switched networks elsewhere.

Donald Davies' team had completed a small network at the NPL's site in London and had started working on its upgrade. Tymshare had a commercial network linking its time-sharing mainframes to each other and the outside world though this was far more centralized than the ARPANET. The French had visited the US in 1970 and had seen the early ARPANET in action. They had two packet-based networks in the offing known as Cyclades and RCP. In 1971, the COST II/European Informatics Network was started as a kind of civil, Europe-wide ARPANET. As it was an intergovernmental body, its progress was painfully slow and the operating network only finally surfaced around 1976. ARPA had also funded a network to link the campuses of the University of Hawaii to its central computers. As linking these by cable was impractical, radio transmissions were used. The resulting network, known as ALOHANET, was operational by the end of 1970.

All these networks had their own way of working. Their own protocols and layouts. It was only a matter of time before there would be a requirement to link two machines that resided on different networks. To move the topic of 'inter-networking', that is to say linking networks, forward a new group was formed, the 'international network working group' or INWG. It was initially suggested that Stephen Crocker, who led the original ARPANET Network Working Group, should take the helm. He declined, suggesting that the role should be passed to one of the other founding members of the NWG, Vincent Cerf.

Given that this was an international effort that must take into account nationalistic and political consideration as much as technical ones, there was no way that a single approach could be mandated across the board. For example, it would not be politically possible to force the British and French networks to accept IMP machines prepared by BBN. Likewise, ARPA was highly unlikely just to drop their approach and accept what the British or French used.

It was Cerf that came up with one of the fundamental concepts that led to a solution: the gateway. A gateway device would be installed at one or more points on each of the networks. Messages would be able to leap between networks only by passing through these gateways. The networks would remain as they were. The gateway would look after any translation that was required to get one network to understand the information flowing through another. In other words the complexity of getting one network to communicate with another would be handled at the gateway not by the host computers.

This however gave the ARPANET a problem. The reliability of the network, the way it ensured that data were transferred successfully from one host to another, was bound up in the IMPs. If a packet went astray, it was the IMPs that sorted out the mess. If a message was sent through a gateway to a network that did not use IMPs there was no way to ensure that the transmission was successful. Messages effectively disappeared into a black hole once they had passed through the gateway. There were no IMPs in Britain or France. How could communication work between the ARPANET and networks that did not have IMPs? A new way of ensuring reliability had to be found. The days of IMPs were numbered.

The concepts surrounding inter-networking started to take shape during a meeting of the INWG at Brighton on the south coast of England in September 1973. It turned out the French Cyclades network already incorporated the answer to the IMP problem: Expect the network to be unreliable and make the hosts look after reliability instead.

Cerf and Kahn returned to the US with a clear outline of the way forward. Their paper, 'A Protocol for Packet Network Interconnection', was published in IEEE Transactions on Communications in May 1974. It put forward the notion of gateways. In order to make sure the gateways on different networks would understand each other, a new standard protocol was required. Cerf and Kahn obliged with what was to become known as Terminal Control Protocol (TCP). A key feature of TCP was that all packets, from whatever source, would be further enclosed in an kind of envelope, formally known as a 'datagram'. The envelope information would include the source and destination address and could be used by the gateway to determine whether a packet was to be transmitted outside its current network.

In order to get the new generation of inter-networks working, the old IMPs had to be removed from the equation. This would leave the old programs that used NCP on a very shaky ground as there would be no means of detecting and correcting failures. There was no option but to replace these programs on the main hosts with a version that used the new TCP. The main host computers would have to start doing the work, originally placed in IMPs, of splitting and reconstituting messages and coping with the vicissitudes of long distance phone lines. Thankfully a lot of water had gone under the bridge since the original decision was made to avoid putting the load on the hosts. Far less resistance came from local teams when placing the computing load of operating the network on the main computers. At least by this stage, networking had been accepted as a concept.

TCP continued to be refined. The biggest change came in 1977 when it was split into two separate protocols. TCP's offspring was called Internet Protocol, or IP. IP was the wild child and focused on throwing data around with abandon. It had no care for accuracy or completeness. TCP would remain the responsible one. On the sending side, TCP would carefully split messages into packets, carefully wrap an envelope around them and hand them over to IP with a grimace of hope. It would also make sure it kept a log of each departure in case something went wrong. IP would, with great energy but with minimal finesse, do its best to transfer the envelopes to the target computer. On the receiving side TCP would send an acknowledgment back to the sender and then make an attempt to reconstitute the message from the fragments of data arriving. If the sending TCP had not received an acknowledgment within a reasonable time, the missing packet would once more be placed in the hands of IP for retransmission.

The benefit of having a second less demanding protocol is that many applications do not need the guaranteed delivery offered by TCP. In voice transmissions for example a loss of 5% of the signal would hardly be noticed by humans. Attempting to catch up with lost fragments of conversation would be futile as it would be too late to playback the recovered snippet. That is why Internet phone services use 'voice over IP' not 'voice over TCP/IP'.

Whilst the ARPANET was maturing, networking had spread in the commercial world. Both DEC and IBM had their own proprietary ways of linking computers known as DECNet and SNA, respectively. A plethora of open standards, such as X25, were also in place. No one protocol had ascendancy over any other. In order to improve TCP/IPs chances of surviving in this crowded marketplace, DARPA (as it was by then called) funded the development of TCP/IP software for UNIX. This was included in the Berkeley version of UNIX in the mid 1980s at no charge. As UNIX was well on the way to becoming the favored environment for academic computing, this ensured that TCP/IP would at least be given a wide audience in universities and helped speed its acceptance. It also meant that no DARPA-funded research group had any excuse for not using it.

Whilst TCP/IP was the only way for users of the ARPANET to communicate with external networks, the old NCP still worked for communication within the US research community. A number of ARPANET sites were slow to move over to TCP/IP as they had little incentive to do so. Eight years after TCP was defined and 5 years after IP was split off, the laggards were given a little push to encourage them to make the transition. DARPA arranged for the NCP transmissions to be blocked for a day. A few months later, NCP was blocked for 2 days before finally being disabled for good on 1st January 1983.

Not long after the switch, operational military traffic was separated into its own network, unsurprisingly called MILNET, leaving the original ARPANET for educational and research purposes. Its meager capacity, about the same as a single modern dial-up modem link, was soon supplemented by that offered by the US NSFNet, created to link the US National Science Foundation's high speed computing efforts. The NSFnet was intended to allow normal universities to gain access to the NSF funded super-computing centers. When it was paired up with the ARPANET, the number of computers that could communicate with each other using the resulting unified network exploded. It was however restricted to the university sector.

Commercial interests were kept out of the network because the NSF would only fund activities related to basic research. The NFSNet network had an 'acceptable use policy' that made it clear that commercial outfits should keep out of its way and find some other channel for communication. In 1989, the capacity of the NSFNet was boosted to what would today be called a domestic broadband connection. This made the ARPANET, still with the same old dial-up modem capacity, look somewhat insignificant and in 1990 it was switched off for good. The NSFNet's capacity continued to grow, by about a factor of 30 in 1990 and 1991 alone. This led to the NSF becoming somewhat irked that it seemed to be spending its money on a data network and not on its beloved basic research. It was also coming under increasing pressure to open up the network to those that did not inhabit an ivory tower. In 1993, it came up with a way to shift the responsibility of running the Internet onto the private sector. Commercial Internet Service Providers would create their own Internets to support the TCP/IP protocol. These would then all be linked together at certain nominated locations. The result would be a single huge network that anyone, commercial or non-profit, could link to. It would be operated and paid for by the ISPs which would in turn receive payment from organizations or members of the public that wished to gain access. The NSF could stand back and return to its roots in supporting computing and networking research. At last the Internet had been unleashed.

The World Wide Web

The Internet is not, in itself, very useful to the man in the street. The Internet is just a number of computers connected using TCP/IP. People can't even interact with TCP/IP directly. They can however build on top of it to do useful things. It is the application protocols that sit on top of it that allow people and computers to do useful work. Some have been mentioned already: FTP for transferring files, TELNET for remotely logging into a machine. Email is normally transferred using something called SMTP, the simple mail transfer protocol, which again is normally built on top of TCP/IP.

At the end of the 1980s, these were the main tasks performed over the Internet. About 40% of traffic was using FTP to shift files around, with TELNET and SMTP having 5–10% each. It's therefore safe to say that, at this time, life on the Internet was not colorful or exciting. All a user could do was type a command and receive some plain text in response. Things were about to change.

In the non-networked world, using a PC was starting to become less drab. In the early 1990s, Microsoft Windows was starting to become widespread. Icons, windows and mice were popping up everywhere. PC users were also starting to come across a new way of interacting with information known as hypertext. At first it was used primarily in the help section of applications. With hypertext, an explanation would be displayed just like in a word processor but certain terms would be highlighted in blue and underlined. When the user moved their cursor over the highlighted area and clicked their mouse, a new document would be displayed which was related to the highlighted term. It was thus possible to navigate through trees of information to get to the data that the user was really interested in.

The idea of hypertext was not new. It had been proposed in the mid 1960s by Ted Nelson, one of the band of self-styled techno-prophets that stalked cyberspace at the time. It had been used by Doug Engelbart in his work that led to the development of the mouse. It reached the edge of the mainstream in the 1980s when Mac users became able to create their own hypertext databases using an application called 'hypercard'. One computer programmer had even written his own hypertext like application, to aid his own sieve-like memory, in the early 1980s. His name was Tim Berners-Lee. By the end of the 1980s he was working at the CERN, international particle physics lab near Geneva looking at ways to collect, structure and allow access to the huge amount of information that was created annually by the large group of researchers working there.

The researchers were not a stable group. Workers would typically only spend around 2 years working with the particle accelerators at the site before returning to their original institutions. Normally their work would be documented, placed somewhere on a computer network and never looked at again. Not because no-one was interested but because no-one knew where it was. Even if they did know where it was it was often in a format incompatible with the one that they used.

In March 1989, Berners-Lee put forward a proposal for a system that would create a repository of information that could be linked and searched. It should be remotely accessible, non-centralized, work with any type of computer and cater for 'old' data formats. It wouldn't so much be a single entity that held all the information but more a method for getting all the current repositories to work together. He saw it as a kind of networked hypertext system. At the time, CERN had a 'Buy don't build' policy, where software would be bought-in from outside companies rather than run the risk of a software fiasco by attempting to build it internally, so Berners-Lee spent some time attempting to find a product already on the market that would fill the need. There were plenty of hypertext systems available but none that were network friendly. When he suggested that the stand alone versions could be adapted to work across networks he was swiftly rebuffed with varying degrees of courtesy.

The proposal was the latest in a long line of attempts at CERN to solve the same problem, all of which had drifted towards an inevitable anticlimax. CERN management chose to ignore his proposal lest it turned into yet another tedious misadventure. The following year, the document was reworded by Robert Cailliau, a colleague of Berners-Lee who had been at CERN nearly 20 years, in an attempt to attract the management's interest. The proposal was circulated another twice with no response. In the vacuum, a pilot implementation was furtively initiated by the scheme's supporters in October 1990. No formal approval had been given and no resources allocated.

This was of course the proposal for the 'World Wide Web'. In technical terms, the web is just another type of application that sits on top of the Internet's TCP/IP network. It required yet another new protocol (hypertext transfer protocol – HTTP) as none of the original set – FTP, TELNET, email – fitted the bill. This is why when you type in a web page address in a browser the letters 'http' appear at the beginning of the line.

The data held on the web were to be formatted using something called Hyper Text Markup Language (HTML). This was a heavily cut down version of SGML (Standard Generalized Markup Language) originally intended for use in typesetting equipment and later appropriated for other uses. An HTML document in its raw form would look something like this

```
<HTML>
<HEAD></HEAD>
<BODY>
 <H1>THIS IS THE HEADER</H1>
 <P>This is a normal paragraph</P>
</BODY>
</HTML>
```

The actual text to be displayed would be enclosed by a number of 'tags' such as <HTML> and </BODY>. Almost all the different types of tags come in pairs with an opening tag <H1> being followed eventually by a closing tag </H1>. Each set of opening and closing tags has a type of layout associated with it, such as bold typeface or heading, which should be applied to all the information between the tags. In the example above <H1> indicates the text should be displayed as a heading in a large font. <P> indicates the text enclosed should be displayed as a normal paragraph. As you can tell its not that easy to make sense of 'raw' HTML so a program must be used to convert it into a more readable format. This program is of course known as a web browser.

It's unlikely that the HTML files to be displayed will be on the computer displaying it. This would severely limit the usefulness of the set-up. The target data are far more likely to be somewhere out on a network. In order to get at it, the browser must format a request (using the new HTTP protocol) and send it over the network (using TCP/IP) to the computer that holds the information. On this computer, which must also understand TCP/IP, there is another program, known as a 'web server', which receives the request from the browser (in HTTP) decodes it and returns the information requested to the browser (formatted in HTML). The browser can then display the information.

In defining the World Wide Web, Berners-Lee made three leaps. One was defining a reasonably simple data format: HTML. At the time, SGML was accepted as being far too unwieldy for most uses. A second was defining the HTTP communication protocol. The third was defining a way to request information such that as many types of information as possible could be retrieved. This request format is known as the URL and is the string of text typed in at the top of a browser. All three strides forward had to be made at the same time for the system to become widely accepted.

In October 1990, Berners-Lee started work on a browser for his NeXT workstation. Few people had a computer as powerful as a NeXT workstation to play with and a more rudimentary non-GUI 'line-mode' browser was knocked up by Nicola Pellow, a student on placement from what was then Leicester Polytechnic. Those lucky enough to have the obscure but powerful NeXT workstations on their desk could use Berners-Lees's whizzy 'WorldWideWeb' browser. Everyone else had to use the unpleasant but functional character-based browser developed by Pellow. Given the basic facilities available to the great unwashed, there was no great rush to use the new tools. Within CERN, Berners-Lee continued to have a hard time firing people's interest. In the early days, his and more especially Robert Cailliau's evangelizing had to be done whilst attempting not to catch the eye of CERN management which still hadn't given its approval for them to spend their time on the scheme. The software, such as it was, was surreptitiously put on the Internet for download from outside CERN. The Berners-Lee/Cailliau roadshow went international in an attempt to generate interest in the putative technologies. They attended any conference that would permit them to demonstrate their ideas and engaged with academics on both sides of the

Atlantic. Their efforts were rolled out to users of CERN throughout 1991 with the World Wide Web being formally announced to the user community in December's edition of the organization's computer newsletter. Slowly but surely over the next year, interest grew, first outside CERN and then within.

As the Web was taking off, Berners-Lee cajoled CERN management into agreeing that the intellectual property rights associated with the World Wide Web should be placed in the public domain. That is to say that any interested party could use the protocols and techniques without fear of being sued for patent or copyright infringement. This was key to the later success of the web. Other similar efforts had been strangled by such concerns. The most notable example was the 'gopher' system developed at the University of Minnesota. Once the university suggested asking for royalties on the use of 'gopher' from commercial entities, it was swiftly abandoned by its users and its carcass left to rot.

This freedom from commercial pressures allowed interested parties to get involved in the effort of popularizing the Web. Robert Cailliau visited the Helsinki College of Technology during 1991 and inspired three students to build a web browser as the project for their masters degree. The department they were studying in was known as the 'OTH'. In a burst of flawed creativity they named their effort 'erwise': together they would form 'OTHerwise'. Yet another dreadful pun. It was the first of a stream of browsers built outside CERN to be released in 1992 that included such names as ViolaWWW and Midas. They were all targeted at the UNIX workstation. The world wide web was clearly catching the imagination of bored and talented computer students everywhere but only if they had powerful hardware on their desktop to play with.

Mosaic and The Browser

Undoubtedly, the browser-building group that made the biggest impact formed itself in late 1992 at the National Center for Super Computing and its Applications, or NCSA, at the University of Illinois at Urbana-Champaign. Marc Andreessen was just another bored and talented computer student. Coming from a relatively modest background Andreessen had to take a job to pay his way through college and was hired by the NCSA to work on the modeling of three-dimensional graphics. He was taken by the potential of the old 'FTP/TELNET' Internet and the ability of the Berners-Lee web to make it easier to use by the technically challenged. He managed to goad an NCSA staff programmer, Eric Bina, to join him in building a browser that would be far easier to use than the previous batch. The new browser would be based on the now widespread GUI approach with 'point-and-click'. With permission from their boss, Andreessen and Bina set about building a browser to include a number of innovations. For example, the original CERN HTML specification did not include the ability to display pictures, it was intended as a dry academic tool. Pictures required a lot of network capacity to transfer and Andreessen would later be 'balled-out' by Berners-Lee for including then. Graphics did however make the web far more interesting for the ordinary user. The result of their efforts, Mosaic, was released in January 1993 and was an instant success. Andreessen and Bina originally wrote Mosaic for UNIX workstations but it was quickly ported to Microsoft Windows for the PC and the Apple Mac by other members of NCSA staff.

Mosaic turned out to be public relations success for the NCSA. Managers, right up to the center's director, became interested and what had originally been a hackers enterprise very quickly took on the aspect of a bloated bureaucracy. As the developers had been paid by NCSA when they created Mosaic, it was the property of the organization. The original free, and occasionally unstable, version of Mosaic continued to be available to download using the Internet. The code however was licensed to a number of companies so that they could extend it into their own commercial products. One such licensee was called Spyglass Inc.

The same year that Mosaic was released, Andreessen graduated. Having become somewhat jaded by the antics of the management at the NCSA, he moved to Silicon Valley to work on unrelated ventures but it was not long before the Web would ensnare him once more. At work one day in February 1994, he received an email:

> Marc. You may not know me, but I'm the founder and former chairman of Silicon Graphics. As you may have read in the press lately, I'm leaving SGI. I plan to form a new company. I would like to discuss the possibility of your joining me. Jim Clark.

Silicon Graphics was a successful designer and manufacturer of UNIX workstations that specialized in computer graphics for film and television. Jim Clark had fallen out with the then management of the company and was thus 'looking for new challenges'.

The first proposal for Jim Clark's new venture was a Nintendo gaming network. This proved unacceptable to the backers Clark had lined up and the idea was dropped. Andreessen, almost as a throwaway comment, suggested that they could create a Mosaic-beating browser. Clark liked the sound of the idea, dropped his recalcitrant backers and put $3 million of his own money into the venture. This was however only a fifth of his net worth at the time.

Seven of the original developers were hired away from NCSA and moved to the new company, to be known as Mosaic Netscape, in Silicon Valley. The company was formally incorporated in April 1994 and by October the browser was on the streets. For copyright reasons, the old Mosaic software could not be used and had to be re-written from the ground up. This did not stop the new enterprise from getting into a spat with the University of Illinois. In an out-of-court settlement the University received $1 million and 'Mosaic' was dropped from the company name.

The browser software was made available free to non-profit organizations and at a modest fee for commercial organizations. This kind of income however would not make a fortune. More profitable was Netscape's web server. That was the program that must run on the central servers to service all the requests coming in from browsers. This, as it would mainly be required by companies, was a full price software product and allowed Netscape to generate some genuine revenue.

In August 1995, less than 18 months after being formally incorporated, Netscape Communications was floated on the stock exchange. On the first day of trading Jim Clark's original $3 million stake in the company was worth $566 million. Andreessen was worth $58 million on paper. The dot.com bubble was starting to inflate.

At around the time that Jim Clark was sending his original email to Andreessen, Microsoft started on its journey to come to terms with the Internet. In the beginning, Bill Gates was dismissive of the Internet and the Web but after his first demo of the original Mosaic he underwent an epiphany. Action had to be taken. Unfortunately for Gates, Microsoft had no browser in the works and it would take too long to get up to speed with the technology. The checkbook was brought out and a browser was licensed. The license was obtained from none other than Spyglass, the company that had in turn licensed the original Mosaic from NCSA. The program was packaged and re-badged as Microsoft Internet Explorer 1.0. Like Netscape, this would be free to download.

For many months, there was a fair battle on an even playing field. It was as difficult for potential users to obtain a copy of Netscape as it was Internet Explorer. This changed in August 1995, the same month as the Netscape float, when Internet Explorer was shipped as a free application within Microsoft Windows 95. It was already present on the computer's desktop as soon as the operating system was installed. It would be available whenever a PC was switched on. Netscape stood little chance of competing with a free product that was already installed on the dominant operating system for PCs. Its market share plummeted and in 1998, the company was taken over by AOL.

The technology of the Internet (TCP/IP) and the world wide web (HTML and HTTP) has not changed a great deal since. Microsoft Internet Explorer remains by far the most widely distributed browser but, as we will hear later, alternatives are starting to make a comeback.

Ethernet

Two computers running TCP/IP software do not a network make. Messages somehow have to leap from one box to another. Introducing a wire that links the two computers helps but still won't make the computers understand each other. Both computers must use the wire in the same way. You guessed it! What that needs is another set of protocols.

This problem had to be confronted at the same time as all the other networking issues. The team at BBN solved the issue once with its IMP to IMP protocol. This was completed and functioning before the delivery of the first IMP to UCLA in late August 1969. The IMP link needed a dedicated mini computer and did work in addition managing the wire link, or, in the case of the ARPANET, the phone lines.

The same issue was confronted a few years later at Xerox Parc where Bob Taylor had settled after his spell at ARPA in the late 1960s. They were building the ALTO 'office of the future' computer and needed to link these both to each other and to expensive new 'peripheral' devices which were being developed. The most costly of the new devices, because it was a research prototype, was the first experimental laser printer.

To help build the new PARC office network, an old ARPANET hand, Bob Metcalfe, was hired from Harvard just as he was completing his PhD, or at least that's what he thought. Unfortunately, Metcalfe, in his younger days, had a strong will, a strong sense of his own destiny and a strong vocabulary to match. A few minutes into his PhD examination, he was told that the thesis was 'insufficiently theoretical' and that it would have to be rewritten. He had in other words annoyed his academic supervisor to such an extent that he had blocked Metcalfe's PhD. 'I wasn't playing ball with him, so he didn't play ball with me', as Metcalfe would recall. At least his time at PARC would allow him to update his thesis for a resubmission.

When he arrived at PARC, he was shown a number of approaches for linking the Altos that had either been tried or were in the works. These included one approach, developed by Charles Simonyi who later became the head of applications development at Microsoft, known as SIGNet which stood for 'Simonyi's Infinitely Glorious Network'. Unsurprisingly, given the egos involved, Metcalfe dismissed them all and set to work on a new approach.

The previous approaches had several drawbacks. They required a large number of wires and a large amount of hardware to be able to function. The number of machines that could be attached to the network was limited as was the geographical dispersion of the computers it linked. The new network had to avoid all these problems and still be cheap to set up, easy to maintain and contain as little high technology as possible.

Whilst still at Harvard, Metcalfe had done some work for ARPA. On a visit to Washington related to ARPANET business, he had stayed the night at the home of Stephen Crocker, the original chair of the Network Working Group who coined the phrase 'Request for Comments', who by that time had become an ARPA program manager. Unable to sleep, Metcalfe selected the most soporific volume of conference papers he could find and sat down to read himself to sleep. The volume included a write-up on the ARPA funded ALOHAnet radio network at the University of Hawaii.

ALOHAnet was what is known as a collision detect network. All sites would listen to a defined, common radio frequency. When one site wanted to communicate with another it would broadcast data packets on this frequency. When a site was transmitting, all other stations would remain quiet. The target station could then pluck its packets out of the ether. Should a second station start to transmit at the same time as the original, everyone must back off for a random time interval before trying again. It was in other words necessary for collisions, two stations broadcasting simultaneously, to be detected and explicitly catered for.

Back at PARC, Metcalfe recalled the principles of ALOHANet and set about designing a network along its principles of operation. Instead of using radio waves, the PARC network would use a single wire. Data packets would be squirted onto the wire and retrieved by the target computer. As every computer was attached to the same wire, it would be necessary for the each computer to listen out for messages intended for it and ignore all the others. Should two computers attempt to communicate at the same time they would both have to abandon transmission and try again later. The resulting system was christened Ethernet as it could work over many physical mediums not just wire.

Metcalfe left PARC in the mid 1970s, having successfully resubmitted his PhD to Harvard which had been augmented by a statistical treatment of collision detect networking, and within a few years had become an Ethernet evangelist. He persuaded Xerox, DEC and Intel to back the technology as an open industry standard against more proprietary systems that were available to achieve the same goal. On the back of this, he founded the company 3Com in 1979 to offer Ethernet technologies. This move turned out to be very well timed as the IBM PC that emerged in 1981 had no network capabilities. 3Com was the first to offer a network card for the platform and by mid 1985, it had the lion's share of the market. Today it has moved onto other things. Ethernet became so popular that it had become a commodity and the profitability dropped. Almost all computer networks, from large server farms down to desktop PCs, use it in one form or another to manage the physical wires that link them together.

Because the principles of Ethernet apply equally to any physical medium, it was natural for it to be a candidate for use in linking computers wirelessly. The original Ethernet specification (known as IEEE 802.3 because the IEEE commenced work on it in the second month of 1980) was extended to apply to signals sent over radio waves. In a manner of speaking, it was ALOHANet coming home. The resulting wireless networking standard (IEEE 802.11) and its variants can now be found operating in coffee bars and hotels everywhere allowing the mobile masses to keep their link to the all-pervasive Internet.

6 Security

The world is a dangerous place. Across the globe, individuals are exposed to threats at every level from wars between nations and international terrorism right down to being ripped off by petty criminals and investment bankers. It should come as no surprise then that the digital world has its fair share of felons, delinquents and malefactors.

Digital Adversaries

The most celebrated digital adversary in the popular imagination is the 'hacker'. Hackers come in many forms, not all bad. In the technical community, the term is used to describe anyone who has been possessed by the need to explore, examine and exploit the deepest recesses of a system. They do this not for payment or to get rich, though its nice if this occurs as a side effect, but either out of plain intellectual curiosity or to demand the respect of their peer group. Eckert, the engineering force behind the ENIAC and early UNIVACs was a hacker. Marc Andreessen and his co-workers on the original Mosaic browser were certainly hackers.

The energy and focus that they displayed in pushing forward the frontiers of technology can however be directed to more malignant ends. A more common perception of the typical 'hacker' is a disaffected youth, a technically literate version of the spray-painting vandal, with a desire to get their own back on society for being spurned so cruelly at the auditions to Pop Idol. They can be seen cackling with malicious delight late into the night, swigging back high caffeine cola as they unleash a torrent of calamity on a sleeping world.

Fortunately, successful evil hackers are few and far between. Most of the youths that answer the description above come under the category of 'script kiddies'. They are drawn to the counter-culture image of being a hacker and fighting against society with all its inequities but they tend not to be very good at the technical stuff. Their attempts at spreading mayhem either fizzle out immediately on leaving their own damaged computer or crash everything they touch meaning that they cannot get very far to do real damage. Possession of fireworks does not make you an explosives expert.

Evil hackers tend to have lost interest in generating kudos within their own circle by the time they reach their mid 20s. By this age, they tend to be more interested in making money and those still bent on mischief have become small-time criminals, either acting alone or in small groups. They're out to get your credit card details or other personal details that they can use to generate cash. To pull off this kind of attack does require a reasonable level of technical skill. In the western world, it is normally more lucrative for them to sell their skills to legitimate companies than to risk getting caught doing something naughty and being thrown into jail.

A more serious adversary, and one that is becoming more interested in diversifying into the digital realm, is organized crime. As with lone criminals, the aim is to make money through obtaining credit card and other personal details though clearly the resources available will be far greater and any attacks executed with greater ruthlessness.

Companies are also open to digital crime though many of their concerns are different from those of individuals. Just like individuals, they like to keep their affairs private. To keep a secret, an individual only has to keep his or her own mouth shut. To keep a secret, a company must ensure that all employees keep their mouths shut. Most of the time, the employees' best interests are aligned with the companies. Who after all wants their company and, by extension, their employment to be undermined in some way? Well, when you think about it, quite a few people. Generally those that are not too attached to their employment: people who are working out their notice, are facing redundancy, have been passed over for promotion or have been embittered in some other way. The digital world offers many ways for information, from the banal to the enlightening, to be passed to outsiders either for profit or shear bedevilment. Companies have to secure themselves against attack from within.

Attack from outside is of course also possible. Companies are always on the lookout for information on the plans of their competitors. A poorly secured corporate network gives industrial spies another path to their target to add to their work-a-day methods of bribery and blackmail.

The most clued up and well funded adversaries in the digital realm are the governmental intelligence and policing organizations such as the CIA, FBI, NSA in the USA; MI6, MI5 and GCHQ in the UK, Mossad in Israel, FAPSI, FSB and GRU in Russia, DGSE in France, BND in Germany, CSE in Canada. The most formidable tool that they have available is believed to be the ECHELON surveillance network. Run jointly by the secret intelligence organizations of the USA, UK, Canada, Australia and New Zealand, the network attempts to listen to all radio and satellite communication on or around the planet. Whilst the network was set up to monitor activity in the Soviet Union and the former Warsaw Pact, it is now notionally targeted at searching for global terrorist activity. There are however a number of unconfirmed incidents where information obtained from signal intercepts was passed to commercial organizations for them to use to their advantage. A former CIA director has even stated that the system was used to 'level the playing field' when non-US companies were using bribes to influence contracts.

Individual Concerns

The main security concern for individuals must be to keep their personal details out of the wrong hands. Once criminals have obtained basic information about their target's life (e.g. name, address, bank accounts, electricity supplier, etc.), it is possible to start to take over their identity. From a bureaucratic point of view that is. Bank loans and credit agreements can be arranged in the target's name without their knowledge or agreement. Criminal offenses, such as fraud or traffic violations, can be committed in their name. The first thing the target would know about it would be when the authorities turn up on their door step. It's very difficult for the individual to claim that they were not the culprit as all the information on the relevant documentation would all be correct. It's also very difficult to stop such attacks once they have begun as the criminals have the same details available to them as the individual.

Slightly lower down the scale of concern is the desire to keep credit card details private. Again these can be used to inflict financial loss on an individual but at least once the fraud has been discovered it is straightforward for the card to be revoked. Generally the credit card company will absorb most of the financial loss and will just issue a new card. In order to avoid the hassle though it is wise to put in place procedures that safeguard this information.

People also don't like the feeling of being watched. They like to go about their business without the feeling that everyone knows their little secrets. Many couples conducting affairs would rather they could keep their assignations to themselves. Most people would rather embarrassing medical conditions were kept under wraps. Few people would like their exact level of personal debt to be public knowledge.

On the other hand, society has decided that engaging in certain activities nullifies a right to privacy. These are generally criminal in nature and include child abuse or conspiracy to commit an act of terrorism. In order to detect these however, communications must be monitored, which has the unfortunate consequence that extra-marital affairs, disgusting medical oddities and rampant gambling are also routinely raked over. The former leads to a safer world, the latter leads to extortion and blackmail. As a result, there is a constant battle between making law enforcement easier and maintaining personal privacy.

In the free world, people have come to expect privacy, they have also come to expect to be able to do what they want, when they want. Within reason that is. They do not expect to be at the mercy of some capricious neighbor who on a whim shuts off their electricity or water supply or blocks their driveway with a car. In the digital realm, this translates into ensuring that when some service is required, be it a website to book air tickets or a bank ATM for obtaining cash, it is available for use. A number of the digital adversaries, primarily the evil hackers and the terrorists, are less interested in financial gain and more in making their presence felt. Widespread irritation is in itself a success.

Corporate Concerns

Commercial organizations have similar concerns to individuals but as they survive or die based on their financial performance, anything that will detract from profit making needs to be minimized.

Companies are even more wary than individuals of being exposed to fraud. They do not want to find themselves shipping expensive goods to a false customer. They need to be sure that customers are who they purport to be and that orders, when placed, will be paid for. In other words, they need some means of identification and authentication.

They need their systems to repel unwelcome outside influence. Free of charge orders that are mysteriously created in the middle of the night, the digital equivalent of shoplifting, are not welcome. They also want to keep their internal secrets away from prying eyes: be they product development secrets or rows between board members.

One part of a business that is particularly appealing to criminals is its customer database. This may well hold credit card information along with names and addresses and buying habits of thousands of customers. Organized criminals would thus make a far greater return on their efforts by targeting this information than they would by attempting to obtain credit card information during thousands of individual attacks.

A classic piece of aggressive commerce is for one company to pretend to be another, a technique sometimes called 'passing-off'. An impostor chooses a name similar to that of an innocent, quietly trading company and then advertises widely. A small proportion of the innocent company's customers are bound to make a mistake and call the impostor who would happily accept their orders. If the customer is lucky, they will get a very similar, or indeed better, service from an unexpected company. If the customer is unlucky, they won't get any product at all and will engage in a long and bitter dispute with the original company.

The passing-off may be done to increase market share. In 1889, Almon Strowager was an undertaker in Kansas City. The story goes that his rival's wife worked in the local telephone exchange which at the time was still operated by humans with plug boards and patch cables. Strowager became convinced that calls destined for him were surreptitiously being rerouted by the telephone operators to his rival's business. He invented a device to allow phone users to be connected automatically without the need for human intervention and gave us the first automatic telephone exchange.

Passing-off may also be done to destroy the reputation of the target organization. Back when Thomas Watson Snr was working at NCR, it was common for the company to demonstrate competitor's machines next to one of their own. Unfortunately, the competitor's machine had often been doctored to malfunction. Either way passing-off is a bad thing for the target company and it would be wise to take steps to ensure it does not happen.

An attack that can be even more damaging is one which renders the company unable to trade, either temporarily or permanently. These come under the banner of 'denial of service' attacks and deluge an organization with unprecedented numbers of requests. This could be either huge volumes of emails or a very large number of requests to a website. Communications from real customers wishing to do business would be lost in the maelstrom and the customers may chose to take their trade elsewhere. If a business is close to the edge of failure, a denial of service attack could be all that is required to push them into insolvency.

So what would be the goals of a personal or corporate security policy?

First of all, services should not be interrupted. The main aim of this is to keep any nasties that may be about well away from any computers. In addition, there should be some means of coping with a denial-of-service attack though for most individuals and businesses, except the likes of eBay and Amazon, loss of email or a website for 24 hours would not be catastrophic.

Secondly data must be shielded so that external agents cannot read it either whilst resident on a computer or whilst in flight across a network. Keeping private information private stops embarrassment as well as fraud.

Any entity that is being dealt with should be able to authenticate itself to ensure that it is a friend and not a foe and any messages they send should be checked to ensure that they have not been tampered with or been corrupted in flight. Ideally a log should be kept of all activity so that, should something go wrong, there can be a witch-hunt after the fact to find out who was to blame.

Most of the threats posed in the digital realm have equivalents in the real world. Computers and networks however make such attacks easier to perpetrate. First of all it is possible to automate a digital attack. One person can only rob a single bank or break into a single office at any moment in time. With a computer attached to the Internet, it's possible to automate an attack such that it is perpetrated while the miscreant is asleep.

In the physical world, robbing a bank or breaking into an office requires travel. This in itself limits the number of attacks that can be carried out. The Internet is a global network and it is just as easy for a petty criminal in Kiev, Johannesburg or Colombo to attack a target in London or New York as it is for a Londoner or New Yorker. Indeed a person of the required skill level is more likely to be paid to secure the system in London or New York than to attack it. This isn't the case everywhere.

Finally, the Web makes it easy for intrusive techniques to be dispersed very quickly. Normally within hours or days of a new means of attack being demonstrated, a set of imitations will be unleashed. In the old days, it would take months and years for one group to learn the techniques of another. More than ever speed is of the essence.

Viruses

Bad things can happen to PCs. One minute they obey their user's every whim, the next they turn into an obstreperous misbehaving bully. Files can be deleted, applications don't do what they are told, the system may even shut down without warning. The PC has just been struck by Malware.

Malware, malicious software, is the general term for programs with an evil soul. These are the programs that swore at teachers and bunked off school. They do no good and get in everyone's way.

The most widely known type of malware is the 'virus' even though they rarely cause serious problems in the 21st century. For malware to be a true virus it must piggy-pack on other software just like real viruses need a biological host to survive. In the 1980s, the most common virus was the file-infecter. This was piece of renegade code that would attach itself to a useful executable program, that is, one that can be run on its own such as a spreadsheet or word processor. When the useful executable was run, the virus portion would spring into life and wander off to look for other files to attach itself to. As these programs were run, they too would search out other targets to infect, and so on. When an infected program was copied to another computer it would start the cycle again. Thus viruses would make their way across rooms of PCs. Often the virus did something more than merely replicate itself such as delete a file or make a noise. The file-infecter virus had a whale of a time until Windows 3.1 appeared around 1992 where suspiciously bloated executables caused the operating system to crash. This stopped all their fun.

A similar type of malware was the boot sector virus. This took advantage of a special area of both hard drives and floppy discs known as the boot sector which was read into the computer's memory whenever the disc was used. The renegade code would lodge itself in the boot sector of a disc and replicate itself onto the boot sector of any other disc it encountered. As a floppy made its way from one computer to another, the virus would spread. With the disavowal of the floppy disc in recent years however the risks are much reduced.

The last type of virus is the macro virus. Macros are lists of instructions that can be recorded and then played back repeatedly in order. They live inside word processor documents and spreadsheet files but do not come to life until the document or spreadsheet has been opened in the relevant application. The most common kinds of macro, those created by Microsoft Office products, are created using a programming language called 'Visual Basic for Applications' or VBA. It's possible to use VBA to do far more things than is really necessary for replaying word processing or spreadsheet activity. It is these powers, and various foibles that have been unearthed in the Microsoft Windows operation system over the years, that has kept evil hackers knocking out viruses in recent years.

The most notable macro virus was the Melissa virus that struck in 1999. This was a macro within a Microsoft Word document that was sent as an attachment to an email. When an unwary user opened the attachment, Microsoft Word opened the file and kicked off the macro. The malicious code read the first 50 users from the Microsoft Outlook email address book and copied the malevolent message on to all of them. A number of these people would in turn open the attachment and the process of dissemination could continue. Within a few generations, the volume of email traffic created seriously affected the performance of the whole Internet. The man who wrote the virus, one David Smith, was arrested within a week of the virus striking and was eventually jailed for 20 months and ordered to stay away from all computer networks unless he had a court's permission.

As a result of attacks like Melissa, the way that application software works has been changed. Whenever a word processor or spreadsheet opens a file that contains a macro, the user should be asked to either enable or disable it. Unless the user knows what the macro is for, it would be wise to select 'disable'. Modern virus checkers also monitor macros in documents for known viruses.

Worms

File-infecter and boot sector viruses have largely been extinct in the wild for nearly a decade. This leaves the relatively manageable macro viruses as the only virus threat that computer users should be on their guard for. A much more serious, and by general users, much less understood form of malware continues to pose a significant threat: the worm.

The worm is a piece of code that can exist and can replicate on its own without the need for a host. A worm attack occurred in May 2000 along very similar lines to the Melissa Macro Virus. Instead of an email containing a Macro virus in a word document, the ILOVEYOU worm contained a small piece of program code written in a Microsoft Language called 'Visual Basic Script' or VBScript. VBScript was originally created by Microsoft as a reply to Netscape's 'JavaScript' language. This was intended to allow web page developers to do things above and beyond that which could be done with standard HTML. Just like VBA used in Melissa, VBScript allows the programmer to cast spells to rouse the darker recesses of the Microsoft Windows operating system that would be better left undisturbed.

When an infected email arrived, the recipient was invited to 'Kindly check the attached LOVELETTER coming from me'. The attached file, called 'LOVE-LETTER-FOR-YOU.TXT.vbs' was actually a VBScript program to wreak havoc on the users PC. Before it set about doing its damage however it read the Microsoft Outlook global address book and sent a blizzard of emails to everyone listed. Each email of course contained a copy of the malicious VBScript. Having ensured its own survival through propagation, it set about copying itself to various directories on the recipient's PC. It overwrote picture files, MP3 and executables with copies of itself so that once invoked they would re-infect a cleaned PC. The worm would then set about overwriting the files

187

on any networked file stores it could find. Any PC that used these file servers then also ran the risk of becoming infected.

Many business had to shut down during the attack as this worm would delete vital files and leave the computer inoperable. The simplest response was to shut down PCs until the security software companies updated their virus checkers to handle the threat. The author of the worm, which came to be known as 'the love bug', was an employee of the Manilla-based China Bank called Reomel Lamores. He was swiftly traced and arrested but was eventually released as the Philippines had no suitable law at the time under which to charge him. He remains largely silent on the issue except to say that it was all a big mistake.

Three years later in August 2003, another landmark worm appeared. This was known as LOVSAN or MSBlaster. MSBlaster was even move invidious than Melissa and the Love Bug in that it did not require any human intervention to spread its mischief. The previous two attacks both required forgetful or dim-witted users to double click on unsolicited email attachments. MSBlaster did not even require them to go to that trouble.

As has been mentioned in previous sections, Internet-ready computers always communicate using the protocol TCP/IP. For TCP/IP to work, the target system must have some kind of process 'listening' for requests. TCP/IP can't go and wake up a program and get it to perform a task: it must be running already, waiting for action. On UNIX operating systems, these listeners are often known as 'daemons' and they run on top of the operating system, they do not run in the so-called 'kernel'. Microsoft Windows however is a more monolithic beast where many more functions are closely interlinked. This is a result of the fact that they are all provided by Microsoft. MSBlaster took advantage of the one of the services provided by Microsoft Windows 2000 and XP known as 'DCOM RPC' – don't worry what this is or does. As soon as a computer infected by the worm was switched on it started to send out TCP/IP requests to random computer addresses. On arrival at a target computer it would ask for the 'DCOM RPC' listener and then issue requests it couldn't understand. This resulted in a 'buffer overflow' which, to cut a long story short, means the 'DCOM RPC' listener dropped its guard and would do anything asked of it. It had in effect been hypnotized. It was of course then asked to install a copy of the worm on the hypnotized machine, start a new listener, known as a remote shell, that allowed an attacker to do anything they wished on the target machine and, at certain times, deluge a Microsoft website with meaningless requests.

Before long the network traffic created by the random searches for uninfected computers started to clog up the Internet. The effect of this was so serious that MSBlaster had largely been cleaned up before it even got time to launch the denial of service attack on the Microsoft website.

The culprit for the MSBlaster worm was never identified or caught (there being no trail of emails like in the previous two cases) even though there is a bounty of $250,000 on his or her head. There were however a number of arrests in the US and Romania related to copy-cat attacks where the worm was copied and tweaked before being released once more into the wild.

These three malware attacks are probably the most notable of the last decade. They have a common feature: all were targeted against Microsoft products. Users of computers running non-Microsoft operating systems were largely immune from all three. They would notice a slower network as more and more Microsoft Windows based computers became affected. As VBA, VBScript and 'DCOM RPC' are all unique to Microsoft, the malign code would just not be understood by any other operating systems.

Indeed the MSBlaster worm program contained the text:

I just want to say LOVE YOU SAN!!

billy gates[SIC] why do you make this possible ? Stop making money and fix your software!!

It should be stressed however that viruses and worms are not unknown on other platforms.

Trojan Horses

A third kind of malware is the Trojan Horse. The term Trojan Horse comes from that legend with the highest cliché count in history: the fall of Troy. Troy was a city on the coast of modern-day Turkey. It was thought to be entirely mythological, like Atlantis, until its remains were found by a German businessman turned archaeologist in the 1870s.

According to legend, the Trojan king's son, named Paris, had been promised the hand of the 'most beautiful woman on earth' by the goddess Venus. He was told to journey to the Greek state of Sparta to find his promised love, Helen. Unfortunately there was a minor catch in that Helen was already married – to the King of Sparta. Paris was welcomed as a guest by the Spartan ruler but when the king was away on business, Paris managed to persuade Helen to elope with him back to Troy. On his return, the Spartan king noticed his wife was missing and took umbrage. He persuaded other Greek states to join him in an attack on Troy to regain his wife. An invasion fleet was launched. Helen's was the 'face that launched a thousands ships' it would be said.

After 10 years of siege and battle, the Greeks were growing weary. In order to bring matters to a head, a large wooden horse was constructed and a number of Greek warriors concealed inside. The horse was placed near the gates of Troy while the Greek invasion force, as if in submission, packed up and sailed over the horizon. The Trojans believing that the Greeks had given up and 'victory' was theirs, spilled out of the city to inspect the gift left behind. Two people were suspicious. A priest named Laocoon proclaimed that we should all 'beware of Greeks bearing gifts'. Cassandra, Paris's sister, also proclaimed that she was unsettled. Cassandra had been given the gift of foresight by the god Apollo who had taken a shine to her. Unfortunately she did not reciprocate and in a huff, Apollo cursed her prophesies to be ignored for all time. (That's why a 'Cassandra' is a doom-monger that no-one takes any heed off.) As a result, both Laocoon's and Cassandra's reservations were overridden and a hole was punched in the Trojan city walls to make way for the wooden horse. The Trojans set about celebrating their victory over the Greeks with considerable gusto.

After night fall, with Troy's inhabitants snoring in a drunken stupor, the Greek fleet returns to shore. The warriors concealed in the horse break their cover and open all the city's gates. With the Trojan defenses well and truly breached, the Greeks set fire to the city and the fleeing Trojans are either massacred or enslaved. Suffice it to say that you don't want to fall victim to a Trojan horse.

On a computer, a Trojan horse is a piece of malware that has somehow breached the computers defenses and is able to wreak havoc from the inside. As we saw with MSBlaster, it's possible for programs such as a Trojan horse to make their way onto a computer unbidden. It is however far more likely to have been actively installed by the users. Installing any software on the computer runs the risk that it contains malicious code. Most computer users reasonably assume that software from companies such as Microsoft, Lotus, OpenOffice or Google will not do them any harm. Unwisely many also trust small 'free' utilities, pirated versions of commercial products and the inevitable animations of dancing cats downloaded from web pages.

Once a user has selected to install a program, there is no saying what will happen. One common type of Trojan constantly monitors keyboard and screen activity for signs that you are about to enter credit card information or log on to a banking website. The keystrokes you enter can be stored and transferred across the Internet at a later time. This kind of Trojan Horse is also known as a 'key logger' for obvious reasons and comes under the banner of 'spyware'.

One of the most worrying Trojan horses for Microsoft Windows is known as 'Back Orifice'. Once installed on a computer, this starts one of those TCP/IP listener programs so that it can accept commands from an outside agent. It's written in such a way that it can effectively take over your computer. A remote user can even switch on cameras or web cams and microphones to watch and listen to what is going on. They can copy and update files or monitor web activity including those precious credit card details and web bank account passwords.

The easiest way to reduce the risk of being exposed to Trojan Horses is to be very careful what software you install. Software however comes in many shapes and sizes. The Google or MSN search toolbars that are installed in web browsers are still software. Key logging spyware can even be implemented as an add-in to Microsoft Internet Explorer without the need for a separate program.

Few software packages these days actually come as a single large program. They often come as a set of thousands of small 'components'. Each component performs a defined function such as adding a number of days to a date or defining the behavior of a button on a toolbar. They can, of course, also be used to implement malware and do nasty things. Microsoft Internet Explorer allows components known as ActiveX components to be embedded in web pages. Depending on the computer's configuration, these ActiveX components can be automatically downloaded to the computer without the user being notified (normally they will be shown a dialog box to confirm the download but it's unlikely they'll understand it). The ActiveX component then interacts with the rest of the computer in any way it wishes. Java applets can also be downloaded in a similar way but these are kept quarantined in a much more stringent manner.

A few years ago, all computer users had to worry about were viruses arriving on a floppy disc. With the arrival of networks, the threat increased dramatically. The time-scale over which new threats become widespread has changed from weeks and months to hours and days. First viruses and malware could only propagate as fast as a diskette could be moved. Then they spread as fast as emails could be sent and opened. Now they zip across networks close to the speed of light without the need for any human intervention.

Ciphers and Secrecy

With so much unpleasantness floating around the Internet, it's pleasing to know that many techniques have been developed to help protect computers and their users. One of the most fundamental is the use of codes and ciphers to protect and authenticate information. This is not as simple as its sounds. As long as people have been attempting to communicate secretly there has been an effort to break into scrambled messages. Encryption, the science of obscuring information, has two opposing camps. On the one hand are the cryptographers. They attempt to come up with schemes to garble information in such a way that the uninitiated can't make sense of it. On the other are the cryptanalysts. They attempt to break the schemes the cryptographers come up with.

Encryption has been around as long as there have been people with sensitive information. That is to say a very long time. The Romans recorded many codes and their uses. Right through medieval times and beyond there were instances of both codes being used and codes being broken. Charles Babbage, he of the Analytical Engine fame, was known to break the codes of anyone who could attract his interest to a sufficient degree. His most notable achievement was to break the Vigenère Cipher which had previously been known as the 'chiffre indéchiffrable' or undecipherable cipher. (As Babbage did not publish his work, a Prussian army officer called Friedrich Kasiski is often credited with the break though he only discovered the method 9 years later.) As has been mentioned, during World War II, codes and ciphers were broken by both sides by one means or another. After the war things went quiet. That is not say that nothing happened but that no-one was allowed to make a noise. The NSA (USA), GCHQ (UK) and similar organizations applied pressure to ensure that any promising cryptographic scheme was kept hidden.

One code enthusiast who managed to keep working on encryption during this period was Horst Feistel. Feistel was born in Germany but emigrated to the US in 1934 at the age of 19. When war was declared, he was placed under house arrest but was released in 1944 when he became a US citizen. Before long he was at work in a US Air Force research center looking at the encryption-related problem of 'Identification Friend or Foe' – how to know if an approaching aircraft is a genuine friend or a foe that's just masquerading as a friend. He went on to work at the Lincoln Laboratory and MITRE Corporation before winding up in the late 1960s at IBM's Thomas Watson Research Center in New York State. Here he came up with the concept of what became known as a Feistel Network.

As with all modern cryptography, the details are a bit dry for anyone but the most impassioned. The basic principle is to convert the message to binary and then split the binary into equally-sized short blocks. Each block is then split into a right half and a left half. The right half is pushed through a 'mangler function' which behaves differently depending on the value of a number known as the 'key'. This is then mashed with the original left-half to form a 'new' right half. The whole process is repeated 16 times with the right half from the one step taking the place of the left hand on the next pass.

The remarkable thing is not that this produces a message that is unintelligible, which is obviously the case, but that by simply reversing the process you can return to the original message. The whole thing works and is secure for a number of different mangler functions.

Knowledge of this ridiculously convoluted process is not what makes it secure; indeed the process is widely published. The security comes from the 'key' that is put into the mangler function. Each different value of key will make the mangler function behave differently so unless both the encryption and the decryption are performed using the same key the result will be a binary mush.

IBM published this approach as its 'Lucifer' encryption scheme in the early 1970s and when the US government started to look for an encryption standard, it was a natural candidate. By 1977, the final DES (Data Encryption Standard) was published, a modified version of the

Lucifer Scheme. As this was the scheme selected by the US government, it was quickly adopted across the board.

Public Key Cryptography

There was however a problem with DES. It was a problem that afflicted all similar encryption mechanisms. To be able to communicate between two points, it was necessary for both the sender and the receiver to have the key. One side having the key was not enough, it had to be used in both encryption and decryption. This is known as symmetric encryption. By the 1970s, there was an entire industry supporting the distribution of encryption keys in such a way that they would not be compromised. The cost of this was huge. If you wanted to communicate securely with a new organization you would have to physically send a trusted person holding the key. Using the normal phone or mail channels would not be good enough as they were not truly secure.

The outlines of a solution were first published by a group of researchers at Stanford University, one of the few university-based research groups looking into encryption at the time – it was primarily thought of as an area for secret government work. The group consisted of Martin Hellman and Whitfield Diffie. Hellman had worked with Feistel at the IBM Thomas Watson research center in the late 1960s before moving into academia. Diffie had been a freelance computer security specialist before joining Hellman at Stanford. Together they focused on what was known as the 'key exchange problem'.

In 1975, Diffie came up with the notion of an encryption mechanism with two keys, one used for encryption the other for decryption. This was to become known as 'asymmetric' encryption: when the sender and receiver of the message no longer had to use exactly the same key. The encryption key could be freely published. As it could only be used to garble data, it would not be of any use to an eavesdropper trying to make sense of what was already encrypted. The decryption key must however be kept private.

Such an approach would allow complete strangers to communicate securely without the need to physically exchange keys first. This was a great stride forward. The only drawback was there was a hole in the method. It would only work if you could find something called a 'one-way function' that met certain criteria.

194

'One-way' functions are mathematical expressions that are easy to solve in one direction but almost impossible to solve in the other. An example of a two-way function might be:

x multiplied by 4 = y

Given any value of x, say 3, it is possible to work out y, in this example 12. If you were told that y was 12, the only possible value for x would be 3. This function works two ways.

One of the simplest examples of a one-way function is the remainder left over during a simple division. Lets take the example:

X divided by 4 = Y remainder Z

Given a value of X, say 14, you can say that Y is 3 and Z is 2. Given that Z is two, you have no idea what the value of X is. It could be 2, 6, 10, 14 etc. Squaring a number is another one-way function. Finding the square of a number can be done with pen and paper. Finding the square root is a bit more tricky.

A physical example of a one-way function is the cracking of an egg. You can crack the egg but once you've done this there is no way back to having a complete egg again. This explains why such expressions can also be known by the charming moniker of 'humpty-dumpty' functions.

Unfortunately, Diffie and Hellman couldn't find a humpty-dumpty function that would fit their narrow criteria and after several months of effort moved onto other activities. It was left to a group of researchers on the other side of the USA at MIT to track down the illusive beast.

The MIT team consisted of Leonard Adleman, Ronald Rivest and Adi Shamir. Rivest was looking for a challenge and found it in the paper published by Diffie about the possibility of asymmetric ciphers. He managed to persuade the others to join in the hunt for a suitable one-way function and they set about proposing numerous solutions. Rivest and Shamir threw ideas into the air, Adleman shot them down. The routine of excited proposal followed by jarring disappointment continued right through 1976 and into 1977. One day in April 1977, Rivest was unable to sleep after returning from a graduate student party. As he sat in his living room letting his mind churn, he was struck yet again by inspiration. He had come up with yet another one-way function and, spurred by his natural ebullience and optimism which had been proved wrong so many times before, wrote up the idea late into the night. The following day, as usual, he presented his idea to Adleman for the ritual dissection. This time was different. For once, Adleman couldn't poke holes in it. This was unsurprising as nearly 30 years later no-one is known to have poked a hole in it yet.

The function, once slotted into the public key scheme proposed by Diffie, was named after the initials of the threesome who developed it: the RSA algorithm. At the core of the RSA algorithm is the one-way function that uses something called modular arithmetic, similar to the division/remainder mentioned above, and the factorization of large prime numbers. Prime numbers can only be divided by themselves and 1. If you multiply two of them together you get a large number that can only be divided by itself, one and the original two prime numbers. It is very difficult to take this large number and, without knowing the original primes, work out what two numbers formed it. Should someone come up with a means of factoring the product of large numbers swiftly, the RSA algorithm will lose its security. For all we know someone already has.

GCHQ

Whilst the RSA team was coming up with their preposterously complicated one-way function, Diffie and Hellman had prepared an alternative means of allowing two parties to come up with a single key without the need to physically send information securely. The result, unsurprisingly known as the Diffie-Hellman key agreement, was the first means of solving the key-exchange problem but was swiftly eclipsed by the RSA approach because, unlike RSA, it required both sender and receiver to be in communication at the same time to generate the key. That is to say, it couldn't be used for sending email where there is no direct communication link at the time the message is sent.

Patents were applied for and granted for both Diffie-Hellman and RSA. Those using the techniques had to pay royalties to the organizations that were assigned the patents (initially Stanford University and MIT). It was announced in 1997 however that both techniques had been formulated years before Diffie, Hellman and the MIT team came across them by one of the secret intelligence agencies. GCHQ, the British government eavesdroppers based in Cheltenham, had 'published' a classified paper on an RSA-like algorithm in 1973. The breakthrough had been achieved by Clifford Cocks who had only just arrived at the institution after graduating from Cambridge University, building on work done by the more long-standing employee James Ellis. In 1974, Cocks explained his approach to one of his old schoolmates, Malcolm Williamson, who had also recently arrived at GCHQ. Williamson, as cryptanalysts do, set about trying to break Cocks' scheme and failed. In the process, he did come up with something similar to the Diffie-Hellman key agreement. It must be said though that while the American researchers founded modern cryptography and built the foundation for reliable e-commerce, GCHQ sat on the ideas and did nothing with them – not even secretly.

Given that GCHQ kept quiet on these developments for more than 20 years, it would not be surprising that they or one of the other secret outfits like the NSA in America had made similar advances in breaking the schemes like RSA but had just kept quiet about it. On the other hand, maybe some individual cryptanalyst working for them had made the advances but the organizations had done nothing with their work.

Cracking the Code

Encrypting and decrypting messages requires a lot of work. That is why computers are normally left to do the job. RSA and similar asymmetric approaches are some of the most intensive ways of encrypting messages and it is thus best to avoid these for large messages. The scheme that is normally applied is for DES or a similar symmetric scheme to be used to encrypt the message based on keys passed between parties using an asymmetric, public key approach like RSA. Keys can still be distributed securely by RSA whilst the bulk of the work is done by the relatively 'fast' DES process.

So how do you go about breaking into a code? The simple codes that were in use up until last century could generally be broken by using something called frequency analysis. With this, the number of times a letter appeared in the cipher text would be counted and compared with the frequency that the letters normally appeared in the appropriate language. In English for example, letters such as 'A' and 'E' are used far more frequently than 'X' and 'Q'. Letters that showed more frequently in the cipher text would be 'A' and 'E', letters that showed up less frequently would be 'X' and 'Q'. Using this approach, simple 'shift' ciphers, where letters of the alphabet are simply shifted a few places left or right, could be broken swiftly unless, that is, the message was very short where the frequency analysis would be built on statistically shaky foundations. This kind of approach breaks down completely with modern encryption as the cipher text does not use characters but a string of binary.

For a symmetric mechanism, the simplest way to get at the plain text, as an unencrypted message is called, is to push it through the appropriate algorithm for every possible value of the key. After each cycle, the potential decrypted message would be checked for characteristics to see if it looked like what was expected. Using DES, all you would need would be around 20 characters of English-like text to know you've almost certainly found the correct key. This is known as a brute force attack and requires a huge amount of computational power. The exact amount of computation required, and thus the time it takes to break into a message, depends on how many possible keys there are to try. All modern encryption mechanisms use numbers as keys, so the length of the key when written in binary can be used to determine how long it will take to crack into a message and thus how secure the message is from an eavesdropper.

When DES was codified in 1977, the key length was set to be 56 bits. This means that there are 2^{56}, or 72,057,594,037,927,936, possible keys. Believe it or not, even in 1977, this was known to be on the short side for true security. It was thought that it was set at this level to allow commercial transactions to have adequate protection whilst also allowing a desperate spook to get into the message eventually. In 1998, an outfit called Cryptography Research built a special-purpose computer using specially designed chips in order to crack DES as part of an open cryptography competition. They spent under a quarter of a million dollars on the machine which could test 90 billion keys every second and could complete a brute force attack on DES in under 4 days.

Four days on a quarter of a million dollar machine means DES is obviously secure enough for normal email chatter or credit card purchases on the Web but is woefully inadequate for diplomatic or large value financial traffic. The DES system was formally disavowed by the US government in May 2005.

An even weaker encryption mechanism was used in the early web browsers. The key lengths used to secure traffic were restricted by the US government to 40 bits. On the machine described above this could be broken by brute force in around 12 seconds. Encryption at this level could only be considered superficial. In the late 1990s, the US government lifted its restrictions and now web browsers are free to use more powerful schemes.

There are many alternative schemes that offer far higher security. Triple-DES encrypts a message using old style DES, decrypts it using a second key and then re-encrypts it using a third. In order to get back to the original message it is necessary to have all three keys played back in the reverse order otherwise you're locked out. It is far more difficult to perform a brute force attack on Triple-DES than the original because you have to try all thee keys simultaneously. This is the equivalent of a single 168-bit key (three times 56 bits) giving 2^{168} possibilities – a number far greater than 1 followed by 50 zeros. It should be noted that adding one extra 'bit' to the key doubles the length of time it would take to perform a brute force attack so a 168-bit key is not just three time more secure than a 56-bit key, it's over a trillion trillion times more secure.

Alternative schemes were proposed by Ronald Rivest (he who put the R in RSA). These include RC2 (RC standing for either Ron's Code or Rivest's Cipher), which is two to three times faster to encrypt or decrypt than traditional DES, and more recently RC4.

A new AES (advanced encryption standard) was announced by the US government in 2001 following an open competition that started in 1997. Originally developed by Vincent Rijmen and Joan Daemen, researchers from Leuven in Belgium, it has been certified by the NSA to secure communications all the way up to Top Secret using 192-bit or 256-bit key lengths. Attempting a brute force attack against a 256-bit key cipher is currently thought to be laughably futile.

Having a long key length does not guarantee security. You have to be careful that the key cannot be guessed by some other means. Normally, keys are created by computers using a random number generator. Unfortunately, it is provably impossible for computers to generate truly random numbers. All they can do is generate a string of numbers that look pretty random. If a key generator is chosen badly it may produce keys that tend towards the lower or upper end of the available range. A brute force attack would then know where to start looking: at the bottom of the range and work up or at the top and work down.

Security by Obscurity

It's very easy to come up with an encryption scheme that's flawed. Even a reasonably well informed specialist can miss serious deficiencies such as a loaded key generator. In order to ensure security, it is wise to rely on openly available methods that have been subject to years of abuse by the international community of cryptanalysts. It is equally wise to avoid schemes cooked up by a closed cabal that are then kept in the dark.

One international authority on cryptography, Bruce Schneier, in his excellent book 'Secrets and Lies' which reviews the whole landscape of digital security, recounts the travails of one security product known as PPTP which was created by Microsoft in the late 1990s. They chose to keep the details of the protocol to themselves.

> They invented their own authentication protocol, their own hash functions, and their own key-generation algorithm. Every one of these items turned out to be flawed. They used a known encryption algorithm, but they used it in such a way as to dilute its security. They made implementation mistakes that weakened the system even further. But since they did all this work internally, no one noticed that PPTP was weak. Microsoft fielded PPTP in Windows NT, 95 and 98 and used it in their virtual private network (VPN) products. It wasn't until 1998 that a paper describing the flaws was published. Microsoft quickly posted a series of fixes, which have since been evaluated and still found wanting.

PPTP was never widely used. The moral of the story can be summed up in Kerckhoff's principle:

> The security of the encryption scheme must depend only on the secrecy of the key, and not the secrecy of the algorithm.

Those in the cryptographic community rail against 'security by obscurity'. By using a widely published and studied set-up, security can be expected. By using secret, proprietary voodoo, all you can do is keep your fingers crossed and hope for the best.

Digital Signatures

What has been discussed so far is the type of encryption that stops an eavesdropper from listening in on a conversation. There is however another use for encryption: to prove who it was that sent a particular message.

When it comes to digital signatures it doesn't matter if the message can be read by eavesdroppers or not, the point is to demonstrate that the message could only have been prepared by the declared sender. Once more it is asymmetric (public/private key) encryption that is pressed into service. The fact that only one person or entity knows the private key is what makes digital signatures possible. When a communication has been sent encrypted using the private key, it can only be 'cleanly' decrypted using the public key. If the sender of the message does not know the private key, no matter how the receiver applies the public key they will not get a clean decryption.

In order to avoid the overhead of applying slow and performance sapping asymmetric encryption to large messages, the digital signature is normally only applied to a mathematical summary of the text or data, known as a hash code. These can be computed easily and accurately by both sender and receiver. If the receiver calculates the hash code of a message and finds that it matches the one from a decrypted digital signature, the message is genuine. If the calculated hash function does not match the one sent, then perfidy may be afoot.

Sadly, it is not quite as clear-cut as this. It would be possible for an interloper with dubious intentions to publish a fake public key in the name of the sender. They could then prepare a message, create the hash code and use their own fake private key to create a digital signature. The digital signature would check out because all the keys were valid. The problem lies with the trustworthiness of the public keys.

In order to prevent this kind of attack, it is necessary for everyone's public keys to be certified by a trusted third party. The certification process take the form of, you guessed it, encryption. This time by the certification authority using their private key. The true sender's details can be obtained by applying the certification authorities public key. This does not solve the problem entirely. It just reduces it to making sure that a single certification authority public key is genuine.

Access Control

The most basic way of stopping bad things happening to a computer, or any resource that is accessed through a computer, is by slapping password access on it. Passwords are everywhere. They're needed to get into PCs. They're needed to get onto servers. They're needed to get into email accounts. They're needed to get into ERP systems. They're needed to get into individual files. They're needed to get into databases. They're needed to get onto network file stores. Unfortunately in the 21st century, passwords are not entirely secure.

Early batch oriented computer systems didn't need a password. To use a computer you had to be standing next to it with a pile of punched cards under your arm. It was only with the advent of time-sharing that user authentication and security became required. Early time-sharing systems would merely hold a list of users and raw passwords. These would be checked against the user name and password entered when someone attempted to login to the computer. Should someone get hold of the password file however things looked pretty grim. It would be very easy for them to login and abuse the system. In the 1970s, instead of storing the raw password, they started to hold a password that had be chewed up in one of those hash functions. When a password was entered by a user it was also chewed up. If the digested remnants of the entered passwords matched the entrails held on the user list, access was granted. If they didn't match, the user was kept out. Should a malefactor get hold of the password file there was little they could do. They would only be able to see the remnants of a password that had been munched through a one-way hash function.

As computers became more powerful, it became possible to throw an entire dictionary through the one-way hash function and compare the values with those in the password list. Hacker utilities have been created to automatically scan for passwords in the most efficient manner. First they'll start with common passwords like 'password' or '54321' before moving on to common words like 'Monday' or 'Golf'. Next will come the more obscure words, 'Horseradish' or 'Nebula' and then words with the Os replaced by zero and Ls by ones. Simple passwords will fall within a matter of minutes. More obscure ones, including those with numbers, may take hours.

One answer is to extend the password to include more letters and to demand the use of non-alphabetic characters thus making the dictionary attack take longer. Unfortunately, most computer users would either forget the password regularly, demand a return to the good old days or both.

An alternative way to authenticate users is to expect some kind of physical access token. This is after all what most office buildings use to assess the right to gain entry. Access tokens are even more useful when used in conjunction with a password. This is in effect what an ATM card and PIN are. One or other is not enough: you won't be able to get cash without both. The drawback of access tokens is that it's possible to forget or mislay them. By and large, they can also be forged in one way or another by those who are suitably desperate.

A special group of physical access tokens come under the title of biometrics. This includes fingerprints, retinal eye scans and face geometry. Obviously, they have the benefit of being difficult to steal and being impossible to misplace. With carefully watched reading equipment, they are difficult to forge. The drawback is that, should a biometric become compromised, by being recorded on some doctored equipment for example, it's very difficult to perform the equivalent of a password change. Biometrics are often seen as a foolproof way to confirm identity. It's agreed in the security community that documentation that includes encrypted biometrics will be more difficult to forge but it is also accepted that it will not be impossible to forge. It is only a matter of time before the keys and the algorithm of such encryption fall into the hands of those who wish to abuse it.

Web Security

Exploring the world wide web is in some ways similar to exploring the high seas in the 18th century. Three hundred years ago, it would have been unwise for an untrained, inexperienced sailor to attempt a voyage without proper equipment, a chest full of armaments and a spirit of adventure. Today, cyberspace can seem an inhospitable and lawless place for the uninitiated. Just as our ancestors did not stay at home and bolt the door, we shouldn't be intimidated just because some latter-day pirates lurk somewhere over the horizon. Today, there is no need for firearms. Generally all you need to do to repel an attack is to recognize it and then ignore it. The general principle of being safe on the web is to 'trust no-one'.

One problem that may be encountered is the unannounced diversion. Should you be struck by the desire to help the US President choose a name for the 'National Thanksgiving Turkey' you could attempt to participate in an online vote at the White House website. You could type www.whitehouse.com into your browser but you would be presented with the website of an estate agent. At the time of writing there was no turkey vote on this site. You could type www.whitehouse.org but you would be presented with an 'alternative' White House site prepared by some people who were clearly very angry. They were remiss enough to miss off a list of turkey names. Finally you could try www.whitehouse.gov which was the website of the genuine White House where you could indeed participate in an online vote to name a turkey.

In other words, just because the name of a website looks right does not mean it is the website you are looking for. Virtually all popular sites will have a similar site with www at the beginning of the name (such as www.wwwwhitehouse.com). Very few of these so-called typo-pirates will take you where you intended.

Abuse of similarly named URLs is often used as part of a 'phishing' attack. In this scenario, an email asking, either apologetically or aggressively, for an unsuspecting member of the public to go to a website to update their bank/credit card/brokerage account details. A hyperlink would be provided which, when activated, takes the user to a website that looks identical to the one the user is accustomed to dealing with. The user would enter their user name and password and, on the following page, be told that the site is unavailable and to try again later. The user name and password would meanwhile have been sent to an attacker who would go off and get up to all kinds of mischief on the genuine site. It's very difficult for the user to spot such an attack as the URLs could be very similar www.MyBank.com versus www.MyBankUpdate.com.

Thankfully there is a way of checking who you are dealing with when using a browser. The approach was originally implemented by Netscape in the mid 1990s and was known as secure socket layer or SSL. It has since been updated and renamed to TLS (Transport Layer Security) which is now an open standard. At its core is a public key certificate that is distributed by the central web server of the site you are looking at. This certificate was created by a certificate authority not by the web servers owner and can therefore be trusted to a greater extent. It could not have been created by the web servers owner as it is encrypted using the certificate authorities encryption key. By basing encryption on this public key certificate you can be assured that the party your dealing with has been certified as the true owner of the key.

When using a browser and SSL/TLS kicks in, a small padlock or key appears (depending on the type of browser you're using) in the bottom right of the browser window. Without a padlock or a fully formed key at the bottom of the browser the link is not encrypted and the party you are dealing with should not be trusted. Unfortunately, the opposite is not entirely true. Just because the icon is in place does not mean a user should trust the site. All the icon says is that the web server's name has been certified with the certification authority not that they are trustworthy. It is down to the user to make that value judgment. You now know that you are dealing with www.dip-and-run.com. Just as in the real world, it is up to you whether it is wise to deal with www.dip-and-run.com.

Cookies

Almost every time you venture onto the web you are being watched. Being spied upon is something that most people don't appreciate. Many websites you pass leave a trail behind on your computer that can be watched from outside. The trail takes the forms of cookies. These are small files that hold information about you and your activities.

Cookies are needed because the web is being used for things it was not intended for. Tim Berners-Lee saw it as a fairly dry way to share technical information. Remember he was not happy when pictures were added into his approach. One thing that was certainly not on the original agenda was to use the web protocol HTTP for having extended conversations between a PC and a server. The HTTP protocol was originally set up to have the memory of a goldfish. Once a page of information had been displayed, both the browser and the web server could forget about the request. The next step would be a hyperlink instruction which had been embedded within the page. Buying a book from Amazon.com does not fit within this approach though. If you added a book to your shopping basket and then continued to browse, the original book would have been forgotten.

To get round this, it is necessary for either the central web server to keep a track of everything that is going on or for each user's browser to remember what's going on in its own little world. Keeping a track of everything centrally takes up a lot of resources and is a bit of a drag which costs the owner of the web server money. Leaving it to the browser to store what's going on in some sort of micro-database, one for each website, seemed far more sensible. And so it came to pass. It is these mini-databases that are known as cookies. Cookies are fairly limited in the format of information they can store. They can't store an image for example. They can however store a fairly large amount of text.

Now just imagine that some enterprising and persuasive soul came up with the idea of selling advertising space on lots of different websites. They would pay a small amount to the owners of websites to display their adverts and hope to sell the advertising space for a larger amount to the usual suspects: media companies, financial companies, shampoo companies, etc. Imagine then that they kept a cookie on all the PCs they encountered that listed all the sites that the PC's browser had visited. They could then target their adverts to the likely audience. A history of visiting child relevant sites would lead to a deluge of toy adverts towards the end of the year. Interest in vehicles and transport would lead to a large number of car adverts. Welcome to the world of online advertising companies such as doubleclick.com. These companies use cookies to monitor users' habits and create databases of activity.

So far, so benign. Avoiding relentless irrelevant adverts can be seen as a good thing. It would however be straightforward for sites to hold other information in the same cookies, such as email addresses, residential addresses, phone numbers and buying habits. These can all be saved at the appropriate juncture in a web transaction. Periodically, they can be downloaded to a central server, linked and cross-correlated and sold on to third parties. Political, sexual and financial predilections would be open for all to see. If you are interested in maintaining your privacy this is not a good thing.

It is possible to disable the use of cookies on a browser but this means that it reverts to its originally-intended forgetful muddle. It also means that you have to type user names and passwords every time you enter a site. Many websites refuse to play with browsers that have cookies disabled. It's probably best to set your browser's security options to clear out its cookie store each time the browser is closed. This strikes a balance between the ability to use sites that require cookies and making it too easy for third parties to watch your activities.

PC Security

So the Internet is pervaded by malign forces: viruses, worms, evil hackers, password crackers, phishers, cookie snoops and IP spoofers. Just as in the real world, where it is not wise to leave doors and windows unlocked, there are some basic security precautions that should be taken.

The most basic and thankfully the most popular precaution is the installation of a 'virus checker' on all PCs. These check-out anything that moves on the computer, looking for things that might be about to cause trouble. Most virus checkers will have a database of potential troublemakers which is then used in the search for baddies. All decent offerings automatically update the database from the Internet without waiting for user prodding. Periodically they will also perform a full system scan which checks everything on a PCs hard disk for a match against the list of known troublemakers. Virus checkers also keep a watch out for network worms so normally there is no need for a separate 'Worm checker'. When malware is uncovered, the virus checker will then advise on the appropriate steps to be taken; be it to attempt a 'disinfection' or to delete the unsalvageable.

The next item is often overlooked. Software that should really be installed on every PC is a personal firewall. This is the main defense against network-borne worms. A firewall sits between the PC and the wild untamed expanse of the Internet and assumes that all traffic in or out is hostile and not to be trusted. It then gives the user the option of allowing certain applications to communicate with the outside world. This is normally a short list and includes web browsers and email programs. Any program wanting to communicate into or out of the computer must get the say-so of the firewall which in turn will ask the user for permission.

One online security firm, Sophos, claimed in mid 2005 that an 'unprotected, unpatched Windows PC', that is without a virus checker or personal firewall, stood a 50/50 chance of being infected by a network-borne worm within just 12 minutes of being exposed to the Internet.

Microsoft has started to provide a basic personal firewall, the Internet connection firewall, with Windows XP. Care must be taken however to ensure that it is activated for each network connection. There are a number of more fully featured firewall products for Windows PCs that can be downloaded for free from companies such as Zone Labs or Sygate.

Trojan Horses, where a program is installed on your PC that allows an outsider access from outside, can be propagated using worms but it is far more likely that they will be have been inadvertently installed by the user themselves. The most common way to achieve this is to send an email with an attachment that includes the Trojan horse software. A suitably crafted email, such as that pretending to come from an bank's technical support desk, has a high likelihood of being actioned by a technically inexpert user. The only real way to avoid being the victim of Trojan horse attack is to delete all unsolicited emails. This is especial necessary if the emails contain an attachment. Those nervous about doing this lest they upset their bank, their employer or a government agency should call the help desk number of the relevant outfit. It is almost 100% certain that unsolicited emails with attachments are malign.

Malware can also be inadvertently downloaded from a website and installed. In many cases, the website will have tricked the user into requesting the download either by placing a false link on a page or by activating the download on the close of a window. Whenever a dialog box is shown that mentions a download or installation it should be closed. Ideally by using the small cross icon in the top right-hand corner. This has less likelihood of triggering the download through misunderstanding. In other cases, the malware will be part of some other small application that the user just likes the look of, for example some fancy 'toolbar', a free game or the animation of dancing cats mentioned earlier. When any program is installed, it is given the power to do what it wants, subject to the operating systems access controls. There is absolutely no reason why a free game program should not send stored passwords, information from cookies or browsing address information out across the Internet. That is not unless you have a personal firewall installed. This would query the communication with the user. Any messages such as 'Should the 'Dancing Cats' be permitted to communicate across the Internet with a computer in Romania?' would indicate that you have done something silly.

This just goes to show that you should trust no-one. Especially when it involves downloading software or entering credit card numbers.

Corporate Security

The same precautions that individuals take should also be taken by companies: virus checkers, personal firewalls and deletion of unsolicited emails. These are however the very least of the concerns of corporate IT functions. Business operates in a different league when it comes to IT security. When an individual's PC plays up it is an annoyance but life goes on. When a business's computer network goes wrong, it directly influences the bottom line.

Keeping viruses and worms out of a corporate network comes high on the list of priorities. As with PCs this is done by using anti virus software on the central email servers and by ringing the network with firewalls.

Firewalls and DMZ

The name firewall came from the early days of rail transport. The steam locomotives would have a coal-fired boiler at the front and a pile of coal at the back. The act of shoveling coal from one end to the other created a lot of coal dust which, given there was a lot of oxygen to react with the carbon, was highly explosive. In order to prevent an explosion in the engine from maiming their passengers, or otherwise spoiling their day, the train company would install a stout metal barrier towards the rear of the locomotive to take the brunt of any blast. This was known as the firewall.

Computer networks in their early days had frequent tantrums where phantom signals got in the way of the smooth flow of information. In order to stop a misbehaving link from crashing an entire network, a set of devices was installed to contain any problems before they spread widely. It was only natural that they would be called firewalls after their steam-age predecessors.

A corporate firewall has one foot in the corporate network and the other foot on the Internet. If network packets want to go from one side of the divide to the other they must pass through the firewall. Just like a personal firewall that runs on a PC, a corporate firewall blocks all traffic except that which has been specifically permitted. The permit/deny decision is taken based on a set of rules which list the types of technical protocol that are permitted and which specific machines are allowed to use them to communicate.

209

There are several types of firewall. One, the packet filter, simply drops data packets that don't meet its filtering rules. Another, known as a proxy server, is commonly used to allow web surfers on PCs within a corporate network to access web pages on the Internet beyond. The proxy server is passed requests from the PCs and then relays them on the Internet, acting as the PC's proxy. The external website only deals with the proxy server which has the task of returning any reply back to the PCs. This way the PCs are safe within the corporate network and do not have to communicate directly with the outside world. The proxy server also gives the company the possibility of watching all web browsing and blocking any sites that it deems inappropriate. Often all web surfing activity is recorded at the proxy server.

Companies need to have a presence on the Internet themselves. The web server where a company's website is hosted must obviously be accessible from the wider Internet with all its bandits and delinquents. It would be unwise to have this inside the corporate network as it would allow the great unwashed to be one step away from every computer in the network. Instead computers that must communicate with the wider Internet are placed in a separate network with its own ring of defenses, known as a Demilitarized Zone or DMZ. Whilst still being owned by the same company, the DMZ is at arms length from it. It has a firewall between it and the wider Internet but it is still considered insecure. So much so that, generally, companies have the policy that computers in the DMZ are not permitted to initiate communications with anything inside their corporate network. DMZ computers are expendable cannon-fodder at the front line in the battle for Internet security.

Virtual Private Networks

Corporates do not exist in a vacuum. They have customers and suppliers. They need to communicate with them in order to receive and place orders. In centuries gone by this would be done in person or by letter. The 20th century was the age of the phone and the fax machine. Since the mid 1990s, it's been possible to allow computers to communicate directly, without human mediation, across the Internet. When you attempt to do this you start to expose yourself to all the rouges and vagabonds that stalk cyberspace. To keep things secure you need to make sure that the entity you are dealing with is who they say they are and that, when they say things that are important, these cannot be overheard.

The answer is a Virtual Private Network or VPN. A VPN allows two parties to communicate across the Internet without being overheard or the risk of an interloper getting in the way. You will recall that the Internet uses the TCP/IP protocol suite for communications. IP is the part of the suite that looks after getting data from one point to another. Unfortunately, is it not inherently secure. In order to make it secure an extension has been defined known as IPSec. This uses the inevitable public key cryptography to negotiate key exchange before encrypting all the data that flies over the public Internet.

A virtual private network can be set up by configuring suitable firewalls to convert the IP traffic that is created inside corporate networks into IPSec traffic for transmission over the Internet. When IPSec traffic reaches a suitable firewall at the target organization, it is then decrypted back to standard IP traffic before being allowed inside the corporate firewall to complete its journey.

VPNs can also be used to allow PCs and laptops connected to the Internet, maybe wirelessly in those coffee-shops or hotels, to communicate with all the resources within a corporate network. The traffic that would be sent using the standard IP protocol has to be converted into the secure IPSec protocol using special VPN software installed on the PC or laptop. This is then converted back to IP traffic once it is accepted by the VPN firewall of the corporate network.

Firewalls are the mainstay of network security but they should not be seen as impregnable. It is possible for either a talented or lucky adversary to get past their defenses. Just as in the real word it's not wise to rely solely on strong locks to look after your possessions. It is wise to watch for incursions and respond accordingly if one is detected. Thus larger computer networks deploy some kind of intrusion detection systems. These include 'burglar alarms' systems which, like in the real world, alerts administrators if they are touched in any way. These can take the form of 'honey pots' which are like burglar alarms but have enticing names like 'BigImportantServer' and simple vulnerabilities that are easy to exploit.

Application security

Organizations not only have to worry about repelling external attacks but must also consider the enemies within. These include everything from organized industrial espionage, where employees are paid to spill the beans on the operational and financial vulnerabilities of an enterprise, all the way down to simple staff incompetence. With the increasing scope of data protection laws and the expectation of client confidentiality, the availability of data must be restricted to only those with a genuine need to see it. Those with no direct call on information should be kept away from it. If such controls are applied, the likes of industrial spies and malign journalists will only be able to see data related to their specific employment not that of the whole of the enterprise.

The most sensitive information is normally held in the accounting, HR and planning systems such as the core ERP system. It would be unacceptable for everyone to have access to the whole system thus each user's access must be restricted to allow them access to only the area of the system relevant to their work. Workers in one plant should not be able to view or update the processing being performed in another plant and vice versa. Accountants should only be able to view and post to the accounts of the companies they have been assigned to work for. HR staff should be able to see the employment records of the workers they are responsible for but not the records of other HR staff.

Implementing this kind of scheme is easier said than done. First, it is necessary to split the operation into distinct organizational units: plants, accounting companies, employee groups, purchasing organizations and so on. Then the computer application must be written to permit or block access to users based on these units. There must be different levels of permission from just allowing data to be displayed all the way up to the ability to write new data. Some users may be able to change documents, such as purchase order but not to create the document in the first place. Others will be able to approve documents but not change them. Each type of action, such as displaying, changing, creating and approving documents, must be considered separately. The application must be able to allow any combination of actions to be permitted within any combination of organizational units. Finally, and most contentiously, each employee must be assigned to a number of organization units and levels of access in such a way that the process does not descend into an administrative quagmire. Often individual employee's responsibilities don't fit neatly within the philosophical notion of an organization imposed by such a framework. Confusion and debate ensue. When key employees go on holiday or fall ill, it quickly becomes apparent that no-one else has the necessary systems access to perform important tasks.

Any updates to authorization profiles must work their way through lengthy and slow help-desk processes.

As a result of these complexities, there was a time, not long ago, when it was normal for only lip-service to be paid to the whole process of application security. This changed with the introduction of the Sarbanes-Oxley Act in 2002. Section 404 of the Act states that each year, a company's management and its auditing accountants must each attest to the effectiveness of their internal 'management controls'. These are the procedures used to make sure that accountants can't commit fraud without being found out. The restrictions on individual users within the accounting systems are pivotal to the effectiveness of accounting controls. If any employee could make any accounting posting to any account whenever they liked, it would be far easier for them to shift money around a company to bamboozle managers and auditors. Restricting their activities cuts down the opportunity for mischief. Any company director found to have contravened Sarbanes-Oxley can be charged in the USA for their shortcomings: not for committing fraud, just for the failure to comply with Sarbanes-Oxley. As a result, senior managers have suddenly become interested in the relatively dry area of application security and there has been a huge increase in the amount of work undertaken by audit and consultancy groups on the topic. When a new application system is being put in place, it has always been necessary to test its operation and ideally the authorizations associated with each user. Now it has become customary to hire an independent group of checkers to review the testing to ensure that it complies with Sarbanes-Oxley. The company's auditors will then audit the checkers to ensure that they have checked the testers. Each group will spend much of their time documenting their work to cover their backs in case lawyers get involved at some later date. The whole process takes up huge amounts of time and results in a cumbersome system that infuriates users. The efficacy of the process in avoiding fraud is unproven but the consultancy companies, who do the testing and checking, are happy enough to be making lots of money.

The Human Factor

Restricting individual users' ability to update their system has another benefit. It reduces the possibility of inexperienced or incompetent users accidentally unleashing havoc. Without any restrictions, a misunderstood command can rapidly reverberate though a system deleting and updating data that an untrained user shouldn't be going anywhere near. Restricting their ability to update a system means their mischief will only impact a relatively small amount of data.

Incompetent humans are in fact probably the greatest threat to effective security. The theoretical basis of security systems, the maths behind the cryptography, the procedures for the use of firewalls, the application security set-up of ERP systems, are pretty sound. It is when humans come to apply it that cracks start to appear. Not all people are motivated to maintain security. Many will be bored by the apparently pointless procedures and skip the more tedious steps. During the Second World War, the German operators of the Enigma cipher machines each day had to select three alphabetical characters at random for use as 'initial rotor settings'. Those who wrote the procedures knew that using the same initial rotor settings every day would reduce the security of the message sent. A number of operators were not so convinced. They used the same initial rotor settings day-in day-out, often ABC or their initials. Once a message had been tied to a specific operator that was known to be lazy, by radio location for instance, it gave the allies a head start in breaking into the message.

Sometimes the operators of secure systems have not been given enough training and are not fully aware of what steps are necessary to ensure security. They make it up as they go along. They don't check things they should check. They skip the boring bits. They also make mistakes far more often than machines do. Unlike machines, they are also susceptible to social engineering. This takes advantage of many people's desires to be helpful and other people's desires to avoid getting into trouble. A carefully worded and carefully delivered phone call to a junior systems administrator will often manage to procure a key password either because the target was trying to be helpful or because they were frightened of later retribution for their intransigence.

It's almost universally agreed that the weak link in computer security is the poor, confused, benighted human.

7 Open Source

GNU

To the avowed hacker, the Artificial Intelligence Lab at MIT contained some of the most desirable pieces of computer hardware available anywhere. To complement the state of the art computers, there had gathered possibly the most talented and single-minded group of programmers and computer scientists anywhere. Well that's what they would tell you anyway.

It was in the spring of 1971 that Richard Stallman, an undergraduate studying physics down the road at Harvard, first wandered over to the AI Lab at MIT to see what was going on. The ARPANET had its first few nodes operational, the microprocessor was about to be unleashed on the world, IBM had started to unbundle its software and the stock market was still recovering from the aftermath of the go-go years.

He hadn't been invited. He just meandered in, looked over people's shoulders and asked what they were doing. His passion for computing was clearly discernible because before too long he had been offered his first summer job there. It would be the start of a relationship with the lab that would last well over a decade and trigger one of the more remarkable personal crusades in the story of computing.

At this time, the Artificial Intelligence community held views about the future of computing that were sharply at odds with those espoused by the early managers at ARPA. ARPA managers like Licklider and Taylor were convinced the future of computers was in the role helping humans perform their work, 'human computer symbiosis' as they put it. The adherents of artificial intelligence thought that, instead of aiding humans, computers would take over from them. Computers would be able to 'think' and make rational deductions.

AI programs where thus not about following a predefined set of instructions, as was done in most business or scientific computers at the time, but about assimilating information and then using it as the basis for some kind of logical reasoning. The traditional programming languages like COBOL and FORTRAN were only suitable for setting down a list of instructions to be followed blindly and were thus unsuitable for AI work. AI researchers had instead come up with a programming language called LISP that was specially tailored to their needs. It was however far more demanding of the computer running it that the traditional languages. During the late 1970s and early 1980s, a one-off computer was designed and built at MIT which was optimized to prepare and run programs written in LISP.

Richard Greenblatt, the designer of this computer, decided that he would like to start up a new enterprise to take advantage of the work he had done at MIT. He didn't want it to be like a normal company but one that would uphold the spirit that had grown up at the AI Lab. There would be no external financial backer to harass and cajole them into doing things they didn't want to do. The staff would largely be hackers from the AI Lab but they would only work there part-time so that they could maintain the commune-like social grouping back at MIT at the same time.

Unfortunately the plan had a flaw. His fellow researchers didn't trust his judgment, well not to the extent that they would risk their futures on it anyway, and a number of them set up a company to do a similar task along more traditional lines. It was called Symbolics. Undeterred, Greenblatt set up his own company, called it LMI, and battle commenced. The first round went to Symbolics who before long had hired virtually all of the original group of hackers from the AI Lab. This left just Greenblatt and Richard Stallman, who had by this time been a permanent member of the lab's staff for many years, from the original group.

Stallman was very angry. 'They destroyed my community', he would later say and vowed to do what he could to ensure that Symbolics would not prevail. Both LMI and Symbolics chose to use the original LISP software from MIT as the starting point for their products. Whenever Symbolics added a feature to their version of the software, Stallman would personally add a similar feature to the MIT version which would then be immediately available to LMI. Keeping this up would be a daunting task given that there was a team of people at Symbolics churning out updates and only one Richard Stallman updating the MIT version. He managed to keep up the pace for nearly 2 years at which point MIT switched over to use Symbolics software. This meant that, whilst he could still update his old system, there would be no group of users within the lab testing it. "I decided I didn't want to just continue punishing Symbolics forever... I decided I would develop a free operating system, and in this way lay the foundations for a new community like the one that had been wiped out."

In order to ensure that the resulting operating system would be of most use, Stallman wanted to create a system that would be easy to move between different types of hardware. He had a look at the products that were available at the time and selected UNIX, already in use in around 100,000 computers around the world, as the most suitable candidate. UNIX however was most certainly not free software, it and its various offshoots were all copyrighted. Stallman would have to write a version from scratch. And so on 1st January 1984, the GNU (standing for 'GNU Not UNIX') project was born.

One of the reasons that UNIX is often described as elegant is that it has a small core, or kernel, that doesn't do too much apart from act as ringmaster. This is supplemented by a plethora of smaller utility programs that do the useful work. Easing himself into the task, Stallman set to work by creating new versions of some of the smaller utilities. The first to undergo the GNU treatment was a version of the obscure tool known as 'yacc'. In order to get as much of the system working as quickly as possible, any previously available free programs would be used as a basis for the new GNU version. A free version of 'yacc', known as 'bison', had been written some years before and was tweaked to meet the requirements of GNU.

Other minor utilities followed and before long he approached the most important of the UNIX programs: the 'C' compiler. 'C' is the programming language that UNIX itself is written in. Having a 'C' compiler would be a major milestone on the way to having a complete operating system. At the time there was a well known compiler called the 'Amsterdam Compiler Kit' also referred to on occasions as the 'Free University Compiler Kit'. It had been developed by an American academic called Andrew Tanenbaum at, unsurprisingly given its name, the Free University of Amsterdam. Stallman asked for permission to use the software in his new free operating system. The reply was not what he wanted to hear. According to Stallman it said, 'the university is free, the compiler isn't'. Tanenbaum had already sold the rights of the software to operations in America and Europe and thus couldn't give it away to the GNU project even if he wanted to. In the end, Stallman wrote the GNU C Compiler or GCC himself. "It was", he says, "the most challenging program I've ever written".

From its early days, it proved to be a success, enabling the formation of the 'Free Software Foundation', an organization to promote and distribute GNU software. Its wide distribution led to users sending feedback with suggestions for improvement. Over time, with an ongoing optimization effort to incorporate the suggestions, the GCC would become known as one of the best performing compilers available for many platforms.

Stallman was on a crusade to provide free software to anyone who wanted it. As he is happy to re-iterate at the least provocation, the emphasis was on 'free, as in freedom of speech, not free beer'. He was motivated by a desire to ensure that no-one would be denied the ability to use a computer just because they could not afford some proprietary software. They should also be able to adapt the software as they see fit without additional payment or lengthy negotiations. He was keenly aware that unless he was careful, his GNU programs would be taken as they were, adapted and then sold on in a proprietary manner. This would defeat the purpose of the exercise. To stop this happening he came up with a concept that he called 'copyleft', as opposed to the traditional concept of copyright. Copyleft, as set out in the GNU Public Licence or GPL, means that the software may be sold but that any changes made to it must also be published and made freely available. The restrictions of Copyleft would then follow this updated version of the program. The GPL, which all GNU software is distributed under, also states that the underlying source code, of both the original and any changes made, must always be made available to allow other programmers to further build on the work.

By 1990, the GNU project was nearly complete. Most of the UNIX utilities had been recreated by a growing band of both paid and volunteer programmers. All of the programs were made available freely under the GPL. The last remaining major hole in the product was the kernel. Stallman had been putting off making a start on it as kernels are notoriously difficult to get working let alone working well. At the time, he did not know that someone else was about to stumble into filling the gap for him.

Linux

When UNIX first made it out of Bell Labs into the academic community in the early 1970s, it was published in its entire form, both the working machine code programs and the underlying human readable source code that was used to generate the machine code. This made it ideal for university lecturers such as Andrew Tanenbaum in Amsterdam who could illustrate how the system worked by taking their students through the source code. All this stopped in 1979 when, with version 7, AT&T made it clear that the source code was going underground and would no longer be available.

Tanenbaum who had for years been teaching a course on the practical aspects of operating systems, abandoned it because there was no decent examples of open operating systems available that his students could get their teeth into. After a number of years concentrating on the theory, Tanenbaum decided to create his own small but perfectly formed operating system that he could use to teach students. It would be intended purely for educational use to replace the UNIX that had been obfuscated years before by AT&T and Bell Labs. He started work in 1984 and by working in the evenings in his own time had a functioning version available in 1986. The new mini operating system would naturally enough be known as MINIX. It was gradually improved over the following years and by the end of the 1980s was used widely in the teaching of computer operating systems in universities across the world.

Tanenbaum also wrote and published a book that explained the inner workings of MINIX called 'Operation Systems: Design and Implementation'. Given that both the software and the book were created with education in mind, it's not surprising that it became a widely used textbook in university courses. In 1990, a copy of the book had made its way into the hands of a Finnish computer science student called Linus Torvalds studying at the University of Helsinki. Torvalds was interested in the inner workings of computers. He had been hooked by his grandfather's Commodore Vic20 microcomputer, programming first in BASIC and then the much more demanding assembly language. By the late 1980s, he had progressed to the unique charms of a machine known as the Sinclair QL but had not made the leap to the far more common IBM PC. The QL was highly idiosyncratic and has never been described as a mainstream machine. As a result, when he arrived at university in 1988, Torvalds did not have a serious computer to poke around. He didn't consider the affordable PC offerings available at the time to be worth the bother. A PC running Microsoft DOS was more likely to corrupt a technical student than educate them. A UNIX workstation would be far too expensive.

Tanenbaum's book brought news that there was another option. MINIX was a usable UNIX system that would run cleanly on a PC with one of Intel's 80386 processors. The 80386 had been available for over 5 years and by 1990 was becoming affordable. Torvalds decided the time was right and with the combination of a student loan and Christmas money he put down the deposit on a PC. He sent off for the MINIX discs (which couldn't be placed in the back of the book as there were 14 of them).

Between the discs' arrival in March 1991 and September of that year he concocted a series of increasingly involved experiments, starting with a basic 'task switcher' and progressing via a basic terminal emulator to a very basic implementation of a UNIX kernel. A member of the university staff, Ari Lemmke, heard that he was working on an operating system and set aside some space on one of the university's FTP sites that allowed anyone on the Internet to download the program code. It was at this point that the development gained its name. Without much thought, Torvalds had christened it 'Freax': Free + freak + the obligatory X because it was based on UNIX. Lemmke obviously did not think much of it as he chose to use Torvalds' working name – one that Torvalds himself had declined to use lest others think him an egomaniac. This was 'Linux' : Linus + X.

During this time, Torvalds had been taking part in the discussions of the MINIX community on a kind of email-based notice board called USENET. Each subscriber to a USENET 'newsgroup' receives a copy of emails posted to it. It's meant for broadcasting information to all the subscribers who take part rather than for individuals having a chat. The shy Torvalds was reticent about letting the outside world see his creation lest they take a disliking to it. It was only on the 5th October 1991 that Torvalds felt confident enough to post the following to the MINIX newsgroup:

> Do you pine for the nice days of minix-1.1, when men were men and wrote their own device drivers? Are you without a nice project and just dying to cut your teeth on an OS you can try to modify to your needs? Are you finding it frustrating when everything works on minix? No more all-nighters to get a nifty program working? Then this post might be just for you:-)

The posting went on to announce the availability of Linux Version 0.02. At peak around 40,000 people around the world read the MINIX newsgroup. They were of course what would kindly be described as 'computer enthusiasts'. Given the size and nature of the group, it's unsurprising that interest in Linux grew quickly. At the point of the October posting, Linux was in a very basic state, it could not handle floppy disks or network connections. The hackers who monitored the newsgroups saw this as a challenge rather than a drawback. Many saw things that were missing that they would like to see in an operating system and sent suggestions to Torvalds on how to go about it. As they could install Linux on their own machines and, because the source code was publicly available, they could update the programs as they saw fit, many built their own suggestions into the system and then sent the updated source code back to Torvalds.

Unlike MINIX, which Tanenbaum refused to update in any significant way in order to keep it clear and uncluttered for its original educational purposes, Torvalds accepted many of the suggestions. These were incorporated into the Linux core and a new updated version of the operating system was quickly placed on the FTP server for anyone on the Internet to download.

The same process was followed for bugs. Any bugs that were uncovered would be notified to Torvalds who could check them out and attempt to fix them. The more experienced users could suggest fixes to the source code themselves.

As time went on and work progressed, Linux picked up a vocal critic. None other than Andrew Tanenbaum, the academic who wrote the original MINIX. He posted a pointed entry to the MINIX newsgroup at the end of January 1992 entitled 'LINUX is obsolete'. His main two grouses were that Linux did not use something called a 'micro-kernel', as his book espoused, and that it was focused entirely on the PC and in particular the Intel 80386 chip and was thus 'not portable'. Unsurprisingly, Torvalds reacted strongly, accusing MINIX of having a number of 'brain-damages [sic]' and pointing out that it was Tanenbaum who made money from MINIX (you had to buy the discs) whilst Linux was only a hobby and thus wouldn't be perfect. Looking at the exchange now, Torvalds comes across as a student who was being petulant because he didn't like what he heard. Tanenbaum comes across as a pompous academic refusing to accept a suboptimal yet reasonably functional real-world compromise. The two sides continued to sling mud at each other for over a week. At times, the exchange descended into petty childishness. Prof. Tanenbaum pointed out that Torvalds should

Be thankful you are not my student. You would not get a high grade for such a design

This received a response from one defender of Linux who said

That's ok. Einstein got lousy grades in math and physics.

There were a number of more mature and balanced responses, such as:

Many if not most of the software we use is probably obsolete according to the latest design criteria. Most users could probably care less if the internals of the operating system they use is obsolete. They are rightly more interested in its performance and capabilities at the user level.

I would generally agree that microkernels are probably the wave of the future. However, it is in my opinion easier to implement a monolithic kernel. It is also easier for it to turn into a mess in a hurry as it is modified.

Regards, Ken

The author was none other than Ken Thompson, one of the Bell Labs programmers who had written the original UNIX over 20 years previously. Eventually the fuss died down and in order to stop trampling on the toes of the MINIX clan, a new newsgroup was set up to focus exclusively on Linux.

The Linux of early 1992 used what is known as a command line interface. This is not very exciting. It allows users to type commands on a keyboard and watch raw text on the screen. Since the advent of the Apple Mac 8 years previously, this was only acceptable to 'computer enthusiasts' who were interested in operating system design. Everyone else would want a graphical user interface. Thankfully, a solution was at hand. During the 1980s, the 'X' consortium had been born. This defined a single way that all the different flavors of UNIX would deal with graphical programs. In order to stop the usual bickering that was a hallmark of the commercial UNIX world, the 'X' specification was freely available and non-proprietary though it took a lot of effort to get it working on a specific platform. By the time that Linux was able to make use of it, in early 1992, it was already available on the Intel 80386. It was called Xfree386 and by May the LINUX kernel had been tweaked to work with it. Networking was added by the end of 1992 but it would take until March 1994 before Torvalds would feel that Linux was in a state where it could justify the label 'version 1.0'.

It was around this time that Torvalds went on a visit to Australia. He popped by the capital Canberra and stayed with one of his hacker associates Andrew Tridgell. They paid a visit to a local aquarium and stopped by a pen that contained a number of fairy penguins. As Tridgell recalled, "There's a little sign up saying don't put your hand in the pen. And of course Linus ignored that, and put his hand in, and one of the fairy penguins gave him a very friendly little nip – just a little inquisitive 'I wonder what that tastes like?' – type nip." Torvalds supposedly already liked penguins but the cute fairy penguins, which only grow to about 15 inches in height, obviously made an impact on him because he chose the penguin, as drawn by one Larry Ewing, as the Linux mascot. According to Tridgell, in his mailing list justification of the choice, Torvalds included a 'story about this penguin in Canberra that mauled him – it was a six foot penguin by this stage.' On pointing out the unjustified hyperbole, Tridgell was informed that he had 'no sense of the dramatic'.

Just because the software had made it to version 1.0 did not mean it was complete or bug-free. The bug reports, fixes and suggestions for improvement continued to roll in. To manage every single update would be far too much for a single individual. The way of dealing with the deluge only emerged gradually. Torvalds had started out dealing with each update himself. A number of his correspondents stood out as both frequent and trustworthy. Trustworthy in that their suggestions were only rarely dropped or changed before making it into the kernel. In short, they knew what they were talking about. As the pace of updates picked up and Torvalds came under pressure the suggestions for updates from the trustworthy 'lieutenants' received less and less scrutiny before being accepted. Each week, the stream of comments and suggestions increased just a little bit more. Torvalds would only be able to deal with a certain number of requests and would drop the rest. Users grew frustrated that their communications were being ignored and would email one of the lieutenants asking for their opinion. If the lieutenants thought that the idea was sound they would act on it themselves and forward the solution to Torvalds. As it had come from one of the lieutenants it had a far better chance of reaching the kernel. The deluge grew. Eventually, virtually the only way to have an update accepted was to send it via one of the lieutenants. At no point though was authority delegated. Torvalds always had the final say. It was the lieutenants' competence that held the system together. As many have said, the Linux community operates along the lines of a benign dictatorship.

Torvalds' days at Helsinki University were numbered though and by 1996, he had moved to Silicon Valley to work for a start-up company called Transmeta that made radical low power microprocessors intended for use in mobile devices. His contract did state that he could work on the Linux kernel part-time but by 2003, he left the company saying that, "I've been feeling a little guilty about how little 'real work' I've been doing lately". He joined a not-for-profit organization, the 'Open System Development Lab', that meant he would be paid to work full-time on the Linux kernel.

Distributions

Linux itself is just the kernel of an operating system. From its very earliest days, it needed a surrounding ecosystem of utilities to allow it to do anything useful. Writing the utilities from scratch would be a huge amount of work. This is why no-one bothered. In 1991, when the Linux kernel was just starting out, there was already a complete set available freely in the form of the GNU project. Linux as used on computers today should more properly be known as GNU/Linux as it is the combination of the two working together that form a workable system. Neither GNU nor Linux on their own is very useful. There was even a failed attempt to have the combined entity renamed 'LiGNUx'. That said it is not just GNU that is used along with the Linux Kernel to create a complete system, for example X Windows is often used with it as well.

In the early days, getting Linux working on a PC involved the tiresome chore of doing the rounds of all the FTP sites retrieving all the component software. First was the Linux kernel, then there were the GNU utilities, the X Windows server and any other software for networking and the like. The user also had to ensure that all the software was of the correct versions. Any incompatibilities, for example an old Linux Kernel with a new X Windows release would do nothing except cause frustration. To try and reduce the hassle involved, the practice of creating a single 'distribution' that contained all the necessary software was created. The Manchester University Computer Center created 'MCC Interim Linux' in February 1992, within weeks of the Tanenbaum argument. A similar effort at Texas A&M University was followed by the 'Softlanding Linux System' or SLS which had a far greater scope and attracted many to try Linux for the first time. The effort of keeping all the different components in step however proved too much and the reputations of the early distributions took a battering.

A number of people started alternative distributions in an attempt to solve the problem. Ian Murdock took the approach of trying to generate a community that would look after a new distribution. Taking the first three letters from his wife's name, Deb, and his own, Ian, he formed the name Debian. The Debian community started in August 1993 as a co-operative effort to create a stable comprehensive distribution and continues today as one of the more 'pure' non-commercial distributions. The distribution market place grew to become quite crowded and has started to fragment into different groups. A new entry Ubuntu, meaning 'humanity to others', emphasizes its inclusive foundations and beliefs. Madriva, formerly known as Mandrake, was founded in France in 1998 and focuses on making Linux easy to use on a desktop PC. Red Hat started as a general distribution for use on both PC and server but has since 'split' with the PC market being served by its Fedora brand and the original 'Red Hat' distribution being focused on serving large enterprises. A similar business-oriented organization formed in Germany in 1992 to be called SUSE (Software und System Entwicklung) and was bought by Novell at the end of 2003. The transaction occurred with IBM's assistance, allegedly to ensure that Red Hat did not end up with the corporate market all to itself.

Another distribution, Caldera, took a different path. It started off as an internal project within Novell but, after management changes, the effort was canned. Two of the employees that had been working on it chose to go it alone and with financial backing arranged by the recently ousted CEO of Novell set up their new business towards the end of 1994. Whilst SUSE and Red Hat followed the spirit of the GPL by offering paid-for services to go along with a free software product, Caldera started adding their own and other companies' proprietary software to a Linux base. An early innovation was their 'Looking glass' desktop. This sat on top of the basic Linux operating system and provided a user experience similar to that offered by the then new Microsoft Windows 95. This was not released under the GPL and meant that it could not be used by the other distributions without payment. This was certainly starting to subvert the aims of the original GPL and Caldera suffered the verbal wrath of a fulminating Richard Stallman, as-ever unwilling to compromise on his principles of free software.

Desktops

The problem of coming up with a pleasant user experience was not restricted to Caldera. A German student Matthias Ettrich had attempted to build a graphical word processor on Linux as part of his studies but found that there was no obvious mechanism for building it without using proprietary software. After a search of the free software sites on the Internet, he came across something called Qt (pronounced the same as 'cute'). This was a toolkit to simplify the generation of programs that operated in a mouse-driven, graphical manner with the likes of menus and 'drag and drop' functions. It appeared to be very simple to create programs using it but it had a drawback. It was not truly free software in the sense of the GPL. Qt was the work of a Norwegian software outfit called Trolltech. Whilst Trolltech was founded by Linux enthusiasts, they also wanted to make a living and expected to sell their produce. They did however offer Qt at no cost to those using it for non-commercial purposes. Ettrich suggested building a graphical desktop environment to be known as KDE based on Qt in an announcement in October 1996 and received a mixed response. The diehards of the free software set assailed the new group because of their inclusion of proprietary programs and also because a number of them didn't approve of 'this sissy 'GUI' thing' as Ettrich would later characterize it.

A rival camp was set up to build an alternative graphical desktop. This would be based on some earlier development done as part of the effort to build a GNU image processing package. As this work was done under the GPL, it would be freely available for all to use. The KDE alternative would be known as GNOME and work would start in 1997 with the first official release in March 1999. During the period between Ettrich's announcement and GNOME hitting the streets, KDE was ahead in the race and it became a major feature of the Caldera and SUSE distributions of Linux. Whilst KDE was published under the GPL, the Qt programs that it needed to run were not and Red Hat refused to carry it in its distribution, no doubt losing customers in the process. The bitterness started to dissolve in 2000 when Trolltech released a version of Qt under the GPL allowing it to be included in all Linux distributions with a clear conscience.

Open Source

The ambiguous relationship between profit-making business on the one hand and the communities that built and maintained software such as Linux on the other had to be cleared up. There was obviously a range of views but the insistence that everything should be entirely 'free' was putting areas of the commercial world off. A 'freeware' summit was called. It would bring together the heads of the various popular free development tools to hopefully agree a common approach. It met on 7 April 1998 in Palo Alto, California. The only figure missing was Richard Stallman from GNU. It was believed that commercial software was such an anathema to him that his presence would only disrupt proceedings. He was not even invited. After considering a number of possible names for their movement including 'sourceware' and 'freed software', they settled on the new moniker 'Open Source'. The term would be applied to all their efforts and give the clear message that the underlying source must be made available to all users without the need for payment. The then head of the Debian Linux Distribution, Bruce Perens, was tasked with drawing up the 'Open Source Definition' a document that would set out the beliefs and behaviors that would distinguish the open source movement from its more traditional alternatives.

The first major company to embrace this new Open Source philosophy did so partially as an act of desperation. By the beginning of 1998, Netscape's business was structured very differently from what had been original intended when Jim Clark and Marc Andressen had set out 4 years previously. With Microsoft shipping Internet Explorer with Windows 95 for free, there was really no market for a paid-for Netscape browser. The company kept afloat by selling the server software that serviced the requests from browsers. In a bold move, the source code for the Netscape Communicator browser was placed on the web for all to see so that the browser would become open to the wider community of developers. To mark the move, the browser would revert to a name that had been used within Netscape for some time: Mozilla. Mozilla was in fact the company mascot, a paper effigy of a dinosaur that had watched over the development of the original Netscape browser in 1994. The source code was available from www.mozilla.org not www.netscape.com. A further indication that the program was no longer Netscape's sole property.

There was an initial flurry of interest as the worldwide community of hackers gloated over the first corporate conversion to Open Source but this turned out to be short-lived. Work did not grind to a halt entirely but it took some years before the project could build up enough momentum to be able to make its first major announcement: the release of the Firefox browser at the end of 2004. This browser would become the first serious competitor to Microsoft's Internet Explorer for years.

Netscape's problems in 1998 were partly brought on by the open source movement. Its main business, the selling of web server software, was under threat from a derivative of the web server that the Netscape team had left behind at the NCSA back in 1994. To complement the original browser that the Mosaic team at the NCSA had developed, they had rustled up a basic example of a web server that could service the

'HTTP' requests that the browsers sent out. On UNIX, this type of process is called a daemon and so it was unimaginatively titled 'HTTPd'. A number of individuals and organizations used HTTPd to support their early attempts at websites. As with all software, there were a number of problems that needed to be fixed. Details of these were sent to the NCSA but disappeared into a void. The exodus of technical talent to Netscape had left the NSCA with nobody to support HTTPd. One of those users hoping to receive a version including a number of security patches and performance improvements was Brian Behlendorf, the 'chief engineer' of the tiny HotWired web magazine. Behlendorf and others in a similar position became tired of waiting and got together to update the abandoned program themselves. They improved and extended it and called their project 'Apache'. The project operated in a similar manner to the Linux kernel effort with suggestions of fixes and improvements being applied to a central instance. By the beginning of 1998, when Netscape published its browser on mozilla.org, nearly 50% of the web servers on the Internet ran Apache. Microsoft's offering, IIS, ran 20% and Netscape's offering, 'NetSite', the product that was keeping them afloat financially, trailed in a poor third place.

The reason for the popularity of Apache was not just that it was free but that it was of a very high quality. This was not lost on IBM. IBM had their own web server at the time called Domino Go. It had a market share of well under 1%. IBM also had a number of other products that needed to work alongside a web server but the risible market share of Domino Go meant that these had difficulty in the marketplace. Instead IBM dropped Domino Go and backed Apache. All its web-related products were re-branded under the WebSphere umbrella with the open-source Apache web server serving as a foundation. This not only meant that IBM could reduce its development costs but that overnight IBM would now have half the web using their preferred web server.

The conversion of IBM to the open source cause changed the company's image somewhat within the hacker community. It had by no means given up its old profit making ways but it was no longer Hacker Enemy Number One. Further evidence of IBM's commitment came at the end of 2001 when it released its Eclipse development platform to the Open Source community. The development platform is the software that programmers use on a day-to-day basis to get their work done. It includes the likes of program editors and debugging tools. The Eclipse platform was the successor to IBM's VisualAge set of tools and development was well under way as an internal project when the announcement was made that $40m worth of work was being transferred to the public domain.

Another company that started to embrace the open source way of working was Sun Microsystems. Originally a vendor of high specification UNIX workstations and servers, their market niche had been eroded over the years by the general increase in the power of commodity hardware. In 1999, they purchased a long established German productivity tool company called StarDivision and their productivity suite StarOffice. In 2002, they released the underlying code for StarOffice to the open source community as OpenOffice. This is an office suite, very similar in function to Microsoft Office, with the likes of a word processor, spreadsheet and presentation software. Unlike Microsoft Office it is available at no cost to the end user. Microsoft Office has many advanced features that are not replicated in OpenOffice but most users have probably never heard of these functions let alone used them. OpenOffice represents a perfectly functional office package that is perfectly acceptable to almost all users. (This book was written using OpenOffice 'Writer'.) Those meanwhile who cannot work without being 'helped' by animated bouncing paper clips will have to stick with Microsoft Office.

Open source software does not preclude making profits. The profits however must come from some other source than selling software products. Sun still sells a version of StarOffice which has more features than OpenOffice and is backed up by commercial support and training. Individuals will use OpenOffice. Organizations will more likely choose to pay for the supported StarOffice. IBM uses Eclipse as the basis for its Websphere studio products. Again by adding features to the openly available version and offering support, training and consultancy it can justify charging a fee for the product.

A number of companies have grown up to provide commercial software along open source principles. These can be used as an alternative means of creating commercial IT systems to complement the three more long-standing approaches of mainframe big-iron, Java application server and Windows .Net. Open source databases can be obtained from companies like MySQL and ProgreSQL which both allow free access to their products but also offer commercial support agreements. Open source Java application servers include JBoss and

JOnAS, again both being freely downloadable but with commercial support available. By using these open source technologies, it is possible to build an application using a freely available operating system (GNU/Linux), database (MySQL/ProgreSQL) and application server (JBoss/JOnAS). All the underlying source code is freely available. Systems built from open source components may not yet be as robust as certain commercial offerings but they are far less costly and yet can perform much the same job.

Open Source will not however take over the world entirely. It is best suited to what might be called commodity software. That is types of software that have a long history, are well understood and can be applied widely. It is not surprising that the main use of open source in the early years was for operating system software. GNU/Linux is based on the 35-year-old UNIX system. It has a large community supporting it because virtually all computers can make use of a UNIX like operating system. Likewise, office packages have been available for the PC since the early 1980s and virtually everyone uses a word processor or a spreadsheet at one time or another. This means there is a large community interested in building and supporting an offering. At the other end of the scale, it's difficult to imagine an open source community forming to build software for managing an obscure piece of factory equipment. The group of people who will benefit from such efforts are limited and thus the time of technically clued-up individuals will be directed to more widely applicable software.

Open Source advocates put forward several reasons why their method of developing software is better than the more traditional approach. One oft quoted phrase was first coined by Eric Raymond in his essay 'the Cathedral and the Bazar'. It states that

given enough eyeballs, all bugs are shallow

This means that, given the large number of people that are exposed to the program code of an open source project, all problems will soon be unearthed. In traditional commercial systems development, the more obscure areas of a system's program code would only be visited by one or two people who may be of limited experience and knowledge. These few individuals may be more likely to attempt to cover up problems, and to succeed in doing so, than an undisciplined bunch of hackers operating in an open forum.

Open Source projects are also almost always conducted under the understanding that they will follow openly agreed standards. They are more likely to attempt to change a standard itself rather than just subvert it for their own ends. A number of commercial organizations on the other hand have become known for attempting to hijack standards by creating their own incompatible versions in order to increase their own profits at the expense of others.

UNIX Wars

Berkeley

GNU/Linux was one of many different operating systems based on UNIX that had been created over the years. HP first released their version called HP-UX in 1982, DEC released Ultrix in 1984 and IBM released AIX in 1986. Programs written for one flavor, as the disparate versions have become known, will often not work on any of the others. This incompatibility was a common complaint applied to UNIX in the 1990s and the arguments over which version was more powerful and reliable became known as the UNIX wars. During the 1980s, a separate, non-commercial version of UNIX grew in popularity. This became known as Berkeley UNIX.

The original UNIX evolved at AT&T's Bell Labs in the early 1970s and by 1974 a version had been installed on a large DEC computer at the University of California at Berkeley. A graduate student, Bill Joy, wrote a few utilities for the system, including a compiler for the language Pascal and a basic editor 'ex'. These were bundled into an add-on package and given to any interested parties as the first Berkeley System Distribution (1BSD). A year later in 1978, Joy had written an improved editor, 'vi', that would later become infamous within the UNIX community for its uniquely counter-intuitive mode of operation, and something called the 'C shell'. These were added to the previous package and distributed as 2BSD.

As the original DEC computer started to show its age, Berkeley moved to a new DEC 'VAX' computer and re-wrote large amounts of the UNIX kernel to take advantage of its features. At this point, the program code underlying the BSD version of UNIX started to diverge from the original AT&T version. Much of the original AT&T program code was still used but in a heavily modified form. This meant that AT&T would still have to be paid a license fee even though its version of UNIX would perform very differently from BSD. 3BSD was released at the end of 1979.

At this point DARPA (as ARPA was now known) started to fund the work at Berkeley to provide a common operating system platform for its research across America. This included the then new TCP/IP networking protocols for the ARPANET. As a result, from this point on, ARPA-funded research was conducted on computers using BSD as their operating system. It was around this time in 1982 that Joy left Berkeley to co-found Sun Microsystems.

As the license cost of the original AT&T version of UNIX started to creep up, Berkeley came under pressure from the user community, generally universities, to attempt to replace all the program code that originally came from AT&T. This was done over a period of years in a manner not dissimilar to that adopted by the GNU project. Well it was almost done. It turned out that six files were potentially 'contaminated' by AT&T code but these were not easy to re-write. Berkeley chose to release what they had as BSD Net/2 and leave the rest to the community of users to sort out. Within a few months, the six files had been rewritten by a developer called Bill Jolitz. The resulting software system which, like Linux, is very UNIX-like but has no program code written by AT&T has spawned a number of distributions. Three of these FreeBSD, NetBSD and OpenBSD are all still available free and all are maintained by communities that operate along open source lines.

Santa Cruz Organization

Whilst all this was going on, a couple of companies were looking to make money from UNIX. As far back as 1979, Microsoft had licensed the underlying source code for UNIX from AT&T. Their version was re-branded to Microsoft Xenix. In the early 1980s, before IBM came knocking with discussions about their all-new Personal Computer, Xenix was seen inside Microsoft as their standard operating system offering. Unlike the eventual MS-DOS product which was sold to end consumers who used PCs, Xenix was only ever sold to other companies who would have to put in the effort to make it work on the particular type of microprocessor they were interested in.

One of Microsoft's partners in this effort was a small UNIX support company that had been founded by a father and son team in 1978 called the 'Santa Cruz Operation', more often called SCO. SCO ported Xenix to the Intel microprocessors that powered the IBM PC. It was marketed widely and was, before long, the flavor of UNIX installed on the most computers (largely because the other flavors of UNIX ran on far larger, far more powerful machines). As the 1980s drew to a close, Microsoft switched its interest to OS/2 and particularly the development version of OS/2 that would eventually become known as Windows NT. Microsoft gave SCO the ownership of Xenix in return for 25% of the company stock. In 1989, Xenix was renamed SCO UNIX and it remained the main version of UNIX for the PC platform well into the 1990s. Microsoft severed its links with the UNIX world and, by and large, left SCO to follow its own path.

Around this time AT&T had finally decided to divest itself of UNIX. The original product and copyrights were split up, shuffled around and in the mid 1990s, at the end of chain of transactions, ownership finally came to rest with SCO. During the turmoil of the dot com bubble and bust, SCO was itself split up and the UNIX assets sold on to a company (the Caldera Linux distribution) that was eventually renamed back to 'SCO Group'. A few months later, in 2003, the new chief executive, Darl McBride, launched a number of bizarre lawsuits.

The first was against IBM initially for $1 billion but then raised to $3 billion and finally $5 billion. It was claimed that IBM had placed 'AT&T' UNIX code in Linux and that, as the owner of the copyright to 'AT&T' UNIX source code, SCO Group was due license payments from every copy of Linux installed anywhere in the world. At around the same time, letters were sent by SCO Group to many of the larger users of Linux warning them that they might be at risk of legal action.

Red Hat, one of the larger distributors of Linux joined the tussle and sued SCO Group for unjustifiably spreading fear, uncertainty and doubt amongst its customers and thus disrupting its business. IBM, not to be out done, counter-sued listing numerous allegations ranging from breach of contract to patent infringement by SCO Group. Novell, the company that had sold SCO the UNIX assets in 1995, claimed that they hadn't sold the whole operating system, only certain rights to future royalties.

By the end of 2005, SCO Group was suing IBM, Novell, DaimlerChrysler and AutoZone and it was in turn being sued by IBM, Novell and Red Hat. The SCO Group versus IBM trial is due to start in February 2007.

Few independent commentators can understand SCO Group's position. Legal action on such a scale is ruinously expensive for such a small operation. It also distracts the management of the company from doing much else. The merits of the case are clouded to say the least. In order to explain the goings on, a number of conspiracy theories have emerged.

One suggestion was that SCO management hoped that IBM would buy the company out rather than engage in a public relations and legal fiasco. If this had come off, SCO shareholders would have made a significant profit. If this was the intention, IBM didn't take the bait.

Another theory centers on Microsoft who would very much like Linux and Open Source to go away. Microsoft abandoned its Xenix in the late 1980s but for some reason chose to pay a substantial license to SCO as the lawsuits started to fly in 2003. It has no UNIX product on the market. It claims that it wants the rights to use UNIX programming interfaces but the rights to these were mainly ceded to The Open Group, along with the UNIX name, in 1993. It's been reported that for some reason, Microsoft's license payment was far in excess of that made by Sun Microsystems which has used the AT&T UNIX source code widely for many years. It's also been admitted that Microsoft 'introduced' a venture capital firm called BayStar to SCO. A few months later, BayStar arranged for SCO to receive a $50m capital injection.

There was a time when the SCO lawsuits threatened the acceptance of GNU/Linux in the corporate world but due to large indemnity funds that have been made available by the likes of IBM and Novell, the legal bickering is now seen more as an entertaining sideshow.

Patents

With the threat of direct legal action receding, the opponents of open source have taken a different tack. Patents have been used for centuries to protect intellectual property but have an uneven history within the world of computing. In the late 1960s, one Duane Whitlow was looking to write a new sort routine for the IBM/360 to improve on the notoriously slow version that was provided for free. During his investigations, he 'discovered' an undocumented processor instruction that would significantly improve the performance of the process. At the same time as using the instruction in his 'Syncsort' product, he applied for a patent on it. The patent was granted and no-one else, not even IBM that had designed, built and sold the computer, was permitted to use it. With so much computer time in the early 1970s spent sorting, large computer users beat a path to his door and by 1975 Whitlow could claim that over half the largest 50 companies used his sorting product.

The most infamous patent of recent times is the Amazon '1-Click' patent. In September 1997, the management of Amazon.com, the online retailer, submitted a patent application for a 'Method and system for placing a purchase order via a communications network'. Amazon supported two means of placing an order. The first was the 'shopping cart' approach where items were placed in a virtual basket and then, when the user had completed selecting their purchases, a check-out routine was invoked where credit card information was confirmed. This has become the traditional approach used across the web. The second, the '1-Click' approach, involved the automatic ordering of any items that were put in the shopping basket using pre-stored credit card information. There was no explicit check-out routine. It happened automatically in the background. It was the second approach that was claimed to be unique. The patent was granted and within a month, Amazon.com was suing its competitor BarnesAndNoble.com for patent infringement for their website's 'express lane'.

To those working with the web, this technique was plain obvious and could only be described as an innovation of the lowest order. One of Amazon.com's original developers, Paul Barton-Davis described the patent as 'a cynical and ungrateful use of an obvious technology.' The publisher Tim O'Reilly described it as a 'land grab, an attempt to hoodwink a patent system that has not gotten up to speed on the state of the art in computer science.'

In theory, it should be possible to overturn 'bad' patents but this means lawyers have to get involved and the process is thus both extremely expensive and unpredictable. In the end, the Amazon '1-Click' patent was overturned but the process took 4 years.

The existence of a patent is normally enough to make sure that all except the most resource rich avoid a particular area. Open Source developers are not resource rich. In most cases, they are working in their own time for the common good and cannot spare the time or cash to get involved in legal battles. Scatter-gun patenting is thus an effective means of cramping their style.

This may be one reason why Microsoft, which filed just five patents in 1990, is expected to have filed around 3,000 in 2005 alone. Open Source is not the only driver for the filing of more patents. Increasingly, it is seen by large companies as a defensive measure. If they hold a large library of patents and are found to have infringed a competitor's, they should be able to find an instance where the competitor has infringed one of theirs. Under such circumstances, it is likely there would be a cross licensing agreement and the issue would disappear. If one of the companies however did not have a library of patents, it would be the victim of 'death by a thousand lawyers'. For the large companies, it's a version of 'mutually assured destruction'. It's unfortunate but as the CEO of SAP puts it, 'These are the rules of the game!'

Well the rules of the game in the USA anyway. The European Patent Office does not accept the concept of patents on software or business processes.

8 Integration

The computers of the 1960s and early 1970s were insular beasts. They kept themselves very much to themselves. They just sat in their own isolated computer center munching on punched cards and magnetic tape. If any information had to get from one computer to another, a magnetic tape would physically be sent between computer centers. Normally setting up a single computer on its own would deliver enough benefits to justify the cost. The costs and complexity of getting several computers to communicate freely and quickly wasn't necessary or even considered. The drift towards a more connected world had however been kicked off by a defining event in a previous decade: the Berlin Airlift of 1948.

Berlin Airlift

Following the end of World War II, Germany was split into four sections administered by France, America, Britain and the Soviet Union. The capital Berlin, located at the heart of the Soviet section, was also split into four sections.

On the 1st January 1947, the British and Americans merged their zones for economic purposes to form a new single entity known as Bizonia. The French zone would soon join them. Like most of post-war Europe, the economy of the new zone was in tatters. The legitimate economy barely existed. The prices of goods had been 'managed' by the German government since 1936 and were well below a realistic level. As a result, there was no incentive to produce any goods for sale. The few goods that were manufactured were exchanged in barter for other physical goods rather than cash. Many firms even hired a barter specialist known as a 'compensator' whose job it was to contrive deals where a proportion of the company's output could be traded for the raw materials it required. Few workers would waste their time at their official jobs because the salary they earned was of little use. After all, there were no goods in the shops to buy with the Reichsmarks they earned. Instead, many would absent themselves from work and spend their time bartering for food and clothing.

With this background, the Allies decided to replace the discredited Reichsmark with a new stable currency, the Deutsche mark. At the same time, government price controls were dropped. Within weeks, the economy was rebounding. Goods started to appear in the shops, workers went back to their jobs and business learned to trade normally once more. The old black market barons were left with piles of worthless Reichsmarks. The Soviets meanwhile were not happy. They claimed that the British and Americans were scheming behind their backs to form a new German nation. This was against the agreements made at the Yalta Conference at the end of the war. It was at least partially true in that Bizonia was being administered by a council made up of German representatives, with allied oversight. In a theatrical outburst, the Soviets sealed the border between their zone and the British and American Bizonia supposedly to stop the new currency causing instability within their sphere of influence.

The people of West Berlin were thus sealed off from the rest of the world and left to fend for themselves. In the words of General Clay, the military governor of the American zone, it was "one of the most ruthless efforts in modern times to use mass starvation for political coercion". The British and Americans (the French were distracted by political machinations at home) were left with a number of unpleasant choices. These included abandoning the population of West Berlin to the Soviets on the one hand or fighting their way through to Berlin with armored convoys on the other. Neither of these options were particularly appealing. The choice taken was to attempt to supply Berlin by air.

Something many thought was too demanding to be achieved given that Berlin needed at least 4,500 tons of cargo to be delivered every day just to survive.

On 26th June 1948, less than a week after the Deutsche mark had hit the streets and the borders had been closed, the Berlin Airlift began. At first, 70 aircraft supplied around 225 tons a day. Clearly inadequate. More and more aircraft were called on to join the effort with American craft being relocated from the Pacific to help. By the end of July, a new senior officer, General Vandenberg, who had run a similar operation supplying American troops over the Himalayas during the War arrived to take over. He didn't like what he saw

> A real cowboy operation. Few people knew what they would be doing the next day. Neither flight crews nor ground crews knew how long they'd be there, or the schedules that they were working. Everything was temporary. I went out to the Wiesbaden Air Base, looked around, then hopped a plane to Berlin – confusion everywhere.

He quickly set about putting in place operating principles to improve the situation. Aircraft should arrive at three minute intervals, no more, no less. If an aircraft couldn't land at Berlin on its first attempt it should fly straight back to the West so that it didn't foul up the next aircraft's flight plan. Pilots would fly by instruments at all times. This would set up a rhythm to the operation that would not be disrupted by weather. Pilots were not allowed out of their aircraft at Berlin. They would arrive, have their aircraft unloaded and then fly back to the West immediately.

The unloading and distribution of cargo at Berlin was under the command of Master Sergeant Ed Guilbert. He set up his own set of procedures. Cargo should be strapped together in large bundles to get it off the aircraft quickly. The payload manifest, or list of cargo, should be transmitted to Berlin, normally by telex, before the aircraft arrives so that plans could be made to move the goods to where they could be used as quickly as possible. Given that the cargo started its journey in many different countries and could be carried by chartered aircraft of many nationalities, all manifests were to be in English and had to be sent in a common format. Moving the cargo quickly also avoided the need for a large warehouse operation.

The cargo passing through the Berlin Airports grew steadily from a daily average of around 2200 tons a day in July 1948, about half that necessary for subsistence, to 4760 tons a day in October. By the following year, the average was up to 8000 tons a day and, in a special effort for the 'Easter Parade', 13,000 tons were delivered over a 24-hour period during the Easter weekend in March 1949. This was three times that needed to feed the population of West Berlin. Clearly the blockade of Berlin had been a failure. Six weeks after the Easter Parade, the Soviets relented and opened the border of their zone to allow for road and rail access to Berlin for the first time in over 10 months and within a fortnight, the Federal Republic of Germany, West Germany, had been created from the American, British and French sectors.

Standards

By the mid 1960s, the US railroad and haulage industries were starting to sink into their own form of confused 'Cowboy operation'. Each operator used their own documentation so that as a consignment made its way across country, it would gather a pile of incompatible shipping notes. There would be occasions when the cargo documented as leaving the original starting point was not the cargo that was documented as arriving at the destination. The cargoes would just turn up at depots with no prior warning leading to confusion and delay. Stepping into this quagmire was the Transportation Data Coordinating Committee (TDCC). It was convened by none other than Ed Guilbert the man who had looked after the ground logistics of the Berlin Airlift. The TDCC was formed in 1968 to come up with data structures that would take the place of the 1948 common manifest format but for application across the entire logistics and shipping industries in the USA. Instead of being transferred by Telex, the messages would be sent electronically between computers. The computers would be programmed to output and receive messages without the intervention of humans. There would be no need to print out messages and then re-key them into a different computer. The communication would be automatic. This became known as electronic data interchange or EDI. The process of definition, refinement and agreement took a long time and it was not until 1975 that the TDCC finally published its first set of EDI data format standards.

A separate effort by the American National Standards Institute (ANSI) commenced in 1979 to define common EDI structures for all industries, not just logistics. The effort built on top of the work of TDCC and became known as the X12 standards. X12 and TDCC formats were not identical but they shared a common basis and professionals conversant in one standard would generally be able to make sense of messages formatted using the other.

A similar enterprise was taking shape on the other side of the Atlantic but given the larger number of players, it led to even more acronyms. In 1974, the UK's trade data interchange (TDI) was published intended for the electronic transfer of customs data to the appropriate government agency. Before long, this had been adapted to be used in the British retail industry as TRADACOM. Germany had their SEDAS format. France had their GENCOD. The Netherlands had TRANSCOM. Sweden had DAKOM. Not to be outdone, industry groups started to set up their own standards: ODETTE for automotive, IATA for air transport, SWIFT for financial payments and so on. Anyone wishing to communicate across frontiers or between industries had a problem. Very few of the standards shared a common base.

This gave rise to a great international effort to come up with some common foundation. Under the auspices of the United Nations, the UN/EDIFACT (United Nations Electronic Data Interchange For Administration, Commerce and Transport) committee was formed. The UN/EDIFACT standard was intended to merge as many of the competing standards as possible and since its inception in 1985 has become a common platform for much EDI across the world though national and industry peculiarities have not been eradicated. In particular, ANSI X12 remains very popular in North America.

EDI in Action

So a company wants to order some material from its supplier. It has the option of picking up the phone or sending a fax to place the order. Let us say instead that they choose to use EDI since both they and their supplier have the necessary equipment.

The first step is the creation of a purchase order in their own computer system. This can either be manually by typing it in or through a material requirements planning (MRP) process which works out what needs to be bought and then orders it automatically. The creation of the purchase order will trigger the sending of a message to software known as an EDI translator. This converts the information from the company's internal format into that used for EDI transmissions, normally an appropriate EDIFACT structure. Once the message has been reformatted, it needs to start making its way towards the supplier. In traditional EDI, the message is sent to a mailbox at a third party known as a VAN or value added network. The VAN accepts messages and forwards them on to the mailbox of the supplier, be it within their own network or on that of a competing VAN. Periodically, the supplier will check with its VAN to see if any messages have arrived in its mailbox. If a message has arrived, it is read into the supplier's EDI translator, converted out of EDIFACT into some less cryptic format and passed on the appropriate computer to create a sales order.

Normally the transmission would have taken between an hour and a day depending on how often purchase orders are processed by the EDI translators. If set up correctly and the supplier mailbox is checked frequently the message can flow through the system in a matter of minutes.

Whilst EDI speeds up the flow of information, reduces manual processing costs and increases accuracy, there is a downside. The leading VANs, IBM and a subsidiary of General Electric called GEIS, are not charities and charge for each message passing through their network. Not only do they charge a fee per message but there can also be fees for the rental of the mailbox and a fee based on the total amount of information transferred. The customer and supplier also have to communicate with the VAN. For low priority traffic, this can be done through a dial up telephone connection using a modem, just like Internet connections in years gone by. For high priority traffic, this would require a leased phone line to the VAN, the cost of which can be considerable. The companies also have to obtain EDI translator software and, even more costly, someone skilled enough to use it.

To get an EDI system working, both companies have to spend time agreeing the exact meanings of each item of data which again takes time and costs money. The large and undefined cost of getting an EDI system working meant that it was only suitable for the largest of organizations with high processing costs to reduce.

The Arrival of the Internet

With the opening up of the Internet to commercial organizations in the early 1990s, the VANs could be made redundant. Business partners could communicate directly across the Internet without the need for an expensive services provided by third parties. Almost no trading partners made the leap. One reason was that the VANs provided secure and reliable communications. The VAN operators went to great lengths to stop the outside world getting free access to their networks so their users could be assured that no-one would be able to eavesdrop on their trading. The Internet at the time was like the early days of the Wild West with few really understanding the security implications. The Internet was also not seen as reliable. While IBM or GEIS account managers could be dragged over hot coals for a failure in service, no-one could be blamed if the Internet was a bit slow. Another important consideration was that, just as it takes 'two to tango', it takes two business partners to make an EDI transaction. If one organization is ready to move to new technology, it won't be able to make the leap until the company at the other end of the transaction chooses to make the same leap. As a result, traditional EDI using VANs kept growing well into the late 1990s.

The Dot Com hype did start to have an impact. The cries of 'business revolution' started out based on little more that a series of web pages where customers could log in to a system and place orders. This was little different to phoning a call center or sending a fax. A human had to perform the task, albeit one at the customer and not the supplier, and could make mistakes when they did so. It was in many respects a step backward from the automation offered by EDI and had little impact on its adoption. In recent years, the boosters of the web revolution have been having another go at creating a bandwagon by declaring the imminent arrival of 'Web 2.0'. This is an umbrella term for the next stage in the technological evolution of the web page though it has no specific definition. Whilst useful, it was quickly branded 'Bubble 2.0' by The Economist newspaper as a warning not to get too carried away in overestimating its scope or its depth.

Once the web pages had failed to change the face of commerce, it was the turn of 'B2B' portals and exchanges to have a go. The notion behind these was that business in need of a service would log their requirements on a B2B website. These would be automatically matched against offers to supply goods and services logged on the website by suppliers. The idea of an exchange, where price transparency is all, makes sense when it is a commodity that is being traded in a liquid market. Unfortunately, the types of commodities that benefit from exchanges, such as stocks and shares, oil and gold, were already traded on real world exchanges. The creators of the B2B revolution had failed to accept that most companies would prefer to deal with a long standing trading partner that they trusted to deliver the goods day-in day-out, rather than a faceless entity that could for all they know be a financially unstable teenager operating out of their bedroom.

A key enabler to moving EDI traffic away from the VANs and onto the Internet was the emergence of XML or eXtensible Mark up Language. XML is a close cousin to HTML that is used in web pages. It is more flexible in that the tags that surround the data can be chosen freely by the user rather than chosen from the list defined by the World Wide Web Consortium. XML is in a way the new age version of the old EDIFACT structures. In EDIFACT, the individual items of data are interspersed with apparently random punctuation marks leaving a meaningless soup of characters. As an example the following could be found in an EDIFACT order message

```
LIN+3+1+123456:BP'
```

It indicates that the information that follows is the third line item of the order. The '1' indicates that this is an order item that the supplier hasn't seen before and should be added to the order. The product in question is 123456 but this is the product code used by the buyer (BP = Buyers Part Number) and will require to be swapped for the supplier's own code. In XML, each item of data is surrounded by tags that attempt to explain what the data is. The example above might look like

```
<LineItem>
 <LineNo>3</LineNo>
 <LineAction>Add</LineAction>
 <Item>
  <ItemCode>123456</ItemCode>
  <CodeType>BuyerPart</CodeType>
 </Item>
</LineItem>
```

This is much more comprehensible to a human. There is the added advantage that additional information can be slotted into the structure without changing the meaning. If an extra field was added to the middle of a line of EDIFACT, the meaning of everything that came after it would be lost. On the other hand, just looking at the above example shows an obvious drawback of XML. It takes around 10 times the size of message to hold the same information as the equivalent EDIFACT. In the 1980s, when EDIFACT was being constructed, a key requirement was to get as much information down a telephone line as quickly as possible. This meant keeping the size of a message to an absolute minimum. The ability for humans to understand the message was of secondary importance. With the vast improvement in communications technology since then, the balance between ease of use and communications capacity has shifted in favor of the human.

The first big shift to EDI over the Internet was announced in September 2002 by the giant American retailer WalMart. They stated that at some point in the future they would be mandating all their suppliers to communicate over the Internet using a protocol known as AS2. This wraps a traditional EDIFACT message in some XML and then sends the whole bundle over the Internet using a secure connection (HTTPS). There would be no need to send the message over a VAN which in turn would allow WalMart to save a lot of money. As time goes on, the number of organizations moving to EDI over the Internet will increase but it requires both the sender and receiver of the message to be ready. Unlike WalMart, not every company is in the position to bully their entire supplier base so the switch over may be quite slow.

An alternative approach to the AS2 chosen by WalMart is ebXML (electronic business XML). EbXML attempts to do much the same thing as AS2, that is sending information securely over the Internet enclosed in an XML wrapper, but because it has been defined by the UN body that manages EDIFACT, it has a greater likelihood that it will prevail over time. Confusingly, ebXML can be used to send most forms of information and is not restricted to XML. It just uses an XML wrapper.

Common Product Codes

When sending messages between trading partners, it's necessary for them to use a common language. That is to say, both sides must be able to take the same meaning from the same string of characters. If the sender sent a message ordering 2 UNITS, does that mean 2 cartons, 2 cases or 2 pallets? There are standard lists of acceptable codes for the likes of country codes, currencies and units of measure. Normally it is the lists provided by the ISO (International Organization for Standardization) that are used. A more tricky issue is the naming of products.

Each company has its own product code which means that a buyer and a seller will often refer to the same item by a different string of letters or numbers. This problem was apparent in the 1970s when retailers started to demand that items had barcodes on them to allow them to be scanned at checkouts. In North America, the Uniform Code Council (UCC) was formed to allocate each physical item a unique 12-digit number. The number became known as UPC (universal product code). In Europe, a separate system, the European Article Number or EAN, was instituted. Each country had their own administrative organization that gave out numbers from a common pool of 13-digit codes. The EAN was gradually adopted as the worldwide standard product code except for the USA and Canada that continued to use their 12-digit UPC. In the 1990s, the 12-digit UPC and 13-digit EAN were merged to form the 14-digit Global Trade Identifier Number or GTIN. The GTIN for a North American product is two zeros followed by the old UPC. The GTIN for all other articles is a single zero followed by the old EAN. Finally, in 2005 the international umbrella organization EAN International renamed itself GS1 and all the national number allocation organizations renamed themselves GS1 followed by their country code. UCC, the American branch for example became GS1 US. It's taken 20 years but at last there is now a single organization allocating common identifiers for products sold worldwide.

Web services

In the future when two businesses choose to start communicating electronically, it is unlikely that they would select traditional EDI as the mechanism. Amongst other things, the cost of the VAN and the incomprehensible EDIFACT structures will put them off. It is more likely that they will choose the greatly hyped technique of Web services. Web services have created a huge amount of noise over recent years, some well informed, some ill informed. As a result, it's often not clear what exactly they are. The dust has not settled on a clear definition but, in short, whilst an old fashioned web page allows a human to interact with a remote computer across the Internet, a web service allows a computer to interact with another computer across the Internet without involving a human.

At its most basic level, web services use the same protocol used by web pages, HTTP. This is the very same one that Tim Berners-Lee dreamed up all the way back in 1991. Instead of communicating across the VANs of old they do so across the Internet. They use human-readable XML rather than the cryptic EDIFACT or X12 data structures used in traditional EDI. Apart from this, they do much the same as traditional EDI. That is to say, they will be used by companies to send orders, invoices and delivery notifications to their trading partners.

They do go beyond EDI in some respects. Each company that creates a web service should publish the details in a publicly accessible electronic directory. Any potential trading partner can then read the details and automatically set up a connection. Protocols (known as WSDL and UDDI) have been defined to help this process but it has yet to be seen if they are useful, or indeed viable, in practice.

It's expected that over the coming years and decades, web services will become far more widespread than EDI. For one thing, the costs will be far lower with no VAN to deal with. Setting up a new trading partnership should be simplified to an extent and the next generation of business software will hopefully be built to cope with web services better than the current generation has been built to cope with EDI.

Many of the problems associated with EDI will return to afflict web services. One partner will want to receive more information than the other wants to give out. There will be disagreements over meaning. Does a stock level take into account customer orders or is it just a count of goods in a warehouse even though they may all have been promised to a customer? Each new pairing between trading partners will have to be tested before it can be trusted. All this takes time and resources and can become very expensive.

Service Oriented Architecture

Communication between computers is not the exclusive preserve of inter-company trading. The number of links between computers within an organization is normally far greater than those to external operations. It should be possible to use the techniques of web services to link applications together within a single enterprise. When web services are applied within an organization as well as between trading partners this is called a 'Service Oriented Architecture' or SOA. In an SOA, all the different applications required for a business, such as accounting, inventory control or production planning, are split out into small mini-applications. They will still all need to work together; production planning will need stock levels from inventory control; goods receipts will need to update the financial stock accounts. Web services will provide the glue to bind them together. The production planning software will use a web service to find the stock levels from the inventory control software. The inventory control software will use web services to make postings to the accounts.

The mini-applications won't communicate with each other directly. They will send all their requests to a central manager process. This central manager will take a request, read its own configuration and determine what to do next. In some cases, the request won't be very interesting and will simply be ignored. In others, the request will be passed on to another application and the response passed back to the originator. It's also possible that a single web service call will kick off a whole string of events in several different applications. These in turn will trigger other web service calls to the central manager. These chains of events and processing steps are known as 'business processes' and can be found in any business whether they use computers or not. They include taking and delivering customer orders, chasing customer payment, and ordering goods from suppliers. The ability to organize and manage business processes has led to the central manager process often being called 'business process orchestration' software. Once a SOA has been implemented, a business' IT system would turn into a shoot-out of web service messages flying between small applications and the central orchestrator.

Benefits

One criticism of the current ERP systems is that they are too large and inflexible for many organizations. Customizing them to do exactly what an organization wants often takes too long or costs too much for it to be practical. It's not unusual for an organization implementing ERP systems for the first time to change the way the operation works to fit the ERP system rather than attempt to adapt the ERP system to their operation. Using smaller applications, smaller building blocks if you like, will allow the organization to refine its systems to work in the way it thinks best rather than the way its software happens to dictate.

The process orchestrator will allow the smaller applications to come together to mimic the operation of a single large ecosystem but without the loss of flexibility caused by large monolithic software such as ERP systems. The business process can be adapted to fit specific needs without the need to reprogram large chunks of the system. This will greatly improve the flexibility of the organization and its ability to respond to changes both external and internal.

Within each of the different systems employed by businesses, such as ERP and CRM, there is already a high degree of automation. To make a business process flow from its start to its end often requires a leap from one system to another. This is normally either disjointed or achieved manually. The process orchestrator can be used to link all the different applications together to complete a process without any manual transfer tasks. Any tasks that must be achieved manually, such as notifications and approvals, can also be automated using the 'workflow' capabilities of the orchestrator where emails are sent to individuals asking them to perform an action that can't be achieved automatically by a computer.

Web services are being specified to work in the same way no matter who supplies the hardware and software. This kind of 'vendor independence' has been claimed many times before and has rarely been achieved. If Web services do manage the feat, they will reduce the cost and time taken to get complex systems working compared with attempting to match up multiple inconsistent systems.

Web services will also finally allow the reasoning behind the corporate portal to become apparent. In the late 1990s, most companies had an Intranet. These were a series of websites that contained information that would be of interest to those working within the company. Often they contained little more than an online phone book and management's exhortations to work harder. In the last few years, these have been converted to more modern sounding 'portals'. Sadly the content of the portal remained almost identical to that available on the earlier Intranet though it was produced using flashier technology.

The concept behind the portal was that it would become the one-stop-shop for information for a company's workers. Not only would the usual meeting-room booking and phone book screens be available but it would also be possible to view stock levels, create a customer order, view accounts and create purchase requisitions. The users would only have one place to look to perform any task and would only need one user id and password to access it. Unfortunately, it proved more costly to link the portals to the underlying applications than it did to enable the applications to create web screens themselves. Instead of a one-stop-shop, users were treated to a cavalcade of different web screens each with their own login and security procedures. You could always call up the log-in screen to the individual applications from the portal though.

Web services are supposed to make it far simpler for a single master user-interface, the portal, to retrieve information from lots of different areas and display it in a standard tidy format. Once this has been achieved, the portal will finally have come of age and could become the central access point for an organization's information.

Web services will allow information to flow more swiftly than a traditional computing environment. Even in the 21st century, most links between computers only operate once a day. This goes back to the days of batch processing on mainframes when information flowed at the speed of magnetic tape. The practice has endured because it is far cheaper to prepare and manage an interface that runs once a day than it is to create one that quickly links two applications built on different technical foundations. Web services should reduce this problem considerably by offering a common framework for all applications to work within. This is where the term 'on demand' has sprung from. Once an event has been triggered, the start of a process, such as a purchase or an order cancellation, it is possible for its effect to ripple through the organization almost instantly.

It would ripple through not only the organization itself but also that of trading partners. Given that web services are Internet friendly, the event triggered by the customer of one organization can easily and immediately make the leap across the divide to its suppliers. There is no need to wait for a nightly interface to run. Changes in requirements become visible throughout the supply chain almost immediately.

Drawbacks

So a web service oriented architecture is more flexible, speeds up processing, helps us to take advantage of the latest technology and makes the world one big happy family. It must be a good thing, right? Well it has its drawbacks too.

Web services are sold as allowing business processes to be performed automatically. Before rushing to implement web services, potential customers should pause to consider how much automation has already been achieved by their large monolithic ERP systems. They will probably find that most of their processes are automated anyway. Whereas in an SOA the business process is configured within the orchestrator, ERP systems come pre-programmed to deliver a similar result. Production planning programs have been written to communicate with inventory control which in turn have been programmed to interact with the accounting module. SOA orchestrators offer the opportunity to go beyond what is automated as part of standard ERP but it's unclear if the extra costs are justified by the small increase in automation.

An SOA needs a host of mini-applications that cede control to the central process orchestrator. It's not clear where these are going to come from. The large ERP systems used today are programmed to work as a single large lump and attempting to get them to work in any other way has a history of leading to trouble. The production planning module won't work without being able to read stock from the inventory control module which in turn will not function without the accounting module being available. The applications are tightly bound to one another meaning the SOA orchestrator is frozen out of the process. That is not to say that it is impossible to get such a system to communicate with the outside world but it is costly and prone to failure. There are a number of individual applications on the market that could be linked together using an orchestrator. This will strike those who have worked in IT for a number of years as very similar to the 'Best of Breed' strategy that was much talked about in the mid 1990s. The idea behind Best of Breed was to take the best performing application from each functional area and attempt to get them to work together like a single large ERP system. In each specialist area, they could wipe the floor with the ERP software. Working together, the combined monster would be far more powerful than any generalist package. Unfortunately, it was too good to be true and the cost and risks of getting all the largely incompatible software to work together often proved too much. Over time, the good-enough offerings from the ERP software vendors won the day. It's not clear in what way SOA has changed the situation.

Web services are supposed to enable a more 'on-demand' world, yet it's possible to achieve an on-demand world without web services. Much of the increase in speed offered by implementing web services can also be achieved by implementing other more mature technologies. The main reasons that they have not been applied is either that the costs of implementing them outweigh the benefits or that the organization that would benefit from them is too short-sighted to make the leap. Not all business transactions benefit from instantaneous action. Procedures that are associated with set administrative cost, such as invoicing, are normally performed once every so often. When a payment is made between companies both have to pay a bank charge. It makes sense then for payment only to be made periodically, normally once every month. Sending a mini-invoice every time a single item is supplied is pointless. All the mini-payments should be stored and sent together so that the overhead of a single bank charge can be spread between many transactions. The availability of web services won't change that.

The process of describing a web service so that it can be called by a partner system without exchanging program documentation is not new or unique to web services. Something similar to the concept of WSDL, which describes how a particular web service works, has been available for years in the IDL used by Microsoft's DCOM. Before that, it was available in CORBA originally defined in the early 1990s. The ability to quickly start calling a remote service can also be achieved using something called 'J2EE stub generation'. The progress offered by web services is not that notable.

A common problem with computers that work quickly, as any self respecting service oriented architecture would, is that when things go wrong, they go wrong quickly and on a grand scale. It is often easy for a program to spot when something is amiss but not so easy to work out what to do about it. It's normally left to humans to pick up the pieces. There are then questions about how the humans are notified, what do they do when they are notified and what is done to the human if they simply ignore all the problems and hope for the best. Large complex integrated business systems are beyond the understanding of most IT support personnel. Expecting them to chase a chimera through a labyrinth of interconnected applications, none of which they fully understand, will lead to disappointment.

Perhaps the most serious problem with web services won't be seen for some time. With information flowing faster and faster through myriad interconnections that are understood less and less, there is an increasing risk the whole system will become unstable. An example of this was seen at the time of the stock market 'crash' of 1987. Financial institutions used computers, known as black boxes, to assist trading. These black boxes followed an academic model known as 'portfolio insurance'. They would blindly follow a set of rules that they had been set. Within these rules was a situation where, in response to a large fall in the price of a certain stock, the order would go out to sell huge quantities of that stock. It's easy to see that this would lead to a downward spiral of prices. The more the price dropped, the more stock would be sold. The more stock that was sold, the further prices fell. In October 1987, the Dow Jones industrial average fell over 22% on a single day. The crash was not caused directly by the black boxes but it was almost certainly made worse by them. All it took was for normal events to stray into an area where the aberrant rule kicked in. The rest was automated carnage.

Any closely linked complex system runs the risk of instability. When web services or similar have been widely adopted, business will be more closely linked than ever. When lighting struck the Albuquerque plant of the electronics firm Philips that made an obscure chip for mobile phones, few would imagine that it would cause major disruption. After all, the fire that resulted had been extinguished within 10 minutes. Unfortunately the 'clean rooms' used to manufacture the chips had become contaminated. All the chips in production at the time had to be destroyed and it took months for the facility to be cleaned and production to get back up to speed. The two customers for the chips, the mobile phone operations of Nokia and Ericsson, took different approaches. Nokia quickly forced Philips to agree to supply their needs from alternative sites. Ericsson was slower off the mark and failed to find alternative supplies. Its mobile phone division ended up reporting a loss of over $2bn the following year. A seemingly small disruption in one company had serious repercussions for another.

The Future

The concepts of web services and service oriented architecture may quietly evaporate or they may eventually make a successful leap into the mainstream. There is however little doubt that one way or another, the world will become a more connected place. It will be possible for information to flow ever quicker from customer to retailer to wholesaler to distributor to manufacturer to supplier. The cost of gathering and distributing information will plummet. This will have a significant effect on society. There won't be a huge powerful single dislocation but a gradual change that is already well under way. In a sense, it's just the next stop in the journey of the industrial revolution that started with the steam engine.

The operations of companies can crudely be split into two sections: the marketing and the delivery. The delivery can be the provision of a service or the manufacturing of goods and is increasingly becoming a commodity. That is to say that it will not make especially large profits. It can be performed anywhere on Earth by low wage workers to a tolerable level of quality. If the workers start to demand more pay or the quality deteriorates, the delivery can merely be shifted to somewhere else that will be more grateful for the work. This trend started in the 1980s with western manufacturing jobs migrating to Asia but continues in the 21st century with the like of software development and call center operations. The manufacturing moved because of the increasing professionalism and systematization of the logistics industry with the introduction of containerization. The services moved because of the availability of high speed, low cost global communications. This shifting of resources and work has caused anxiety in the 'developed' world but we have to accept that disquiet about, and reaction to, such forces of 'progress' is not a new phenomenon.

Back when Charles Babbage was studying at Cambridge University, in 1811, menacing letters started being delivered to the mill owners of Nottingham. The missives claimed to come from 'General Ned Ludd and the Army of Redressers' though Ned Ludd was never identified and was probably just a cover name. The skilled workers in the textile trade were unhappy, to say the least, that the new steam driven machinery was reducing the skill required to produce saleable cloth. This meant that they were not being paid as much as before. They demanded that the new machines be removed and the old ways of working reinstated. Over a period of months, a campaign of violence swept the counties of Northern England, mills were invaded and machinery destroyed. In response, the government made 'machine breaking' an offense punishable by death (despite a notable speech in the House of Lords by Lord Byron, the father of Ada Lovelace, who stood up for the so-called Luddites). The army was called in and a number of the protesters were captured and hung for their crimes. Over time, the anger dissipated into acceptance but the lesson remains that it's not possible to somehow 'uninvent' technologies no matter how much people want them to go away. The process that today has been labeled globalization cannot be sent into reverse any more than it was possible to forget how to make steam engines in the 1800s. It would be wise to accept the process and find a way of continuing to work whilst it runs its course.

Far less prone to cost pressures than the delivery side of an operation, and thus less itinerant, is the marketing activity which also tends to be far more profitable. The key to profitability is to build a brand that is trusted by consumers. Once consumers trust a brand more than its competitors, it's possible to charge a premium for it. The consumers are willing to pay quite a bit more for that 'peace of mind' of buying a brand they trust. Making a brand more desirable, more sexy, than its competitors also makes it possible to charge more. The underlying product can in truth be quite mediocre as long as the consumers are left with the impression that it is highly desirable or should, in some way, be trusted. The key means of achieving this is of course advertising. Financial services firms, like banks and insurers, and firms in the medical and health market emphasize how trustworthy they are. Jewelry, cosmetics and fashion firms focus on how much more desirable you would be if you used their products.

About half the revenue received by the large packaged consumer goods firms goes into manufacturing and delivering the products they sell. A quarter of the revenue goes on advertising and marketing. The remaining quarter on administration and profit. It matters little to the company where the goods come from or services performed as long as they're available when the customer wants them. These operations are increasingly seen as prone to the influence of globalization. This is also true of administration. It's shifting the balance between marketing expenditure and profit that interests companies today. The delivery and administration is just a hygiene where costs should be stripped out wherever possible.

Companies have already started to jettison the delivery side of their business and focus on the far more profitable marketing side. The businesses that perform the delivery side are doomed to accept whatever small profit margin the commissioning marketing group feels is appropriate. The marketing operation, on the other hand, can make as much money as they can hoodwink out of the consumer.

A leading example of this is airlines. Today, purchasing a ticket from an airline does not mean that you will fly on that airline's aircraft. You may end up receiving the service from a code share partner or a franchise partner that merely has their planes painted in the ticketing airlines colors. The delivery has been divorced from the marketing. The annoying task of flying people from A to B has been offloaded on to a low profit outfit whilst the ticketing airline makes as much profit as the market will allow based on their brand's level of trust and desirability.

To make this kind of scheme work needs technology. Once the ticket has been sold, it's necessary to inform the airline operating the flight. Information has to flow between companies. It's been possible to do this for decades using manual faxing and phone calls or traditional EDI but the advent of simple messaging across the Internet will make it even easier. Given that on the Internet someone in India or China is only a fraction of a second further away than the person next door, the forces of globalization will only intensify. 'Offshore' trading partners can be kept intimately aware of every event that affects their 'onshore' partner's business.

Another change that has already been seen is the flight away from experience. There was a time when having experienced staff was seen as the best way to ensure a high quality of product and a high level of service. The experienced staff had seen it all before and when things went wrong, they knew how to handle the situation and what remedial action to take. There was however a problem with experience as a delivery mechanism: it was expensive and took time to acquire. When the primary goal is short-term profit, experience quickly falls out of favor to be replaced by 'business processes'. Processes proscribe what actions to take under certain circumstances and how to trigger the next event in a sequence. The theory goes that once a process has been defined and the chosen tools have been put in place, any monkey can be taught to deliver the service or create the goods. The monkey, generally chosen more on the basis of cost and availability than any talent or understanding, can then replace the experienced operative.

Unfortunately, when things go awry the monkey can be left confused and helpless. They have neither the knowledge nor the will power to work out what to do. When the processes, which are the only paths they are permitted to go down, do not explicitly cater for the situation that has arisen they can only stop and play for time.

This was the approach taken when mass production was first applied. The process of making a car was analyzed and each individual step codified. Each worker on the assembly line would only have to perform a small defined set of well defined tasks. When something went wrong however they would be helpless and the problem would have to be left to fester. At best the defective product would find its way into a repair loop to be handled by the more experienced line workers at worst it would go all through the processes and be presented to the customer.

The approach has in recent years been extended to call centers and is why they generally give rise to more frustration than happiness. Certain customer requests, the ones that have been anticipated when the center was set up, will be handled efficiently and courteously. Any other requests, the ones that were not predicted when the center's systems were being set up, get nowhere. The low paid and inexperienced person in the call center has no understanding of the bigger picture and would have no power to do anything about it even if they did. Unless staffed by experienced workers that are genuinely empowered, a call center will only be able to cope well with simple requests that never go wrong.

In the future, the flow of information between computers will be managed by business process orchestration software. It will follow a highly structured path between several systems. This will run the risk of falling prey to the same kind of issues. When the simple processes that have been anticipated during the design phase are invoked, all will be well. Should a situation arise that has not been anticipated, at best the process will stop and wait for input. At worst it will continue blindly, creating a Frankenstein's monster that will take considerable effort to kill.

Since their earliest days, computers have always done exactly what humans have told them to do: no matter how malformed or ill-conceived the instructions may have been. They have always done it without question and at great speed. As the speed increases and the computers are networked to create a single large ecosystem, the humans must be more careful than ever to ensure that what they tell the machines to do is not damaging. The opportunity for confusion in the future will be greater than ever. Computers do give us the opportunity to create more and more with fewer and fewer resources. They can design products that would be impossibly advanced for humans to come up with unaided. They are directly linked to the push to improve the quality of life and to extend life itself. Yet we have to be careful how we use them because, as The Farmers' Almanac put it nearly 30 years ago:

To err is human, but to really foul up requires a computer.

9 Bibliography & Sources

Major Sources

- Campbell-Kelly, Martin & Aspray, William *Computer: A History of the Information Machine*, Boulder CO & Oxford, Westview Press, 2004
- Ceruzzi, Paul E. *A History of Modern Computing*, Cambridge MA & London: MIT Press, 2003 (2nd Ed)
- Campbell-Kelly, Martin *From Airline Reservations to Sonic the Hedgehog*, Cambridge MA & London: MIT Press, 2004
- Naughton, John *A Brief History of the Future: the Origins of the Internet,* Weidenfeld & Nicholson, 1999
- Schneier, Bruce *Secrets & Lies, Digital Security in a Networked World,* John Wiley, 2000
- Moody, Glyn, *Rebel Code: Inside Linux and the Open Source Revolution*, Perseus, 2002
- St Andrews University Website of Mathematical Biography (www-groups.dcs.st-and.ac.uk/~history/Indexes/Full_Alph.html)

- Charles Babbage Institute at the University of Minnesota, Minneapolis - Oral Histories (www.cbi.umn.edu/oh)

Additional Sources

- Moseley, Mabot *Irascible Genius: A Life of Charles Babbage*, Inventor, Hutchinson, 1964
- Hyman, Anthony *Charles Babbage: Pioneer of the computer*, Oxford University Press, 1982
- Sobel, Robert *Thomas Watson Sr.: IBM and the Computer Revolution*, Beard Books, 2000
- Sebag-Montifiore, Hugh, *Enigma: Battle for the Code*, Weidenfeld & Nicholson, 2000
- Smith, Michael, *Station X: The Codebreakers of Bletchley Park*, Channel 4 Books, 1998
- Goldstine, Herman *The Computer from Pascal to von Neumann*, Princeton University Press, 1972
- Wilkes, Maurice, *Memoirs of a Computer Pioneer*, MIT Press, 1985
- Hally, Mike *Electronic Brains, Stories from the Dawn of the Computer Age*, Granta, 2005, P40-42
- Lavington, Simon H *Early British Computers*, Butterworth-Heinemann, 1980, P29-31
- Ferry, Georgina *A Computer Called Leo: Lyons Teashops and the World's First Office Computer*, Fourth Estate, 2003
- Murray, Charles, *The Supermen: The Story of Seymour Cray and the Technical Wizards Behind the Supercomputer*, John Wiley, 1997
- Riordan, Michael & Hoddeson, Lillian *Crystal Fire: Invention of the Transistor and the Birth of the Information Age*, W W Norton, 1999
- Cringely, Robert X. *Accidental Empires*, Penguin, 1996, P55-61
- Craig, David *Rip-Off: The Scandalous inside story of the management consulting money machine*, London: Original Book Company, 2005
- Pyatt, Edward *The National Physical Laboratory: A history*, Mauve: Teddington, 1993
- Berners-Lee, Tim "Weaving the Web: Origins and Future of the World Wide Web", Texere, 2000 p1-80
- Cassidy, John *Dot.Con: The Real Story of Why the Internet Bubble Burst*, Penguin, 2002, p51-65
- Hiltzik, Michael *Dealers of Lightning: XEROX PARC and the dawn of the computer age*, Harper Business, 1999, p178-193
- Raymond, Eric S *The Cathedral and the Bazaar*, O'Reilly, 2001
- DiBona, Chris (Ed) *Open Sources: Voices from the Open Source*

Revolution, O'Reilly, 1999
- Botting, Douglas *From the Ruins of the Reich, Germany 1945-49,* Methuen, 1985, 2005
- Sheffi, Yossi *The Resilient Enterprise: Overcoming Vulnerability for Competitive Advantage,* MIT Press, 2005

A more detailed list of sources (including web resources) can be obtained from the book's web site: www.crash-it.com.

Printed in the United Kingdom
by Lightning Source UK Ltd.
120134UK00001B/80